WORD MYSTERIES & HISTORIES

FROM QUICHE TO HUMBLE PIE

By the Editors of
The American Heritage Dictionaries

With Illustrations by
BARRY MOSER

Foreword by
ROBERT CLAIBORNE

Author of
Our Marvelous Native Tongue:
The Life and Times of The English Language

Houghton Mifflin Company   Boston

The slogan "Coke Is It" is a registered trademark of The Coca-Cola Company.

The slogan "You're the Pepsi Generation" courtesy of PepsiCo, Inc.

The quotation on page 176 is reprinted by permission from *Jacqueline* by Ron Galella. © 1974 by Sheed & Ward.

Information about the trademark STAR WARS® courtesy of Lucasfilm Ltd.

Information about the trademark Teflon® courtesy of E.I. du Pont de Nemours and Company.

The inclusion of any word in this book is not an expression of the Publisher's opinion as to whether or not it is subject to proprietary rights. Indeed, no word in this book is to be regarded as affecting the validity of any trademark.

Illustrations © 1986 by Barry Moser.

Book design by Margaret Tsao

Library of Congress Cataloging in Publication Data

Word mysteries and histories.

  Includes index.
  1. English language—Etymology—Dictionaries.

I. Houghton Mifflin Company.
PE1580.W67   1986   422'.03   86-10455
ISBN 0-395-40265-4
ISBN 0-395-40264-6 (pbk.)

Manufactured in the United States of America

TABLE OF CONTENTS

ILLUSTRATIONS AND SELECTED COMMENTARY

Barry Moser

EDITORIAL STAFF

Anne H. Soukhanov *Executive Editor*
Kaethe Ellis *Coordinating Editor, Reference*

The Word Historians

David A. Jost *Editor and Compiler*
Ph.D., Harvard University

Marion Severynse *Editor*
Ph.D., Harvard University
Susan M. Innes *Assistant Editor*
M.A., Boston University
James P. Marciano *Assistant Editor/Research and Index*
A.B., Assumption College

The Consultants

Gretchen B. Armacost
Ph.D., Stanford University

David M. Weeks
Ph.D., University of California
  at Los Angeles

Paul Acker
Ph.D., Brown University

G. N. Clements
Ph.D., University of London

Ives Goddard
Ph.D., Harvard University

Robert M. Good
Ph.D., Yale University

Roberto Miranda
A.M., Harvard University

Production

Christopher Leonesio *Production Manager*
Donna L. Muise *Production Coordinator*
Patricia McTiernan *Editorial Production Assistant*
Margaret Anne Miles *Administrative Assistant*
Cara Murray *Editorial Department Secretary*

Composition Keyboarding

Brenda Bregoli-Sturtevant
Celester Jackson
Ron Perkins

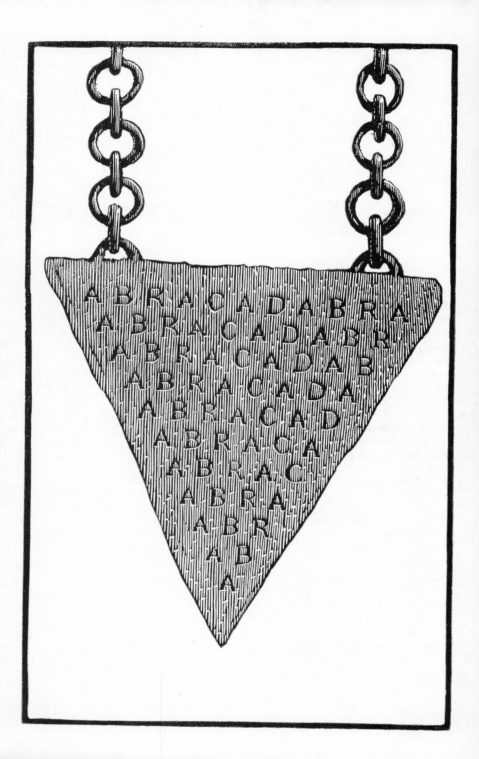

FOREWORD

Having written two books and part of a third on English words, I consider myself something of an expert on them. I was therefore both startled and delighted to discover how much of *this* particular book was new to me. The words in our English lexicon are virtually inexhaustible—and so, evidently, are the stories behind them.

No less fascinating than the stories are the people in them; one wants to know more than the dictionary's bare facts—more, even, than the sketches you'll find here. For instance, Captain William Lynch: was he a peaceable man, driven beyond endurance by the local marauders—or, perhaps, the Dirty Harry of his time, certain that the only way to cope with "lawless men" was . . . to become lawless yourself? We know something about the 4th Earl of Sandwich—notably, that he was what we'd now call a compulsive gambler. But what sort of fellow was the anonymous London wit who first transferred the name Der(r)ick from the hangman to his apparatus? Or the grinning sailor who later transported this bit of (literal) gallows humor from grim Tyburn to the deck of his ship?

Let me now introduce a couple of other "word" personalities whom you won't find in these pages, because the words they gave us are seldom used— rather a pity, under the circumstances. Around 1730 Graman Quassi, a Suri-nam black (his African surname means "born on Sunday"), discovered the medicinal properties of the South American *quassia* tree. The dictionaries tell us no more than that. Yet he was surely a man of consequence among his fellows, as his first name ("grand man") shows. I see him, then, as a witch doctor, respected for his knowledge of potent spells and herbal potions. Torn from his African home and shipped overseas in chains, he continued his medical practice—and, like any good doctor, kept looking for new drugs.

Abracadabra

From later in the same century we have a quite different personality, the French naturalist Pierre Sonnerat, whose mixture of curiosity and ignorance gave us a name for one of the lemurs found in Madagascar. I imagine him as a type of French savant common enough in those days (and still not extinct): fascinated with new things and new ideas—but unwilling to learn anyone else's language. Around 1780 Sonnerat was exploring the then-unknown interior of Madagascar with a native guide. Spotting a lemur, the man pointed to it, crying *Indri!* (in Malagasy, "Look!"). Sonnerat, however, thought his companion was calling out the animal's name—and *indri* it has been, in French and (later) English, ever since.

Words not only introduce us to intriguing personalities; they can take us on a journey halfway around the world in the few moments it takes to look them up. Take *parka*, for instance. Among the Samoyeds, a hunting people of northwest Siberia, it meant "reindeer hide." The word was picked up by Russian trappers and traders and applied to a skin or fur jacket. Later, the Russians passed it to the Aleuts of Alaska (then a Russian possession). When American prospectors and settlers surged into Alaska, drawn by the Gold Rush later immortalized by Charlie Chaplin, they picked up both the garment and the word; Robert W. Service, poet laureate of the Alaskan "sourdough" (look *that* one up in your dictionary!) worked it into his ballads: "Talk of the cold! through the parka's fold it stabbed like a driven nail!" The parka eventually spread to most of the English-speaking world.

Another long voyage begins at the southern tip of Africa, among the sixteenth-century Hottentots. A herding people, they guarded their cattle from nocturnal predators by penning them in enclosures of dried thorn bushes, which they called something like *curral*. The Portuguese picked up the word and passed it to the Spaniards, who pronounced it *corral*. Transplanted to America, it passed from Mexican vaqueros to English-speaking buckaroos—from the South African veldt to Portugal to the O.K. Corral!

We can journey in time as well as space. The mysterious Basques of northern Spain and southwestern France may well be descended from the Ice Age Cro-Magnon hunters whose artifacts have turned up profusely in the region; their language is certainly the sole survivor of the aboriginal tongues of Western Europe, displaced long ago by those of the Indo-European family, of which English is one. Basque *bizarra* means "beard." The Spaniards borrowed it as *bizarro*, with the sense of "handsome, brave," along the lines of their own expression, *hombre de bigote*—literally, "man with a mustache"; actually, "man of spirit." The French and Italians took the word over with the sense of "angry" or even "capricious"; in the seventeenth century, the remote descendant of the aboriginal Basque beard passed into English.

You won't find these tales in this book—but there are plenty of equally bizarre ones in it. Good reading!

Robert Claiborne

PREFACE

The recipe for the more than 500 articles in *Word Mysteries and Histories: From Quiche to Humble Pie* is found in the thousands of letters that the editors of *The American Heritage Dictionaries* have received over the years from our readers. About half those letters contain questions regarding the origins of English words—questions going far beyond mere dates of first occurrence of words in our language and often involving information not usually included in the brief etymologies given in dictionaries. These are really questions about "lexical genealogies": the histories, and quite regularly the mysteries, associated with English words.

Such curiosity is not at all surprising when one considers the fact that the speakers and writers of a language control its development in the long term. Why shouldn't they be interested in the origins of the terms in their language? In the words of Robert Claiborne, from his book *Our Marvelous Native Tongue: The Life and Times of the English Language*, "Language is people: the human comedy and tragedy. The history of English, then, is also a panorama of the living, loving, joking, cursing, arguing, poetizing, working and playing people, who, in their tens and hundreds of millions, in a score of lands and across fourscore centuries, have shaped and reshaped our native tongue into what it is."

If language is people in the sense defined by Robert Claiborne, it is no surprise that many (though by no means all) of the words examined in this book are animate nouns. In delving into the stories behind the *bromides* and *bluestockings*, the *Amazons* and *eunuchs*, the *ignoramuses* and *shysters*, the *lords* and *ladies*, the *admirals* and *generals*, the *privates* and *sad sacks*, the *geniuses* and *idiots*, the *entrepreneurs* and *intrapreneurs*, the *prunes* and *pundits,* and the *wizards, zombies,* and other *unmentionables,* we were impressed not only with the varied linguistic processes in play but also with the human dynamics affecting the language over the centuries. For instance, when a word like *hussy,* once synonymous with *housewife,* takes on a pejorative meaning over time, the users of the language are responsible for the eventual shift in meaning. Conversely, when a word like *prestige,* once associated with deception and trickery, becomes elevated in meaning, the users of the language bring about this semantic shift. When moribund words like *dais* and *car* are revived, the users of the language revive them. When foreign words like *paparazzo* immigrate into English, they are sponsored by the users of English. When *martinets, silhouettes, vandals, hectors,* and *quislings* gain entrée to our lexicon, the users of the language make these eponymous associations and bring the words into currency. And when trademarks such as *Teflon* and *STAR WARS* undergo semantic extension, the users of English are responsible. These are but a few examples.

Insofar as the English language is a reflection of the history of a far-flung, diverse, individualistic, and often unruly people, the histories of the words under discussion in this book reflect in tone, style, and length the individual sets of circumstances underlying the development of the words. For instance, the articles about words such as *apartheid, assets,* and *hearse* differ markedly from the ones about words such as *court, fizzle,* and *funky.* And when origins of words like *jazz* and *posh* are obscure or disputed, we treat them as mysteries. Each article in the alphabetically ordered list is self-contained; that is, the reader does not have to follow cross-references from one section of the book to others in order to understand the background of a word. An index lists the words under discussion in the text. "The Last Word," a brief encapsulation of the history of English, the linguistic processes examined herein, and the scholarly sources consulted during our research, is found at the end of the text.

The Foreword by Robert Claiborne, whose memorable statement "Language is people" inspired us to undertake this book, is the appetizer to *Word Mysteries and Histories: From Quiche to Humble Pie.* Mr. Claiborne, an editor and writer for more than twenty-five years, has had a lifelong fascination for words. This fascination is evident in his many books, among them *The Birth of Writing* (1974), *Our Marvelous Native Tongue* (1983), and most recently, *Saying What You Mean: A Commonsense Guide to American Usage* (1986). Mr. Claiborne contributed to Eric Partridge's classic work on language, *A Dictionary of Slang and Unconventional English,* and is the major American contributor to the second edition of Partridge's *Dictionary of Catch Phrases.* He is now at work on *The Book of Lost Metaphors.*

To the extent that in Ruskin's view "Great nations write their autobiographies in three manuscripts—the book of their deeds, the book of their words, and the book of their art," a volume offering up a soupçon of lexical history, however brief, demands the very best in illustration. We therefore commissioned especially for this book dozens of original wood engravings by the internationally acclaimed artist Barry Moser, whose Pennyroyal Press edition of *Alice in Wonderland* won the 1982 American Book Award for the best illustrated book of the year. His illustrations have graced other diverse works such as *Moby Dick*, *Frankenstein*, *The Wizard of Oz*, and *Huckleberry Finn*. Barry Moser's illustrations represent the element of artistry that Ruskin found inextricably linked to the histories of great nations.

We would like to give special acknowledgment to the work of our colleague Marion Severynse, Ph.D. Dr. Severynse's work on the word history paragraphs in *Webster's II New Riverside University Dictionary* provided a foundation for this book. Her word histories, characterized by William Safire as evincing "the light touch of original scholarship," have been invaluable to us in developing this entirely new work.

Dear readers, it is now time to pick up your *runcible* spoons and join us for a *brunch* of word lore. We hope that you will be *tantalized* and *mesmerized* by the stories behind the *canapés* and the *cordials*, the *garlic* and the *kale*, the *vermicelli* and the *lame duck*, not to mention the *schmaltz* and all the other ingredients from which we have prepared *Word Mysteries and Histories: From Quiche to Humble Pie*.

Anne H. Soukhanov
Executive Editor

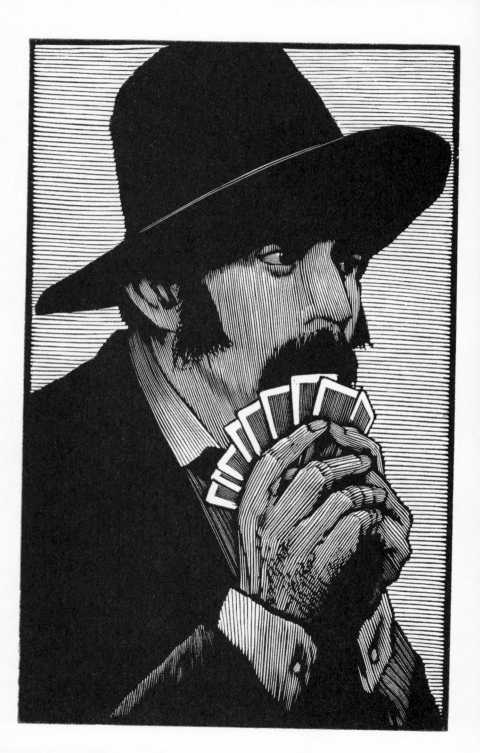

aboveboard   Cardsharps take note: the term *aboveboard*, now meaning "without deceit or trickery," is a compound of *above* and *board*, the latter of which once meant "a table of any kind." *Aboveboard* is a gambler's term recorded as early as the seventeenth century. If the gambler's hands were above the board or gaming table, then presumably he could not surreptitiously change his cards or indulge in other forms of cheating. *Board* still harks back to its original sense of "table" in the expressions *room and board* (*board* being a table at which food is served) and *board of directors* (*board* being a table where a council is held).

abracadabra   "Abracadabra," says the magician, unaware that at one time the thing to do with the word was wear it, not say it. *Abracadabra* was a magic word, the letters of which were arranged in an inverted pyramid and worn as an amulet around the neck to protect the wearer against disease or trouble. One less letter appeared in each line of the pyramid, until only *a* remained to form the vertex of the triangle. As the letters disappeared, so supposedly did the disease or trouble. While magicians still use *abracadabra* in

Aboveboard

their performances, the word itself has acquired another commonly known sense, "foolish or unintelligible talk."

absurd   *Absurdus* in Latin meant "silly" and "irrational," just as *absurd* does in English, but its literal sense was "out of tune." It was used figuratively outside the realm of music and acoustics to mean "out of harmony with reason."

accident   *Accident* unfortunately occurs in general use all too often, but when it first came into English its senses were chiefly technical. If it had retained only these senses, we would probably use the word rarely today. *Accident* goes back to a Latin word that meant "a chance event" and also "a contingent attribute." The second sense was useful to medieval philosophers and theologians in discussing the nonessential characteristics of things. Such characteristics were particularly important in regard to the nature of the sacramental bread and wine. *Accident* was used to refer to their outward physical properties, such as texture, color, and taste. The philosophers and theologians thought that after transubstantiation the essence of the bread and wine was changed though the accidents remained. Physicians also used the word *accident* in various ways, for example, as a term for a disease that was not normal or natural.

These technical senses of *accident* are used rarely if at all by the general public, but the first Latin sense, "a chance event," has associated with it two senses that are heard everywhere and that keep the word firmly entrenched in the language. One sense is "a bad chance event," perhaps illustrating the unhappy nature of many a chance event. The other sense, "chance," is often seen in the phrase *by accident*.

acre   An acre is 4,840 square yards to us, but to a speaker of Old English an *æcer*, the ancestor of *acre*, could have been any number of square yards. Old English *æcer* meant "a field, land," as well as "a particular quantity of land," said in Anglo-Saxon times to be the amount of land a yoke of oxen could plow in one day. Although the size of the measure of land varied in different places and at different times, it was set by statute during the Middle Ages at 4,840 square yards, the amount it remains today. Old English *æcer* is descended from the same Indo-European form as Latin *ager* and Greek *agros*, which both mean "field."

admiral
An American or British admiral probably would not think he had much in common with an emir, "a prince, chieftain, or governor, especially in the Middle East." Historically, however, the words *admiral* and *emir* are both related to the Arabic word *'amīr*, meaning "commander." The connection between *emir* and *'amīr* is easy to see. The close relationship of the two words reflects the fact that *emir* was borrowed into English in the seventeenth century as an Arabic or Moslem title. In *admiral*, however, the relationship to *'amīr* is disguised by the presence of the *d* and the *al*. The *al* is explained by the fact that *admiral* goes back to the Arabic phrase *'amīr a 'ālī*, "high commander." The *d* appears first in the Medieval Latin and Old French forms, from which *admiral* came into English, becoming standard during the sixteenth century.

Admiral does not, however, mean the same thing as *'amīr*. The tie of an admiral to the sea is explained by the fact that in Europe, beginning in Sicily during the twelfth century, a naval commander was designated by words going back to the Arabic word *'amīr*.

adust
Literally and etymologically, *adust* doesn't have a speck of dust on it. *Adust* acquired the meaning "burned, scorched," directly from its Latin ancestor *adustus*, the past participle of *adūrere*, "to set fire to." *Adust* came to mean "melancholy, gloomy," through its use in early medical writings. Dryness, heat, and a burnt color of the body and its components, such as

blood, certain organs, and the skin, were considered symptoms of a melancholy temperament. So a dust cloth and Lemon Pledge® won't help at all if you feel adust today.

algorithm *Algorithm* has a wonderful high-tech sound, as if it had been coined recently for the world of Silicon Valley. *Algorithm*, however, can be traced back to a ninth-century Moslem mathematician, Mohammed ibn-Musa al-Khwarizmi (780–850?). So named because he came from Khwarizm, a region in south-central Asia, al-Khwarizmi is perhaps most important to us because Arabic numerals became generally known in Europe through a translation of his work on algebra. He also wrote a treatise on algorism, the Arabic or decimal system of numeration, in which he was the first to discuss these numerals. *Algorism*, named after him, gave rise to the variant spelling *algorithm*, probably influenced by the word *arithmetic* or its Greek source *arithmos*, "number." With the development of sophisticated mechanical computing devices in the twentieth century, *algorithm* was adopted as a convenient word for a recursive mathematical procedure, the computer's stock in trade. In its new life as a computer term *algorithm*, no longer a variant of *algorism*, maintains the presence of the great Arab mathematician amid all those little bits and bytes.

alibi "I don't have an alibi for not getting you a birthday present," we say without necessarily realizing that we owe the word *alibi* to the language of the law. The Latin word *alibī*, "elsewhere," in its first recorded use as a noun in English meant "the plea of having been elsewhere at the time when any alleged act took place." Perhaps because frail human beings cannot have too many words that mean "excuse" or "apology," we have appropriated this term to mean simply "an excuse," although our speaker may have been elsewhere at the time the birthday present should have been bought.

4

aloof Those who own their own yachts might feel that they ought to remain aloof from those who would otherwise seek invitations for cruises. But at one time the yacht itself could have sailed aloof. *Aloof* is made up of the prefix *a-*, meaning "in the direction of," as in *aback*, and the word *luff*, "the windward side of a ship." A yacht sailing aloof would sail with its bow into the wind. Doing so would keep the ship from being blown by the wind toward the lee shore, for example. The fact that the ship kept its distance from something, such as a shore, when it sailed aloof led to the development of the senses "away at some distance" and "from a distance," which were later extended to become the sense "without community of feeling; distant, indifferent." Two other nautical terms that have seeped into everyday life and have lost their salty tang are *average* and *ahead*—one of the earliest senses of which was "in front of a moving company of ships."

alto Does *alto* mean a male or a female singing voice? No matter which gender you choose you will be correct. An *alto* can be a countertenor, the highest male voice. *Alto*, borrowed from Italian and meaning "high," is first recorded in English with reference to a person with a countertenor voice. Not long after coming into English *alto* was extended to refer to the female singing voice known also as *contralto* because the range of the female alto is similar to that of the highest male singing voice.

Amazon In Greek mythology an Amazon was a member of a tribe of female warriors. The Greeks themselves devised what is probably a folk etymology for *Amazon*, the ancestor of the English word *Amazon*. According to Greek legends, the Amazons cut off one of their breasts so they could use a bow more easily. The word thus appears to be formed in Greek from the prefix *a-*, "not," and *mazos*, "breast," referring to the Amazons' mutilated condition. This explanation, however, is probably not the correct one. It is possible

5

that Greek *Amazon* comes from an Iranian tribal name with the assumed form *ha-mazān-*, meaning "warrior."

ambition A modern politician may be full of ambition, but if he or she had lived in ancient Rome, ambition would have entailed some very practical politicking. The Latin word *ambitiō*, which gave us our word *ambition*, meant "desire for advancement," just as it does today. However, an earlier sense of the word was "a soliciting of votes, canvassing." *Ambitiō* comes from *ambīre*, a combination of *ambi-*, "about," and *īre*, "to go." *Ambīre* could mean "to canvass, solicit for political support," as well as "to canvass for an office, prize, etc." Corresponding senses of *ambitiō* were "a standing for public office" and "rivalry for honors." Related to these senses of *ambitiō* were the senses "currying favor" and our own "desire for advancement." In Middle English *ambicioun* was only negative, as in the statement, "ambition [is] an evil wish to be great," but by Shakespeare's time *ambition* had developed the positive sense "a strong desire for something that gives honor or is advantageous." *Ambition* today can be viewed as positive or negative, but though it may give rise to a lot of work, it does not necessarily involve canvassing.

among Among friends of the English language it could be safely said that *among* is a useful but colorless word without real interest in itself. But *among* contains more than meets the eye of one who does not look into its past. It has been suggested that a predecessor of *among* was the Old English phrase *on gemang*, containing the words *on*, "in," and *gemang*, "crowd"; hence meaning, as a phrase, "in the company of." In an Old English poem the emperor Constantine orders a banner with the Cross on it to be carried *on feonda gemang*, "in the throng of enemies." The phrase became a preposition with the sense "surrounded by."

Amazon

Although there is more to the story of how we got the preposition *among*, one part of it is that the phrase *on gemang* became shortened to the word *onmang*, which in turn became *among*, a seemingly colorless word among the company of its more colorful brothers and sisters.

Annie Oakley Annie Oakley was a sharpshooter with Buffalo Bill Cody's Wild West Show who sometimes used playing cards as targets. Free passes punched to prevent their being sold were thought to resemble Annie Oakley's handiwork. Annie Oakley herself explained this in the New York *World* of June 28, 1922. "A man was brought to [Ban Johnson, president of the American League of Professional Base Ball Clubs from 1900 to 1927] who had rented out his baseball pass. Ban Johnson looked at it, filled with neat holes, and suggested that the man had been letting me use it as a target." The term has been extended to mean "anything with many holes punched in it." In 1934 we find mention of an *Annie Oakley* spinnaker, which was "a . . . balloon of canvas with holes punched in it like a complimentary ticket." The "free" aspect of an *Annie Oakley* is emphasized in the use of the term in the 1940's for a base on balls, or a "free" trip to first base when the pitcher throws four balls.

Antares Antares is the brightest star in the southern sky. Its Greek name *Antarēs* can be interpreted in more than one way: "against Mars," "opposite Mars," or "instead of Mars." Since the planet Mars, which the Greeks called *Arēs*, moves through the sky, it is not always opposite Antares in position. The Greek name *Antarēs* more likely refers to the star's pronounced red color, which sometimes causes the star to be identified as Mars.

antenna A television antenna does not look much like an insect feeler, nor does either one immediately call to mind a sail yard, "a spar or yard on which a sail is spread." All three things are connected, however, in the development of our word *antenna*. The connection between a sail yard and an insect feeler was made by Theodorus Gaza in a translation of Aristotle's *History of Animals*. This medieval scholar was faced with the problem of translating the Greek word *keraia*, meaning "an insect horn or feeler," into Latin. He knew that *keraia* also meant "yardarm, a projecting 'horn' or end of a sail yard," and therefore thought that the Latin word *antenna*, meaning "sail yard, yardarm," was an appropriate translation. In our own modern period *antenna* was extended to refer to a radio aerial wire, perhaps because of its resemblance to an insect feeler. It was then natural to name a television aerial an *antenna* as well.

antic To damage an *antique* would be too serious an offense to be considered a mere *antic*. This sentence is one of the few ways these two words can visit each other, even though they are etymological blood relatives. The source of *antic*, "a ludicrous or extravagant act or gesture," is the Italian word *antico*, which means "ancient." The Italians used *antico* to refer to the grotesque designs found on some ancient Roman artifacts. *Antico* is derived from *antīquus*, the same Latin word from which *antique* is derived. The two words are separate borrowings, and the English words *antic* and *antique* do not share any meanings.

apartheid Although South Africa has not furnished a great number of words that have achieved general currency in British and American English, one in particular, *apartheid*, has gained wide circulation. The first recorded use of *apartheid* as an English term, in the *Cape Times* on October 24, 1947, is an ironic commentary on much of the word's use since then: "Mr. Hofmeyr said apartheid could not be reconciled with a policy of progress and prosperity for South Africa." According to the March 15, 1961, issue of the London *Times*, the word *self-development* was supposed to replace *apartheid* as the official term used by the South

9

African Broadcasting Corporation for "the Government's race policies." And in *Move Your Shadow*, published in 1985, Joseph Lelyveld says that the "word is [now] shunned, even resented by the [National Party's] high priests as if it were an epithet fashioned by the country's enemies." But *apartheid* as a word and as a reality has not disappeared.

The history of *apartheid*, however, offers a possible model for change in this policy, for the word is an example of a mixture and combination of resources, in this case linguistic. *Apartheid* is an English word that came into South African English from Afrikaans, the language of the Dutch settlers of South Africa. They in turn had made up the word from the Dutch word *apart*, "separate," and the suffix *–heid*, which corresponds to our suffix *–hood*. Thus *apartheid* literally means "separateness." The Dutch had earlier borrowed the word *apart*, as did we, from the French phrase *a part*, meaning "to the side."

apron "Put on your *napron*," "pierce the wood with a *nauger*," and "kill the *numpire*" would be everyday phrases had it not been for a linguistic phenomenon illustrated by these three words. From incorrect division of the phrases *a napron*, *a nauger*, and *a noumpere* came the phrases *an apron*, *an auger*, and *an oumpere*. By losing the initial *n*, the words *apron*, *auger*, and *oumpere* (later *umpire*) had their etymological histories obscured. *Apron*, when it was *napron*, clearly showed that it came from Old French *naperon*, "tablecloth," a word with connections to *napkin* and *napery*. *Auger*, when it was *nauger*, gave some indication that it went back to Old English *nafogār*, a compound word made of *nafu*, "wheel hub" (related to *navel*), and *gār*, "spear." An *auger* is thus a tool for piercing and boring holes, like the hole in a wheel through which the axle passes. And *umpire*, when it was *noumpere*, showed clear traces of its derivation from Old French *nonper*, which is made up of *non*, "not," and *per*, "equal," as is someone who is requested to act as arbiter of a dispute between two parties.

argosy

Your mind is tossing on the ocean;
There, where your argosies with portly sail,
Like signiors and rich burghers on the flood,
Or, as it were, the pageants of the sea,
Do overpeer the petty traffickers,
That curtsy to them, do them reverence,
As they fly by them with their woven wings.
—Shakespeare, *The Merchant of Venice*, Act I, Scene 1

The lordly argosy, the largest type of merchant sailing vessel, is named for Ragusa, now known as Dubrovnik, Yugoslavia. In the Middle Ages Ragusa, a great merchant republic allied with Venice, had a flourishing trade with England. In sixteenth-century English the name *Ragusa* was spelled with an *a* preceding the *r*, as in *Aragouse*. In such spellings we see at work the linguistic process of metathesis, the switching of two sounds of a word, in this case the sounds represented by *r* and *a*. Thus when the Italian word *ragusea*, meaning "a Ragusan ship," came into English, the metathesis present in English forms of the city name led to or supported metathesis in the ship name; hence *argosy* rather than the earliest recorded form of the word, *ragusye*. There is no hint of a connection between *argosy* and the ship *Argo*, in which, according to Greek mythology, Jason sailed in search of the Golden Fleece.

arrest

If we overhear the word *arrest* in a conversation, we can reasonably assume that the situation under discussion involves police custody, perhaps a cell. Overhearing the word *arrêt*, the French descendant of the Old French word *arreste*, which was borrowed into Middle English about four hundred years ago, we would not have warrant for the same assumption. *Arrêt* in French has many current senses, including "stopping," "decree," and "impounding," as well as the legal sense of "arrest." *Arrêt* also occurs in numerous phrases such as *trajet sans arrêt*, "nonstop journey," and *arrêt de la circulation*, "traffic jam." We see in the English development of *arrest* a linguistic phenomenon called specialization. As a result of this process, the semantic range of *arrest* has narrowed in general usage. While in French *arrêt* has many senses and enters into many phrases, in English *arrest* is probably most commonly used in its legal senses and does not enter into numerous phrases. If *arrest* had not narrowed in this way, in English as in French we might have "a journey without arrest" and "an arrest of traffic."

asset   Is it ever possible to have enough assets? Whether it is or isn't, *asset* is related to a word meaning "enough." *Asset* comes from the old legal term *assets*, which was not a plural noun (*asset* plus –*s*); in fact, it was not a noun at all but rather an adjective. *Assets* was originally *asetz* or *asez*, an Old French word meaning simply "enough," as does *assez*, the modern French form. *Assets* was used as legal shorthand for "enough wealth to settle the claims made against a deceased person's estate." Because *assets* looked like a plural form and had a collective meaning, the word was mistakenly analyzed by a process known as back-formation as being the base word *asset* with the plural affix –*s*. The singular form *asset* appeared in the nineteenth century to denote a single item in the assets column of a balance sheet, and from that usage the figurative meanings developed.

atlas   The word *atlas*, referring to a collection of maps, is derived only indirectly from the name of the mythological figure Atlas, a Titan condemned to support the heavens on his shoulders. *Atlas*, the title of a work by the great sixteenth-century Flemish geographer Gerhardus Mercator, consisted of two parts, a treatise on cosmology and a collection of maps. Mercator named the entire work after Atlas, a legendary king of northern Africa who was sometimes identified with, or considered descended from, the Titan Atlas. King Atlas was renowned for his learning, especially in astronomy. He was depicted on the title page of Mercator's work holding and measuring a globe; a mapped globe lies at his feet. Mercator's successors retained the title *Atlas* for their collections of maps, and the word became generic for any similar work.

12

attic　Attics have long been the residences of starving authors and mad relatives—inhabitants who may belie the elegant origins of the word *attic*. *Attic* goes back through French and Latin to the Greek word *Attikos*, "relating to Attica or its chief city Athens." In French *attique* referred to, among other things, "a decorative architectural structure placed above another decorative structure of much greater height." This structure usually made use of the *Attic order*, an architectural order having square columns of any of the basic five orders, such as Doric or Corinthian, with pilasters rather than pillars. The English, who also built these structures, borrowed the French term for them. The story of the building enclosed by this decorative structure was called the *Attic story*. *Story* later disappeared from the phrase and left us with the lowercase word *attic*, stripped of its elegant associations, for the top story of a house.

avalanche　An *avalanche* is a natural phenomenon that few people are unfortunate enough to see firsthand. But since avalanches are not uncommon in the Alps, it is not surprising that French dialects spoken in the Alps contain related words for "a fall or slide of a large mass of snow, rock, or other material down a mountainside." The French word *avalanche*, which gives us our word *avalanche*, is related to *avalantze* and *vallantze*, all three words meaning "avalanche." The origin of these words is disputed, but it is thought that they come from the assumed earlier word *lavanca*, "avalanche," which also became the Old Provençal word *lavanca*, meaning "ravine." The assumed word *lavanca* is akin to the Latin verb *labī*, meaning, appropriately enough, "to slide."

average　An average day may not be wonderful, but it might at least be unblemished. The history of the word *average*, however, is full of blemishes and damage. The word *average* came into English from the Old French word *avarie*, "damage to shipping." Its ultimate source is the Arabic word *'awārīyah*, "damaged goods," a derivative of *'awār*, "blemish." *Average* is first recorded in English around 1500 as a maritime term referring in general to any expense, such as a loss from damage, over and above the cost of shipping freight. These expenses were usually distributed proportionally among the interested parties in the venture. It is from the notion of the distribution of a sum to a number of persons that the idea of a mathematical average—the arithmetic mean—developed, and from this sense of a "mean" or "medium" figure that the senses of the adjective *average*, "typical" and "usual," are derived.

ax to grind Grinding axes is no longer a common task for urban or even suburban men and women. Today, many of us may not even realize that *grind* means "to sharpen" in the expression *to have an ax to grind*. When someone with such an ax approaches us, however, we are wary because we do know that they are pursuing a selfish or subjective aim and are unlikely to have our best interests or the interests of anyone else, for that matter, at heart. The expression *to have an ax* (or *axe*) *to grind* originated in the days when many people still sharpened axes. It is said to have come from a story by the nineteenth-century journalist Charles Miner (alias Poor Robert) about a seemingly friendly man who was able by flattery to persuade a young boy to turn a grindstone for him. The story first appeared in the Luzerne, Pennsylvania, *Federalist* on September 7, 1810, under the title "Who'll Turn Grindstones?" and later in an 1815 book entitled *Essays from the Desk of Poor Robert the Scribe*. Because "Poor Robert" was confused with "Poor Richard," the story has often been erroneously attributed to Benjamin Franklin.

Although originated by an American less famous than Franklin, the phrase is nevertheless an Americanism—a word or expression originating in the United States. It was also at first restricted to political contexts. Quotations from James Joyce ("Skin-the-Goat . . . evidently with an axe to grind, was airing

14

his grievances") and George Bernard Shaw ("Distinguished statesmen of different nations . . . each with a national axe to grind") attest that the phrase has traveled abroad and, as we know, is no longer found only in political contexts. So we can be on the lookout all the more for those in politics and out who need help in grinding their axes—and simply tell them that we don't do axes.

ballot The earliest meaning of *ballot* in English is "a small ball used to register a vote," which was also the meaning of the Italian word *ballotta*, the source of the English word. The ball was dropped into a box or other container, and in this manner it was possible to vote secretly. When yea and nay votes were recorded with different colored balls, a black ball was often used to register a negative vote. This practice gave rise to the verb *blackball*, meaning "to exclude someone from membership by a negative vote."

bank I will meet you opposite the *bank* of the river near the *bank* building by the door closest to the *bank* of elevators. In this sentence we recognize three different nouns spelled *bank*. All three are possibly derived from the same Germanic ancestors. The first *bank* was borrowed in the early Middle English period, probably from Old Norwegian, which used the word to refer to natural objects like a bank of clouds or the bank of a river. This *bank* retains those senses and has extended them to manmade objects. Another noun *bank*, "a financial institution," appeared in English in the late fifteenth century as a borrowing of

Book

the Italian word *banca*, "moneychanger's table," via the French word *banque*. Italian *banca* is derived from the ancestor of German *Bank*, "bench," although in the process of borrowing, the meaning became more specialized. The third noun *bank* appeared in Middle English with the meaning "bench" in the judicial sense; it is now used for sets of things arranged in rows, like elevators. This *bank* was borrowed from the Old French word *banc*, a derivative of Late Latin *bancus*. The Late Latin word is ultimately derived from the same Germanic forms that gave rise to the Old Norwegian ancestor of the first English *bank* and to the German ancestor of the second English *bank*.

barnacle   The history of *barnacle* is a tangled and encrusted story. The word does not appear before the fifteenth century in English, into which it came from Old French *bernacle* and Latin *bernacula*, both meaning "a kind of wild goose." The word in English was originally applied only to the bird now called the *barnacle goose*; its application to the crustacean is of considerably later date. Because the bird summers in the Arctic and was never observed to breed, fantastic theories were elaborated to account for its genesis. One theory was that the bird grew from the little shells found on trees or driftwood by the seashore. These shells are what are now known as *barnacles*. The heat of the sun, which Shakespeare tells us bred crocodiles from the Nile, was also supposed to cause the small crustaceans to grow into the large birds.

bastard   *Australians pride themselves on their imperviousness to excitement. The phrase "she's a bastard" is usually regarded as adequate for most dramas from your four-year drought to bush fires.*
                                                      —*The Observer*, December 18, 1960

The useful term *bastard*, which simply means "something bad or annoying," gains what force it still has from the fact that at one time it referred to an individual cloaked in ignominy, though through no per-

18

sonal fault. The origin of the word *bastard,* "an illegitimate child," has been thought to be ignominious as well. In Old French one name for a bastard was *fils de bast,* which may have literally meant "child of a packsaddle." The term *fils de bast* referred to the unsanctified circumstances in which the child was conceived. Travelers used packsaddles as pillows—often, no doubt, as pillows for impromptu marriage beds. The word *bastard,* therefore, was thought to have been formed in Old French from *bast,* "packsaddle," and the suffix *–ard.* More probably, however, the Old French word *bastard* goes back to the Germanic word *banstu,* "liaison; a marriage in addition to one's regular one," from which is also derived the Old Frisian word *bōst,* meaning "marriage." Despite the later ignominy connected with the term, *bastard* in French and in English was originally a quasi-legal term referring to the facts of birth, whether conception took place on a packsaddle or not.

bathroom   "Could you please tell me where the lavatory is?" may sound precious to some when the word *bathroom* will do nicely. But the users of the term *bathroom* may be surprised to learn that it, as well as *lavatory,* is an example of euphemism, the substitution of an inoffensive term for one considered offensive. Euphemistic designations abound for the place where one performs those bodily functions necessary to a healthy daily existence. Some of these euphemisms have been replaced by others over time, as was *privy* by *toilet* in America and then *toilet* often by terms such as *rest room* and *bathroom.* Other euphemisms, such as *comfort station, water closet, little boys'* or *little girls' room,* and the totally obfuscatory *facilities,* will spring to mind. But none is quite as down to earth, yet as euphemistic, as the German expression *Ich gehe wo der Kaiser selbst zu Fuss geht,* "I go where the Kaiser himself goes on foot."

bay   While contemplating the *bays* ("honor, renown") in her life, she sits by a *bay* window overlooking the *bay* while a *bay* horse trots by on the beach below and a nearby hound *bays* at the moon. As unlikely as this sentence is, it illustrates the fact that in *The American Heritage Dictionary, Second College Edition,* we find five homonyms with different meanings and origins that are spelled *bay* and pronounced (bā). These English *bays* derive from words that were, in fact, not homonyms. As a group they illustrate that words can change their "shapes" over time. The following list contains the words to which our five *bays* go back: Latin *bāca*, "berry"; Vulgar Latin *batāre*, "to gape or yawn"; Old Spanish *baia*, "bay (of water)"; Latin *badius*, "reddish brown"; and Vulgar Latin *batāre*, "to gape or yawn," possibly by way of the assumed Medieval Latin word *abbaiāre*, "to utter a prolonged bark." You can see by matching senses that these words are the sources respectively for *bay*, "the laurel, laurel crown, or honor"; *bay*, "a bay window"; *bay*, "a body of water"; *bay*, "reddish brown"; and *bay*, "to utter a prolonged bark."

bead The connection between a bead and the Old English word, meaning "prayer," from which it derives is in the Christian practice, begun in the Middle Ages, of keeping count of prayers by means of beads threaded on a string. Telling one's beads—or saying one's prayers—with the aid of a rosary was such a common way of praying that the Middle English descendant of the Old English word gradually became the word for the counter as well as the prayer that was counted. By modern times *bead* no longer meant "prayer" at all but had been extended to signify other small round objects, such as drops of water.

bed When we lie down in our bed at night, with its box springs, mattress, sheets, blankets, and pillows, we are far removed in terms of comfort from the users of an earlier form of the word *bed*. Our word goes back to the Indo-European root *bhedh-*, meaning "to dig." In prehistoric Common Germanic, the reconstructed ancestor of languages such as English, German, and

Swedish, the word derived from the Indo-European root meant "a garden plot, flower bed," and "a sleeping place." The connection between digging and a place for sleeping lies in the notion that beds, or resting places, were at one time dug out of the ground.

belly If you told your doctor that you had a pain in the belly, he or she might ask where in your abdomen this pain was located. *Abdomen* is now the polite term for the area of the body that lies between the chest and the pelvis and encloses the viscera. The use of *abdomen* for *belly* is an example of euphemism—substitution of an inoffensive term for one considered offensive. *Abdomen* seems to have been a scientific term for the belly since the seventeenth century. *Belly*, though a general term, was at one time used in medical texts, as it was in Sir Thomas Watson's *Lectures on the Principles and Practice of Physic* in 1843, a context in which it would no longer be acceptable. It would seem, however, that *abdomen* cannot claim the whole field. *Abdomen-dancing*, *abdomenbuttons*, and *abdomenaching* would appear to be far in the future.

blackmail Blackmail has nothing whatever to do with the post office. *Black* is used in the figurative sense of "evil" or "wicked." *Mail* is a Scots word meaning "rent" or "tribute." The term *blackmail* originated in Scotland, where Highland chiefs at one time extorted tribute from Lowlanders and Englishmen on the Scottish border in return for protection from being plundered.

blue chip Blue chips in poker are usually the chips with the highest value. It is from this usage that the term *blue chip* is applied to highly regarded stocks. Its first recorded appearance with this meaning occurs in the October 30, 1929, edition of the Baltimore *Sun*. The usage is figurative and the sentiment prophetic: "Agriculture still has too much to reclaim . . . to become a 'blue chip' in the near future."

bluestocking The term *bluestocking* originally referred to one who was informally and unfashionably dressed, wearing, for example, inexpensive cloth stockings, commonly blue or gray in color, instead of fine silk stockings. Such cloth stockings are said to have been worn by a Mr. Benjamin Stillingfleet, who was a member of a circle in eighteenth-century London that met for literary and intellectual conversation rather than fashionable amusements such as card playing. The husband of one of the members of this circle jestingly called it the "Blue-Stocking Society." Since women figured prominently in these gatherings, the term *bluestocking* was transferred, now as a sneer and without reference to the original male wearer of the stockings, to any woman with pretensions or aspirations to literature and learning.

blurb In a lifetime of reading the puffery on book jackets we may never have stopped to think about the origin of *blurb*, the term for this kind of prose. *Blurb*, in fact, does not come to us from another language, nor does it go back to an Indo-European root. The American humorist, illustrator, and author Gelett Burgess coined *blurb* in the early 1900's. He did so on a book jacket meant to be comic that he designed for his book *Are You a Bromide?* (first published in 1906). The cover pictured a well-endowed young woman whom Burgess christened Miss Belinda Blurb. Burgess himself had these words to say about *blurb* in 1914: "On the 'jacket' of the 'latest' fiction, we find the blurb; abounding in agile adjectives and adverbs, attesting that this book is the 'sensation of the year.'" Although we are indebted to Burgess for *blurb*, it is a pity that we could not also have kept some of his other coinages, including *oofle*, "a person whose name you cannot remember," and *tintiddle*, "a witty retort, thought of too late."

bodice If a *body* meet a *bodice*, what happens? *Bodice* is a specialized use of *bodies*, the plural of *body*. The spelling, first recorded in 1679, represents the old pro-

22

nunciation of the plural with a voiceless *s*. A *body* was the part of a woman's dress that covered the torso. A *pair of bodies* was an inner corsetlike garment made of two *bodies* quilted and stiffened to provide support. The word *stays*, likewise a plural, was also used for a similar garment. Since the words *body* and *bodice* both referred to a garment that covered the torso, the terms were used synonymously for a time. Today only *bodice* has kept the meaning "the upper part of a woman's dress."

bohemian   The nomadic people called Bohemians who roamed Europe from late medieval times came in fact from the borderlands of India and Iran and not from the former Czech kingdom of Bohemia. The Europeans, speculating about this people's original homeland, gave them names such as *Bohemian* and *Gypsy* (from *Egyptian*). The French word *bohémien* was also used of "social gypsies"—artists and writers who led unconventional and irregular lives, abandoning their own class of society for a much lower one. Thackeray introduced this sense of the word *bohemian* into English in *Vanity Fair* (1848). The noun *bohemia*, meaning an artistic community or its dwelling place, is derived from *bohemian* and is not directly from the name of the region and former kingdom in western Czechoslovakia.

book   A few zealots have predicted that computers may someday replace books. We think that is extremely unlikely, but if it should ever come to pass, there would be a certain lexical justice to it, since the word *book* itself attests to a previous replacement. *Book* goes back to the Indo-European root *bhago-*, meaning "beech tree." From this root was derived a Germanic word that meant "beech" and also "a beech staff for carving runes on." This word probably developed the sense "letter" and later the sense "writing." The Old English word *bōc* that comes from the Germanic word could mean "something written, such as a document or a treatise." The works were written not on beech staffs but rather on materials such as parchment and in forms such as bound volumes. These advances in technology were adopted by the early English converts to Christianity. Thus a word for a beech staff with runes on it became a word for a bound volume containing letters written in Latin characters. Clearly, the way to preserve at least the word *book* in this electronic age is to gain acceptance for it as the designation for a computer disk.

boss   Americans would stiffen at calling a person in a managerial position their master. The word *boss*, however, which we feel comfortable using, goes back to the Dutch word *baas*, which means "master." *Boss* was used in the early days of the American republic as a euphemism for *master*, probably because *boss*, coming from a foreign word, lacked the negative connotations of *master*. It has served a useful purpose, because even in a democracy somebody has to be the boss.

boutique   You would not go to an *apothecary* for the same products that you would look for in a *boutique* or a *bodega*, yet all three words are derived from the Greek word *apothēkē*, "storehouse." These words came into English by way of Latin, which borrowed the Greek word as *apothēca*. The addition of the Latin suffix *-ārius* formed a new word, *apothēcārius*, meaning "storekeeper"; the neuter plural, *apothēcāria*, meant "the things pertaining to a storekeeper." In postclassical times the Latin words came to refer primarily to the storing and selling of medicines and drugs, and with such meanings the word *apothecary* was borrowed into English. *Boutique* and *bodega* are both derived from Latin *apothēca* and came to English from French and Spanish, respectively. *Boutique* originally meant a small shop of any kind but now refers to a small, fashionable retail store. *Bodega* in Spanish means "wine cellar" or "tavern"; only in American Spanish has it been extended to mean "grocery store" as well.

bowdlerize In our permissive times Dr. Thomas Bowdler would find it difficult to know where to begin if he wished to practice the activity named for him. In his 1818 edition of Shakespeare's works, Dr. Bowdler cleansed the poet's writings of "those words and expressions . . . which cannot with propriety be read aloud in a family." Hamlet no longer uses the expression "transform honesty from what it is to a bawd," but says instead, "debase honesty from what it is." His exchange with Ophelia in which he mentions "country matters" is transformed from fifteen speeches into six.

As Bowdler noted in the preface to his multivolume work, "I can hardly imagine a more pleasing occupation for a winter's evening in the country, than for a father to read one of Shakspeare's plays to his family circle. My object is to enable him to do so without incurring the danger of falling unawares among words and expressions which are of such a nature as to raise a blush on the cheek of modesty, or render it necessary for the reader to pause, and examine the sequel, before he proceeds further in the entertainment of the evening."

In performing such a service to the father, Bowdler was actually taking over for his sister Harriet, who in 1807 had anonymously published her own expurgated Shakespeare. Bowdler's edition was far from anonymous; it sold well and drew critical attention, both pro and con. It is probably because of this critical attention that the suffix –ize, meaning "to treat according to the method of," was added to the puritanical Dr. Bowdler's name, creating the verb bowdlerize, which was first recorded in 1836 and meant "to expurgate offensive material."

boycott Charles C. Boycott seems to have been forced by his strong sense of duty into becoming a household word. Boycott was the estate agent of the Earl of Erne in County Mayo, Ireland. The earl was one of the absentee landowners who as a group held most of the land in Ireland. Boycott was chosen in the fall of 1880 to be the test case for a new policy advocated by Charles Parnell, an Irish politician who wanted land reform. Any landlord who would not charge lower rents or any tenant who took over the farm of an evicted tenant would be given the complete cold shoulder by Parnell's supporters. Boycott, a former British soldier, refused to charge lower rents and ejected his tenants. At this point members of Parnell's Irish Land League stepped in, and Boycott and his family found themselves isolated—without servants, farmhands, service in the stores, or mail delivery. Boycott's name was quickly adopted as the term for this treatment, not just in English but in other languages such as French, Dutch, German, and Russian.

bridal Champagne, not ale, flows at many modern bridal celebrations. *Bridal*, however, is a compound of two Old English words that meant "bride" and "ale." In the days when heartier drink was imbibed, the compound meant "wedding feast," but by late medieval times it was used to refer to the ceremony itself. The word *bridal* as an adjective probably arose from the widespread interpretation of *-al* as the common adjectival suffix.

bromide Several bromine compounds, especially potassium bromide, have been used medicinally as sedatives. In 1906 Gelett Burgess, the same person who coined the term *blurb*, wrote a book entitled *Are You a Bromide?* in which he used *bromide* to mean a tiresome person of unoriginal thoughts and trite conversation, the sort of person who might put you to sleep. "The Bromide does his thinking by syndicate. . . . In a word, they all think and talk alike—one may predicate their opinion upon any given subject." According to Burgess, *bromides* included personages such as Adam, Polonius, and William McKinley. *Bromide* was soon after extended to include the kind of commonplace remarks that could be expected from a bromide, such as "You're a sight for sore eyes."

brunch   "To be fashionable nowadays we must 'brunch.' Truly an excellent portmanteau word . . . indicating a combined breakfast and lunch." This quotation from *Punch* in 1896, which contains the first recorded use of the word *brunch*, is a lexicographer's dream. Not only is a definition of *brunch* given but also its etymology. *Brunch* is a portmanteau word, a term we owe to Lewis Carroll. In *Through the Looking-Glass* Humpty Dumpty uses *portmanteau* to describe the word *slithy*, saying "it's like a portmanteau—there are two meanings packed up into one word" (the meanings being "lithe" and "slimy"). Portmanteau words are also called blends. Words of this type, such as *brunch* or *motel* (from *motor* and *hotel*), sometimes endure. Usually, however, they are evanescent—such as the words *alcoholiday*, *revusical*, and *yellocution*.

bureaucrat   A bureaucrat may seem to have little connection with wool, unless he or she engages in woolgathering. The word *bureau*, however, goes back to the French word *bureau*, which originally meant "a coarse woolen material." Because this material was used to cover writing desks, it came to mean "writing desk" and "office," that is, a place containing a writing desk, as well as "a government department." These three senses were taken into English with the word *bureau*. From French, English also borrowed the words *bureaucracy* and *bureaucrat*, which were formed on the model of words such as *aristocracy* and *aristocrat*.

bus   The word for the substantial object known as a *bus* is formed from a grammatical ending, something that by itself refers to little that is substantial. *Bus* is short for *omnibus*, the Latin form of *omnis*, "all," with the plural ending *–ibus*, meaning "to or for," attached. *Omnibus* was used in the French phrase *voiture omnibus*, "vehicle for all." This phrase appeared in French around 1830 and was both borrowed and shortened to *bus* by the English before the end of the decade. *Omnibus* was also used to designate a waiter's assistant at a restaurant, though whether this usage derives from the use of *omnibus* to mean "vehicle" or if it was an independent use of the word is not clear. *Bus boy* is derived from the shortening of *omnibus* in this sense of "waiter's assistant." But the verb *bus*, meaning "to work as a bus boy," comes from *bus boy*, and not directly from the word *omnibus*.

business   "The chief business of the American people is business," stated Calvin Coolidge in 1925. In expressing these sentiments Coolidge used both an older sense of the word *business*, "one's rightful or proper concern," first recorded in 1525, and a more recent sense, "commercial, industrial, or professional dealings," first recorded in 1727. *Business* over the centuries has had numerous senses, but in many of them one feels the stir and bustle that is present in most of the senses of *busy*, from which *business* derives. If America's business is business, it may be of interest to note that *business* is much more recent as a term for a profitable way of spending one's time than *law* and *medicine*. *Law* was first used to mean "the profession of law" and *medicine* to mean "the practice of medicine" during the Middle English period.

butterfly   Is a butterfly named for the color of its excrement or because it was really a thieving witch? The first suggestion rests on the fact that an early Dutch name for the butterfly was *boterschijte*. This name is as astonishing a phenomenon as the fact that anyone ever noticed the color of butterfly excrement. Apparently, however, when the butterfly was not busy leaving colorful traces of itself, it was stealing milk and butter. This was not because of its thievish nature but because it was really a mischievous witch in the form of a winged insect. So the second suggestion is that this predilection for butter larceny gave rise to the colorful insect's name.

buxom A buxom woman in modern parlance is "healthily plump" and most likely large-bosomed as well. It is hard to believe that such a meaning grew out of the original sense "obedient," but an intermediate stage is probably to be found in the obsolete sense "gracious, courteous, obliging." This usage developed into the sense "lively, jolly," and from there it was a short step to using *buxom* to indicate someone who looked lively and jovial, as ample-figured persons are reputed to be.

caldron You cannot cook a *chaldron* of *chowder* in a *caldron*,
but if you could, you would be dealing with three
words from the same pot. All three go back to the
same Late Latin word *caldāria*, "kettle." *Caldron*, at
that time spelled *caudron*, is the earliest form, appearing in Middle English in the fourteenth century. It
was borrowed from Anglo-Norman, which preserved
the original *k* sound of *c* that occurred in the Latin
form. The other forms of *caldāria* came from the central French variant of *caudron* and reflect the change
of Latin *c* to *ch* characteristic of this dialect. *Chaldron*, from the Old French word *chauderon*, was at
first used in English as a synonym of *caldron*, meaning "kettle," but by the nineteenth century it meant
a unit of dry measure used only for coal. It is therefore not possible to cook a chaldron of *chowder*, the
third word that goes back to Latin *caldāria*. *Chowder*
came into English from the modern French word
chaudière, "pot." It was borrowed in the eighteenth
century with the meaning "fish stew," a meaning it
probably developed in the French spoken in Brittany
and the Maritime Provinces of Canada. *Chowder* is
not the only word for a cooking vessel that has come
to denote the contents instead: *lasagna*, derived from

Cat

Latin *lasanum,* "cooking pot," and *casserole,* from French *casserole,* "saucepan," are two others.

camouflage   *Camouflage,* "the method or result of concealing personnel or materiel from an enemy by making them appear to be part of the natural surroundings," came into English during World War I along with other terms, such as *gas mask* and *tank,* that document the grim reality of warfare. *Camouflage,* which was borrowed from French, has something of an artistic heritage, however. One sense of *camouflage* in French, preceding its military use, was "all that concerns the complete transformation of an actor for the interpretation of a role, including costume and make-up." *Camouflage* did not long remain only in military dress, for even during World War I it had also come to mean merely "concealment," a general sense that *camouflage* already had, and still has, in French. In 1918, only a year after the first recorded use of *camouflage* in English, George Bernard Shaw wrote, "The first necessity of such souls when truth is about, as it always is, is camouflage, or, better still, complete cover."

canapé   *Canapé* and *canopy* can be pronounced alike, but are they related otherwise? One Middle English spelling of *canopy* was *canape,* which makes its relationship to *canapé* easier to see. Our Modern English word *canapé,* however, was borrowed from French in the late nineteenth century, as is revealed by the accent mark and the French pronunciation of the *é* that some people use. Both French *canapé,* which was recently borrowed, and English *canopy,* which was first recorded in English in the late fourteenth century, come from Medieval Latin *canapeum,* which was derived from Greek *kōnōpion.* The Latin and Greek words signified a bed or couch hung about with mosquito netting. The English word *canopy* preserves the idea of a covering; the modern French word *canapé* preserves the idea of a seat and means "couch." French *canapé* also means "appetizer." The appetizer was apparently visualized by the French who invented it as a little seat for a savory tidbit.

candidate   Candidates for political office may not wish to know the origins of the term for them. *Candidate* derives from the Latin word *candidātus*, "a person standing for office," which is from Latin *candidus*, "white," and the Latin suffix *–ātus*, denoting the wearing of something. A Roman *candidātus* wore a bleached white toga (as, perhaps, a symbol of his political purity) when he went to the Forum to seek election to the magistracy. All this is harmless enough and need not bother the three-piece-suit candidates of today. What might disturb our modern-day candidates about the historical company they keep is the knowledge that a white-clad Roman *candidātus* was accompanied to the Forum by *sectātores*, "followers," who helped him get votes by bribery and bargaining.

candy   The simple noun *candy* did not occur in English until the eighteenth century. The word first appeared in the fifteenth century in the compound *sugar candy*, derived through French and Italian from the Arabic phrase *sukkar qandī*, "candied sugar." *Sugar candy* was a particular kind of sugar that resulted from boiling and crystallization. In this form sugar was often served as a confection, and in British English today *candy* is largely restricted to sweets of sugar candy. In the United States *candy* includes confections made of other ingredients besides sugar, such as chocolate, fruit, and nuts. The original sense is retained in the verb *candy*, which means "to coat with sugar."

cannibal   Etymologically speaking, a *cannibal* is neither an eater of human flesh nor a subject of the Great Khan of China, as Christopher Columbus erroneously believed to his dying day. From Indians who lived in what is now Cuba Columbus learned of a people called *Canibales* on the island of Hispaniola. Columbus referred to these people as inhabitants of *Caniba*

33

or *Canima* and thought that *Canibales* meant "people of the Great Khan." The English word *cannibal*, which is said to go back to the name *Canibales*, was used at first only as a proper name for the people discovered by Columbus. *Cannibal* became a term for those who eat human flesh because the Canibales were noted for this unfortunate propensity.

canvass What does a public opinion poll have to do with canvas, or with cannabis for that matter? The verb and noun *canvass*, which have to do with poll taking, derive from the word *canvas*, meaning "the fabric that can be made from hemp." The spelling of *canvass* with an extra *s* comes from an earlier spelling of *canvas*. Our word *canvas*, which came into English by way of Anglo-Norman and Medieval Latin, goes back to the Latin word *cannabis*, "hemp." At a later date *cannabis* itself was borrowed into English, in which it now means "hemp" and "a substance, such as marijuana, made from hemp." *Canvas* developed several verb senses, such as "to toss in a canvas sheet," "to shake thoroughly," and "to examine carefully or discuss thoroughly." It is not known how the verb developed the sense "to solicit." Once this notion was part of the verb's semantic range, however, the verb could develop senses relating to the soliciting of political support, including the sense "to take a poll of public opinion to ascertain and evaluate the degree of one's political support."

caprice When we think of the word *caprice*, hedgehogs and goats don't immediately come to mind. Yet both animals play a part in the history of *caprice*. The word comes to us from the Italian word *capriccio*, originally *caporiccio*, which first meant "fright, a state of being startled, shivering." The Italian word combined two words, *capo*, "head," and *riccio*, "hedgehog," because in a state of fright one's hair stands on end like the spines of a hedgehog. After the word changed in form from *caporiccio* to *capriccio*, the *capr–* part of the word was associated with the word *capra*, "goat,"

34

which it resembled, possibly because being startled is behavior characteristic of goats. Other goatlike behavior then became part of the meaning of the word, including impulsive behavior, which in humans can include sudden changes of mind. *Caprice* came into English through French from Italian with the sense it has today, "an impulsive change of mind."

car *Car* was a moribund word in English until modern technology brought it back to life. By the middle of the nineteenth century *car* was only a poetic synonym for *chariot,* to which it is related. With the advent of the railroad, *car* gained a new lease on life by being used in the United States for what the English call a "railway carriage." The word kept its hold on life by also being used for the part of an elevator that carries passengers or freight, but *car* really came to life after the term *motorcar* was adopted late in the nineteenth century for the automobile. *Motorcar* was soon shortened to *car,* which lost all its archaic and poetic associations in the brave new era of gas-guzzling machines.

cardinal The disparate senses of *cardinal*—"of foremost importance," "a number, such as 3 or 11 or 412, used to indicate quantity but not order," "a Roman Catholic prelate," "a deep red color," and "a North American bird"—are connected by a hinge. "Hinge" is a meaning of the Latin word *cardō,* from which Latin *cardinālis,* "serving as a hinge or pivot," is derived. In Late Latin *cardinālis* developed figuratively so as to refer to something on which something else turns or depends, that is, something that is principal or chief. The Latin *cardinālī,* or "cardinal numbers," were the numbers from which the ordinal numbers were derived. How *cardinal* came to be used for a Catholic prelate is a complex matter, but ultimately it seems to involve a figurative use of *cardō,* "hinge." The deep-red color sense of *cardinal* in English comes from the color of a cardinal's robes, as does the bird sense, for the bird's plumage is similar in color.

career An ideal career would be a steady progression from one set of responsibilities to other, increased responsibilities rather than a mad race from job to job. The pace of a modern fast-track career actually seems to reflect early senses of the word itself. In early use the English word *career*, first recorded in the sixteenth century, had such senses as "racecourse," "a short gallop at full speed," "a rapid course," and "the moment of peak activity." Clearly this was a word that had to do with speed. However, the French word *carrière*, from which *career* comes, originally meant "chariot road." In French *carrière* quite naturally developed the senses "course or progression of one's life" and "one's chosen pursuit," and these senses were borrowed into English from French in the nineteenth century. Thus, they did not develop in English from the "fast" senses of the word. Etymologically, at least, one can get one's career off the fast track and travel at normal speed on the road.

carton Can something as mundane as a carton be related to a sprightly cartoon? Both *carton* and *cartoon* come from the same French word, but because this word was borrowed into the English language at two different times, the forms of the word in English differ. The French word *carton* originally meant "pasteboard, cardboard," and was extended to mean a drawing, especially an artist's sketch, made on such material. *Carton* in the sense "drawing" was borrowed into English in the seventeenth century, at a time when the French syllable –*on* was rendered as –*oon* in English, thus giving us *cartoon*. The English word *carton* represents a nineteenth-century borrowing of the French word. By this time the original sense of "pasteboard" had been extended in French to mean a container made from stiff paper material.

Other pairs of English words are related in much the same way as *carton* and *cartoon*. *Dragon* was borrowed into Middle English from Old French; by the seventeenth century, the French word *dragon* also meant "carbine" or "a trooper armed with a carbine" and was borrowed into English as *dragoon*. *Marron*, "Spanish chestnut," and *maroon*, "reddish brown" (the color of a chestnut), were both borrowed from the French word *marron*. Both *salon* and *saloon* came from the French word *salon*, though one will rarely find the drawing-room crowd in the local saloon, or vice versa.

cat In ancient times the domestic cat did not exist in Europe. Among the Romans the Latin word *fēlis* meant "any of several small carnivorous animals, probably including the wildcat." Among the Greeks the word *ailuros* did denote the domestic cat as well as other kinds of cats, but the only domestic cats mentioned by the early Greek writers lived in Egypt. Thousands of cat mummies found in Egypt give evidence of the cat's importance in that society, and the existence of mouse mummies shows that though cats were sacred, they caught mice nonetheless.

By the fourth century A.D., however, the domestic cat had been introduced into Europe, and new words appeared for this creature: *cattus* in Latin and *kattas* in Greek. The Latin form is the source of the word for "cat" in all the Romance languages, such as French and Spanish. *Cattus*, also borrowed into West and North Germanic at an early date, is the source of the Modern English word *cat*. Some form of the word, perhaps the ancestor of the Greek and Latin forms, was borrowed into the Celtic and Slavic languages at least by the very early medieval period. Although common in Europe, the word for "cat" represented by Latin *cattus* is not of Indo-European origin. It was most likely borrowed from a language of northern Africa, which agrees with the fact that the Egyptian domestic cat probably came from a North African wildcat.

catch Nowadays if a hunter chases a quarry, he or she does not necessarily catch the animal, but it was not always so. *Catch* and *chase* are ultimately the same word but derived from two different dialects of Old

French. *Catch* descends from the Anglo-Norman form *cachier*, which meant only "to chase" and not "to catch." The Middle English word *cacchen*, the ancestor of *catch*, is first recorded in the early thirteenth century. In Middle English *cacchen* seems to have become associated with the native English word *lacchen* (the descendant of which, *latch*, occurs in our phrase *latch on to*), with which it shares many senses, including the sense "to capture." The word *chase*, on the other hand, comes from the central French, or Parisian, form *chacier*, which, like the Norman form *cachier*, meant only "to chase." "To chase" is still the meaning of the modern French word *chasser*. After the adoption of *chacier* in English in the fourteenth century, *catch* became used exclusively to mean "to capture."

cattle A rancher driving his *cattle* to market could technically say that they were his *chattels* or his *capital*, but he would be unlikely to realize that all three words go back to the same Latin adjective *capitālis*, "of the head, principal." *Cattle* and *chattel* go back through medieval French to the Medieval Latin word *capitāle*, "property," which comes from the Latin word *capitālis*. *Cattle* is derived from Anglo-Norman *catel*, which in medieval times meant "movable property" in general. The word gradually became restricted to that sense because livestock was such an important form of property. The further narrowing of *cattle* to refer only to bovine animals occurred in the nineteenth century. *Chattel* represents the central French form *chatel*. *Chatel* was adopted in medieval England as a legal term for "movable property," supplanting *cattle*. *Capital* was also borrowed from French in medieval times; it represents not the regular French development of Latin *capitāle* but instead a French reborrowing of the Latin adjective *capitālis*. The original use of *capital* in English was as an adjective, first meaning "relating to the head" and later meaning "principal" or "chief." *Capital* came to denote "wealth" when it was used to mean someone's principal substance or property.

chair   A chair is fundamentally a humble object, bearing up the weight of the world. The word *chair*, however, has ties with some of the most exalted creations of the human spirit. Our word *chair* goes back through Old French to the Classical Latin word *cathedra*, which meant "armchair" as well as "chair of a teacher." In Late Latin the word *cathedra* developed the meaning "bishop's office or position," from which arose the Late Latin and Old French words that gave us *cathedral*, "the principal church of a bishop's see, containing his throne." Though cathedrals may not come to mind when one sits in a chair, *chair* in English has continued to have elevated senses in its own right—senses such as "episcopal dignity," "the office of a professor," "mayorship," and "chairperson." These senses arise from the fact that no matter how dignified one is, one must sit somewhere, although monarchs do still prefer their thrones.

charming   In a Middle English translation of the Bible we read of "a womman havynge a charmynge goost." How nice even in one's afterlife to be charming, one might think. Another version of this same passage, however, states that the woman has "a feend spekynge in the wombe" (a devil speaking in the abdomen). Clearly this "goost" is not as charming as we thought. "Charmynge goost" really means "spirit of magic or divination," for *charming* in Middle English only had senses relating to charms and magic. *Charming* was first recorded in its present sense of "highly pleasing" in the seventeenth century, at first as a figurative extension of the previous magical sense, which is now almost completely gone. In other words, the force of the power of a charming thing no longer resides in its own magical powers but in our response to it.

chauvinism   If accused of chauvinism, one may be surprised to learn of a link between oneself and a French soldier who served under Napoleon. Nicolas Chauvin would likewise be bewildered to see his name living on as a term for someone wearing gender-colored spectacles.

Chauvin, who received seventeen wounds during the Napoleonic Wars, became in retirement a byword in his village because of his unerring and vehemently expressed devotion to his leader. Chauvin's opinions and behavior soon became known elsewhere, for he was made a humorous character in several nineteenth-century French comedies. Just as *Pollyanna*, a modern literary and film character, became a term for a certain type of person, that is, one who wears rose-colored glasses, so did the character of Chauvin lend his name to an attitude of exaggerated patriotism called in French *chauvinisme*. The English word derived from this French word, first recorded in 1870, was generalized to mean "an exaggerated devotion to one's own group or place." Recently *chauvinism* has narrowed in meaning and become notorious. First it became part of the phrase *male chauvinism*, and then, as if to make a feminist statement, *chauvinism* shed the *male* and acquired the simple meaning "antifeminism."

cheap   We travel by a supersaver fare, not a cheap fare; we buy inexpensive clothing, not cheap clothes; and we don't want to be considered cheap. *Cheap* is an example of a word that has suffered pejoration, the semantic process by which meaning degenerates over time. Before *cheap* could undergo this process, however, it had to become an adjective. Old English *cēap* and its Middle English descendant *chep*, from which our *cheap* derives, were nouns with neutral senses such as "bargain," "price." Middle English *chep* was commonly used in phrases: *god chepe*, "a favorable bargain," *light chepe*, "at a favorable price," and *gret chep*, "low-priced." From the shortening of phrases like these came our adjective *cheap*, first recorded as standing by itself in 1509 and meaning simply "costing little." What costs little may not always be of good quality, and over time *cheap* also came to mean "of poor quality." This new, pejorative sense has not robbed *cheap* of all value: something that is cheap at half the regular price is a bargain and is well worth having.

check If the former Shah of Iran had ever lost a game of chess played for money and had to write a check to the winner, he would have been in a delightful etymological situation, for the three words *check*, *chess*, and *shah* are all related. *Shah*, as one might think, was borrowed into English directly from the Persian title for the monarch of that country. The Persian word *shāh* was also a term used in chess, a game played in Persia long before it was introduced to Europe. One said *shāh* as a warning when the opponent's king was under attack. The Persian word in this sense, after passing through Arabic, probably Old Spanish, and then Old French, came into Middle English as *chek* about seven hundred years ago. *Chess* itself comes from a plural form of the Old French word that gave us the word *check*. *Checkmate*, the next stage after *check*, goes back to the Persian phrase *shāh māt*, meaning "the king is stymied."

Through a complex development having to do with senses that evolved from the notion of checking the king, *check* came to mean something used to be sure of such things as accuracy and authenticity. One such means was a counterfoil, a part of a check, for example, retained by the issuer as documentation of a transaction. *Check* first meant "counterfoil" and then came to mean anything, such as a bill or a bank draft, with a counterfoil—or eventually even without one.

child *Hat, hats; dog, dogs*. We all know how plurals in English are usually made. *Sheep, sheep* is a familiar exception, as is *ox, oxen*. *Child, children* is one of the oddest of the exceptions because *child* has had its plural formed in three different ways over the course of its history. The earliest Old English form, *cild*, "child, infant," formed its plural by adding no suffix, like the Modern English *sheep* and *deer*. Other Old English nouns, however, formed plurals by adding the suffix *–ru*, and in later Old English times a new plural, *cildru*, was used for *cild*. This form developed into *childer*. Still other nouns in Old English formed the plural with the suffix *–an*, which survived in Middle English as *-en*. *Oxen* and *brethren* are modern plurals that show this suffix. In some dialects of Middle English *-en* was the usual plural suffix, and it was added to *childer* to make it conform to other nouns. *Childeren* was probably pronounced (chĭl′drən), as in *children*, the modern spelling of the plural of *child*.

city   Philadelphia, which means "brotherly love" in Greek, may have the correct etymological notion of *city*. *City* goes back to the Indo-European root *kei–*, which meant, among other things, "beloved, dear." The Latin word *cīvis*, meaning "a fellow countryman, citizen," is derived from this root. From *cīvis* comes *cīvitās*, "an organized community" and also "a town or city." In Old French *cīvitās* became *cité*, which became *city* in English. Though not everyone in a city loves his or her fellow citizens, the possibility still exists, if only from the etymological standpoint.

class   Certain things have *class* and therefore are *classy*, while the related words *classic* and *classical* refer to a culture with a lot of *class*. One may be a bit puzzled by these senses, since the word *class* in its references to social status or biological divisions is a neutral word, not in itself denoting levels of quality or of rank. *Class* is from the Latin word *classis*, "a division of the Roman people." *Classis* had an adjective, *classicus*, that originally meant "belonging to a *classis*" but that later meant "belonging to the highest-ranking *classis*," from which the sense "first-class, superior," developed. English *classic* and *classical* are derived from *classicus* in the more general sense. But because the ancient Greek and Roman authors were considered models of excellence and were universally studied in schools and universities throughout Europe until recent times, the terms *classic* and *classical* came to be associated first with ancient Greek and Roman literature of all degrees of excellence and then with anything pertaining to ancient Greece or Rome. As for *class* and *classy*, *class* meaning "great style or quality" seems related to the use of *class* in the adjec-

42

tives *high-class* and *first-class*. Once *class* gained the meaning "great quality," someone or something could be *classy*.

cloud   The weather in medieval England must not have been very sunny, because two modern English words meaning "sky" meant "cloud" in earlier times. *Welkin*, from Old English *wolcen*, meant "cloud" until the twelfth century, as the German word *Wolke* still does. *Sky* comes from the Old Norse word *skȳ*, meaning "cloud." The Old Norse word was borrowed into English with the meaning "cloud" in the thirteenth century and was not used to mean "sky" until about a century later. The word *cloud* itself, from Old English *clūd*, is quite down to earth, for it meant "hill" or "rock" until about the fourteenth century. The ordinary word for "sky" in Old and Middle English was the ancestor of our word *heaven*, which retains that sense in Modern English only in the plural *heavens*. The use of *heaven* as the abode of God is recorded as early as the word itself.

clove   It may seem odd that *clove*, "a section of a garlic bulb," and the spice called *cloves* in English should share the same name, but the two words are not at all related. The *clove* that means "bulb section" comes from Old English *clufu*, a noun related to the verb *clēofan*, "to split," the ancestor of *cleave*, "to split or separate." *Clove* as a name for the spice is really a misnomer. The full name of the spice in Old French was *clou de girofle*, literally "nail of the clove tree." *Clou* is from Latin *clāvus*, "nail." The dried flower bud of the clove tree, which is the part used as a spice, somewhat resembles a small nail or tack. The English shortened the full name of the spice, which explains why its modern form is one word, *clove*.

clue   *Clue* and *clew* were at one time simply two spellings of the same word with the same meaning "ball," especially a ball of yarn or thread, an obsolescent sense of *clew* today. The meaning "guide to a solution" developed from the story of Theseus and the Minotaur. Theseus, a great Athenian hero, had the task of killing the Minotaur, a monster half man and half bull who lived in the Labyrinth, King Minos's maze on Crete. Finding the Minotaur was no problem, but discovering the way out of the Labyrinth would have been impossible if Ariadne, Minos's daughter, had not provided Theseus with a clew—or ball—of string. Theseus unwound the ball as he entered and wound it up as he returned, thus following a sure path out of the maze. Allusions to this "clew of thread" or a "clew to a maze" have been common from Chaucer's day to modern times and have appeared in contexts that referred to various kinds of difficulties. As a result, the figurative import of the word *clew* was gradually lost, and all associations with a ball of twine were broken. In very recent times, especially since the advent of detective fiction, the spelling *clue* has primarily signified the meaning "guide to a solution."

coach *Coach* was used to mean a "tutor" or a "trainer" in allusion to the speed of stagecoaches and railway coaches. In the days before automobiles and airplanes, the fastest method of travel was by coach—at first horse-drawn and later steam-powered. A *coach* in the parlance of a British university is an instructor who brings his students along at the fastest possible rate.

cocoa The confusion of *cocoa*, the beverage, with *coco*, the tree, can be traced to Samuel Johnson's great dictionary, published in 1755. Johnson maintained the distinction between the two words in his own writing, but by some editorial or printing error the definitions for *coco* and *cocoa* appeared together under the word *cocoa*. That was unfortunate, because *coco* and *cocoa* are two different words that refer to two different trees. The cacao tree of tropical America produces both cocoa and chocolate. The name *cacao* comes

from Nahuatl (Aztec) *cacahuatl,* "cacao bean," while
chocolate comes from *xocolatl,* "article of food made
from cacao," an unrelated word in the same language.
The word *cocoa* is simply a variant spelling of *cacao.*
The coconut or coco palm originated in the East In-
dies. Its name is not a native name like *cacao* but
comes from Portuguese *coco,* "goblin," referring to
the facelike appearance of the three holes at the bot-
tom of the fruit.

colonel   The improbable pronunciation (kûr′nəl) for the word
spelled *colonel* represents the triumph of popular
speech over learned tinkering. *Colonel* goes back to
Old Italian *colonnello* from *colonna,* "column (of soldiers)." The officer named *colonnello* led the first
company of a regiment. In English, however, *colonel*
did not come directly from Italian but by way of
French. The French word was at one time spelled
coronel. This spelling represents the fact that in
French the word was affected by a process called dissimilation, in which two similar or identical sounds,
like the two *l* sounds in *colonnello,* become less
alike. Later in literary French *coronel* was replaced by
colonnel because the latter looked more like the original Italian. This French usage influenced English writers to use the form *colonel,* as did their perusal of
Italian military treatises. The pronunciation based on
the spelling *colonel,* however, did not win out over
(kûr′nəl), which was the pronunciation of the older
English form *coronel* based on French *coronel.*

colossal   "What colossal nerve!" one says in exasperation,
without thinking of the Colossus of Rhodes, one of
the seven wonders of the ancient world. This huge
bronze statue bestrode the harbor of Rhodes, with
ships passing between its immense legs. From the
Greek word for such giant statues we get *colossal.* Adjectives that denote hugeness seem readily to be created from the stuff of antiquity, legend, mythology,
and literature as well from the names of creatures in
the animal kingdom. *Brobdingnagian* comes to us

from the land of Brobdingnag in Jonathan Swift's *Gulliver's Travels.* Its enormous inhabitants could hold Gulliver in their hands. From the race of one-eyed, giant Cyclopes of Greek mythology, we get *cyclopean.* The giant king Gargantua in Rabelais's *Gargantua and Pantagruel* gives us *gargantuan. Giant* itself and *gigantic* take us back to a giant race who warred against the Olympian gods of Greek mythology and lost. *Herculean* comes from Hercules, the Greek hero who helped the gods in this battle. And *titanic* recalls the Titans, the gods who preceded the Olympians and also fought them. *Elephantine, mammoth,* and *mastodonic* come to us from elephants or elephantlike creatures, past and present. *Pythonic,* the word with which we wrap this huge matter up, comes to us in its sense "huge" from the mythological serpent killed by Apollo and the large snake that can be seen in our zoos.

comedy   Comedy, like so many of the literary genres of Europe, originated in ancient Greece. Although its exact beginnings are lost, the word *comedy* itself provides a clue to the development of the form. Greek *kōmōidia* is derived from *kōmōidos,* a compound of *kōmos,* "revel, carousal," and *aoidos,* "singer." The earliest kind of comedy thus seems to have been a performance by a singer at the Greek religious revels. These celebrations were part of certain important religious festivals in Greek life and contained elements like mime, masquerades, and choruses that were later stylized and incorporated into a literary and dramatic form. Comedies probably have happy endings because the Greek revels ended in a feast.

comfort   *Comfort,* as a noun and verb, is ultimately derived from the Latin prefix *con–* and *fortis,* meaning "strong." The Latin verb *confortāre* and its descendants in the medieval Romance languages meant "to strengthen." The verb and the noun were borrowed into English from French in the thirteenth century. The senses "to strengthen" for the verb and "strengthening" and "solace" for the noun both occur at that early date. The meaning "ease" for the noun is not recorded until the early nineteenth century, although the meaning "at ease" for *comfortable* developed earlier, during the eighteenth century. Today we can at least take comfort in knowing that these new senses are the normal ones and that the older meanings are obsolete.

computer *Mouse, window, menu, daisy wheel*. To the uninitiated it may be difficult to imagine what common realm these terms could occupy. The magic word *computer*, however, is enough to orient us. *Computer* itself is a word formed in English from the verb *compute* and has a recorded history going back to 1646, when it was used to mean "a person who computes." In 1897 we find the word first recorded as "a calculating machine," although that particular machine, which was "of the nature of a circular slide rule," bore little resemblance to a modern computer. For a recorded use of the word *computer* to describe such a machine, we must wait until 1944, when the July 8 London *Times* stated that "The Mark XIV consists of . . . a rectangular box called the computor [*sic*], which might be described as the brains of the machine."

Many other terms remind us that the terminology of computers, like the word *computer* itself, can be down to earth, even if the terms describe things far removed from everyday life. For example, in computer parlance, a *mouse* is not a small, furry, often annoying creature but a small hand-held device used to move a cursor on a video-display terminal. A *window* can't be washed and looked through but can be used to view a selected portion of a file or image displayed on a terminal. You might ponder a *menu* in a restaurant while the waiter hovers impatiently nearby, but you can contemplate the *menu* on your home computer to your heart's content, then choose the part of the software program that you want to see and use. And don't expect that *daisy wheel* to bloom in your garden or flourish in a vase on your table; it is a round, high-speed printing element that will show you, in a trice, what you and the computer have wrought.

constable Words, like families, can rise and fall on the social scale. *Constable* is a case in point. *Comes stabuli*, the Latin phrase from which *constable* is derived, meant in the fifth and sixth centuries "officer of the stable" or in ordinary parlance "head groom." By the thirteenth century this humble officer had achieved the dignity of being the chief household officer of the great lords and kings of France. In the latter case he was called the Constable of France and commanded the army in the king's absence. *Constable* was adopted by the English in the thirteenth and fourteenth centuries for a number of officers, including the wardens of royal castles and various officers of the peace. Many of these positions have been abolished or are now ceremonial; in British usage *constable* refers especially to what Americans call a *policeman*.

contact "I'll contact them" may still raise eyebrows but perhaps not as high as it did in 1935, when the English author A. P. Herbert wrote, "A charming lady in the publicity business shocked me when we parted by saying 'It has been such fun contacting you.'" Why this particular instance of the common linguistic practice of conversion or functional shift, that is, using one part of speech, the noun *contact*, as another, a verb, should have occasioned such shock is difficult to say. Such a conversion had already occurred in 1834 in a technical context that mentioned the contact between a spark and gunpowder. It may have been in the case of *contact* that the purists' objection was not so much to this particular instance of conversion as it was to the users of *contact* as a verb. The

(continued)

usage seems to have been perceived as being confined to the world of American business. Nevertheless, the word did make its way into most reaches of society, for an Oxford don in the 1950's wrote that "Lord North despatched an emissary to contact Benjamin Franklin." Whatever the ultimate fate of *contact* in the eyes of the purists, conversion will remain an important way of forming new words. What would we do without the verb *telephone* from the noun or the noun *commercial* from the adjective?

continent Can one be *continent* on any *continent* despite the ravages of traveler's tummy, Montezuma's revenge, Rangoon Runs, Hong Kong Dog, or L.A. Belly? Whether one can or cannot, we think of the noun *continent* and the adjective *continent* as separate, even though they are derived from the same Latin word. They were, however, borrowed into English at different times with different meanings. Both words are derived from Latin *continens*, a form of the verb *continēre*, which has the basic meaning "to hold together." One of the senses of *continens* was "moderate, restrained," and from *continens* in this sense the adjective *continent* is derived. This adjective appeared in English during the fourteenth century and from its introduction had the meaning "characterized by self-restraint." But the Latin word *continens* also meant "continuous," and in the sixteenth century, during the great age of exploration and discovery, the noun *continent* came into use for various kinds of land masses. The word at first denoted any continuous tract of land but was also applied to a mainland as distinguished from islands or peninsulas, especially to the European continent in contrast to the British Isles. By the seventeenth century *continent* was used to refer to the land masses we call continents today.

cookie What could be more American than cookies, kept in the cookie jar waiting to be consumed? *Cookie*, however, is only American insofar as the word was borrowed into English in America, but it was borrowed from a word that does not have an English or American English appearance, the Dutch word *koekje*, "little cake," which is the diminutive of Dutch *koek*, "cake." *Cookie* was borrowed into American English apparently from the Dutch settlers of New York. It first appears in 1703 in the statement that "at a funeral, '800 cockies . . . were furnished." This early English spelling of the word differs from our modern spelling, but looks nothing like the Dutch spelling either. In taking *cookie* into English its users may have spelled the word the way it sounded. Aside from the spelling *cockie*, several other spellings arose, such as *cookey*, *cooky*, and *cookie*. The spelling *cookie* may have won out because the word, denoting something small and tasty, is very common in the plural, spelled *cookies*. The commonly seen ending *-ies* may have given support to *cookie* instead of *cooky*, which has the *-y* spelling that is usual in words, such as *cookery*, that have a plural ending in *-ies*.

copacetic   All is not copacetic when we consider how little we know about the origin of the word *copacetic*, meaning "excellent, first-rate." Is its origin to be found in Italian, in the speech of southern blacks, in the Creole French dialect of Louisiana, or in Hebrew? John O'Hara, who used the word in *Appointment in Samarra*, later wrote that *copacetic* was "a Harlem and gangster corruption of an Italian word." O'Hara went on to say, "I don't know how to spell the Italian, but it's something like copacetti." His uncertainty about how to spell the Italian is paralleled by uncertainty about how to spell *copacetic* itself. *Copacetic* has been recorded with the spellings *copasetic*, *copasetty*, *copesetic*, *copisettic*, and *kopasettee*. The spelling is now fixed, however, as *copacetic*, even though the origin of the word has not been determined.

The Harlem connection mentioned by O'Hara would seem more likely than the Italian, since *copacetic* was used by black jazz musicians and is said to have been southern slang in the late nineteenth century. If *copacetic* is Creole French in origin, it would also have a southern homeland. According to this explanation, *copacetic* came from the Creole French word *coupersètique*, which meant "able to be coped with," "able to cope with anything and everything," "in good form," and also "having a healthy appetite or passion for life or love."

Those who back the Hebrew or Yiddish origin of *copacetic* do not necessarily deny the southern connections of the word. One explanation has it that Jewish storekeepers used the Hebrew phrase *kol bĕşedeq*, "all with justice," when asked if things were O.K. Black children who were in the store as customers or employees heard this phrase as *copacetic*.

No explanation of the origin of *copacetic*, including the ones discussed here, has won the approval of scholars, as is clearly shown by the etymology of *copacetic* in the first volume of the *Dictionary of American Regional English*, published in 1985: "Etym unknown."

copper   Copper is associated with ordinary things like pennies, pots, or wire. But the history of *copper* is more romantic for it has associations with the island of Cyprus in the Mediterranean Sea. The English word *copper* comes from the Late Latin word *cuprum*, derived from Latin *Cyprium*, "Cyprian." The ancient Romans called copper the "Cyprian metal" because Cyprus was the main source of copper in the ancient world. The Romans annexed the island in 58 B.C. and mined the copper for their own use.

cordial   "Gold in phisik is a cordial," states Chaucer in the *Prologue* to his *Canterbury Tales*, leaving us wondering perhaps what a cordial is and how it is being used. *Cordial* had its origin as a term used in medicine (*phisik*), and in early use the word's derivation from the Latin word *cor*, "heart," was not forgotten. The first recorded use of *cordial* in English is found in the quotation from Chaucer's *Prologue*, where it indicates a medicine, in this case an expensive one.

Such cordials were supposed to achieve beneficial effect by stimulating the heart, as no doubt do the liqueurs that are also called *cordials*. The heart in medieval physiology was also considered the center of feelings and affections; from this association the adjective *cordial*, meaning "hearty" or "heartfelt," arose.

corn   *Corn* refers to different grains, depending on what part of the world you live in. In England *corn* means "wheat" not "maize," as it does in the United States. In Ireland and Scotland *corn* means "oats." *Corn*, in fact, seems to be an impressionable word, taking on its meaning according to the main crop of a given area. Maize became the *corn* of the New World because of its importance there, leaving *grain* as the term for crops such as wheat, oats, and rye. Although not a case of six of one, half a dozen of the other, *corn* and *grain* do ultimately go back to the same Indo-European root—corn by way of Germanic and *grain* by way of Old French *grain* from Latin *grānum*.

coroner   A coroner would seem to have little to do with royalty unless it was with Pluto, King of Hades. Nevertheless *coroner* comes from Anglo-Norman *corouner*, a word derived from Old French *coroune*, "crown." *Corouner* was the term used for the royal judicial officer who was called in Latin *custos placitorum coronae*, or "guardian of the crown's pleas." The person holding the office of coroner, a position dating from the twelfth century, was charged with keeping local records of legal proceedings in which the crown had jurisdiction. He helped raise money for the crown by funneling the property of executed criminals into the king's treasury. The coroner also investigated any suspicious deaths among the Normans, who as the ruling class wanted to be sure their deaths would not be taken lightly.

At one time in England all criminal proceedings were included in the coroner's responsibilities. Over the years these responsibilities decreased markedly, but coroners have continued to display morbid curiosity. In the United States, where there is no longer a Crown, a coroner's main duty is the investigation of any sudden, violent, or unexpected death that may not have had a natural cause.

costume A costume is a custom of dress, a fact that is partly explained by the origin of both *custom* and *costume* in the Latin word *consuētūdō*, "custom, habit, usage." English borrowed both words from French, but at different times. *Custom* appeared first; it was used about 1200 in the still current sense "habitual practice." *Costume* was borrowed from French much later, in the eighteenth century, as a term from the technical vocabulary of the fine arts. It meant "the features characteristic of a particular historical period represented in painting or sculpture." This was the meaning of the Italian word *costume*, from which the French word *costume* and the later English word *costume* derive. Such characteristic features naturally included styles of dress; as the use of *costume* expanded beyond its original area, its meaning was restricted to clothing styles.

court *"Collar that Dormouse!" the Queen shrieked out. "Behead that Dormouse! Turn that Dormouse out of court! Suppress him! Off with his whiskers!"*

"Never mind!" said the King, with an air of great relief. "Call the next witness."
    —Lewis Carroll, *Alice's Adventures in Wonderland,*
                                                    1865

In Lewis Carroll's courtroom, where the king was judge and the jury box was filled with twelve "creatures"—animals and birds—we may find an analogy to the word *court* itself, which, though referring to the halls of justice and the palace, has its ultimate roots in the farmyard. No doubt some members of the Honorable Judiciary have arrived at a similar analogy based on their observations of the flamboyant behavior of some attorneys, witnesses, plaintiffs, and defendants.

The words *court, yard,* and *garden* all share the same Indo-European root, *gher-* [1]. *Court* came into Middle English through Old French from the Classical Latin word *cohors*, meaning "farmyard" as well as "an armed force; retinue; band." The Old French word *court* developed senses relating to the king, perhaps first denoting his landholdings or the enclosed place where he resided or perhaps with reference to those who hung around that place. Both possibilities exist in the Latin senses of *cohors*, "farmyard" and "retinue," respectively.

Our English word *court* is one of a group of words having to do with government that were borrowed from French into English during the first two centuries after the Norman Conquest. In Middle English *court* referred to, among other things, the king's residence, his establishment, and his entourage as well as to a formal assembly held by him. This last meaning of the word is said to have developed into our present judicial meaning because at one time the king administered justice during his assemblies, although this sense could have come directly from the French. The rise of *court* on the semantic scale from the farmyard to royalty and the halls of justice is an example of the linguistic process called elevation or melioration, a gradual improvement in the meaning of a word— the injudicious behavior of some flamboyant courtroom personalities notwithstanding.

cow Everyone knows that *cow* and *beef* refer to the same animal. A smaller number of people, who have studied medieval English history, know that *cow* and *beef* are a pair of words that illustrate how the English borrowed new words for food after the conquest of England by the more culinarily advanced Normans. From the French language the English adopted words such as *beef, mutton, pork,* and *veal* for table meats taken from animals—the cow, sheep, swine, and calf—that kept their native names.

An even smaller number of people, who have studied Indo-European, know that *cow* and *beef* are derived from the same word. This word has been reconstructed as the Indo-European form *gʷōus*. As individual dialects and languages such as English and Latin developed from Indo-European, features preserved in one language were sometimes lost in another. The Old English descendant of the Indo-European form was *cū*, now the Modern English word *cow*, while the Latin development was *bōs*, "ox, bull, cow." An example of differing development from the same Indo-European form is the fact that in Latin the final *s* remains while in English it does not. *Bōs* had a form *bov-*, which was used, for example, in the possessive form *bovis*, "of a cow." From this form the Old French word *boef* or *buef* is derived. The English word is *beef*.

crisscross   *Crisscross* is a phonetic spelling of *Christ(s)-cross*, which literally means "the cross of Christ." The word originally denoted a mark of two crossed lines resembling the Christian religious symbol. This mark had two main functions: it was placed at the head of alphabets used for the teaching of children, and it was a figure used in place of a signature by uneducated persons. In the nineteenth century the religious association was lost, and *crisscross* was applied to any pattern of crossed lines.

crucial   A crucial election is like a signpost because it shows which way the electorate is moving. The metaphor of a signpost, in fact, gives us the sense of the word *crucial* meaning "of supreme importance; critical." Francis Bacon used the phrase *instantia crucis*, "crucial instance," to refer to something in an experiment that proves one of two hypotheses and disproves the other. Bacon's phrase was based on the notion of a *crux*, the Latin word for "cross." This word had come

56

to mean "a guidepost that gives directions at a place where one road becomes two," and hence was suitable for Bacon's metaphor. Both Robert Boyle, often called the father of modern chemistry, and Isaac Newton used the similar Latin phrase *experimentum crucis*, "crucial experiment." When these phrases were translated into English, they became *crucial instance* and *crucial experiment*, giving us the crux of the word *crucial*.

curfew   A curfew was originally a medieval regulation requiring that fires be put out or covered at a certain hour at night. *Curfew* comes from the Old French word *cuevrefeu*, which was formed from *couvrir*, "to cover," and *feu*, "fire." The rule of curfew was probably instituted as a public safety measure to minimize the risk of a general conflagration. A bell was rung at the prescribed hour, and the word *curfew* has been extended to denote both the bell and the hour in addition to the regulation.

currency   "Funny money" is a nice rhyming term for counterfeit currency; "runny money," or more precisely "running money," could be justified as an etymologically humorous term for the real thing. *Currency* goes back through several stages to the Latin verb *currere*, "to run," which could be applied to things such as liquids. In Medieval Latin *currere* referred to money that circulated from one place to another. Latin *currere* became Old French *corir*, a form of which, *currant*, became Middle English *curraunt*, the source of our *current*. In English as early as the fifteenth century *current* also had a sense relating to the circulation of money; this same sense passed to the noun *currency* derived from *current*. The final stage of development occurred later, when the sense "circulation" developed into the meaning "something, such as coins, that is in use as a medium of exchange," a sense first recorded in the writings of Benjamin Franklin in 1729.

cynosure

Towers, and battlements . . .
Where perhaps some beauty lies,
The cynosure of neighbouring eyes.

—Milton, *L'Allegro*, 1632

The occurrence of *cynosure* in Milton's poem is perhaps the most poetic use of this word, familiar nowadays largely to crammers for the SATs. The history of the word *cynosure* should lead us to expect from it the sublime, as in Milton's poem, as well as the ridiculous. The ridiculous is revealed in the literal sense of the Greek word *kunosoura*, "dog's tail," from which the English word *cynosure* is derived. A dog's tail would hardly attract eyes, however. A cynosure does so for a compelling and elevated reason. The Greeks used *kunosoura* as their name for the constellation now known as Ursa Minor. In ancient times this constellation was always above the horizon in latitudes north of 18 degrees. It was used in navigation because it contained Polaris, the polestar, which appears at the tail end of the Little Dipper and very near the north celestial pole. The word *cynosure* was originally borrowed into English as the name of the same constellation, but was also used figuratively to mean "a guide or center of attention."

D

dais

Dais is apparently a word that English speakers could not do without because it was brought back to life after an untimely death. It first appeared in the thirteenth century as *deis*, from the Old French word *deis*, indicating a table raised on a platform at which honored guests were seated. *Deis* was also used of the platform alone. Although this word died out in England in the sixteenth century, it survived in Scotland with the meaning "bench." In the late eighteenth and

(continued)

Dentist

early nineteenth centuries writers such as Sir Walter Scott revived the word. Although they used the modern French spelling *dais*, the reappearance of *dais* probably represents a revival in English itself rather than a borrowing from French, because the modern French word means only "canopy." The French forms *deis* and *dais* are ultimately derived from the Latin word *discus*, which in medieval times meant "table." *Dais* thus comes from the same Latin word as do *disk*, *dish*, and *desk*.

daisy

Daisy, Daisy, give me your answer, do!
—Harry Dacre, "Daisy Bell," 1892

The word *daisy* contains more than meets the eye. So does the plant to which the name was originally applied. The European plant *Bellis perennis*, known in the United States as the *English daisy*, folds its petals at night, hiding its yellow center, and opens them in the morning with the sun, like an eye that sleeps and wakes. Because of this property, the old English name for the plant was *dægesēage*, a compound word made up of *dæges*, "day's," and *ēage*, "eye," which gives us the Modern English word *daisy*.

dapple-gray

Dapple-gray is probably an alteration of *apple-gray*, which refers not so much to color as to the blotchy dark-gray markings found on gray horses. The origin of the term is not known with certainty. Similar words are found in other Germanic languages: Old Norse *apalgrār* and Middle High German *apfelgrā*, literally "apple-gray." These words had the same meaning and application as *dapple-gray*, but it is not known if either the Norse or the German term is the direct source of the English word. *Dapple-gray* first appeared in the fourteenth century in Chaucer's *Canterbury Tales*. In the same work Chaucer also used the synonymous term *pomely-grey*, which is apparently a partial translation of French *gris-pommele*, "apple-gray," from *pomme*, "apple." It is possible that Chaucer coined the term *dapple-gray*, but the origin of the *d* is still unexplained.

deal   A *raw deal* could never be a *square deal*, but it would be a *big deal* to the person getting it. *Deal* is a term that crops up constantly by itself or as an element of phrases in politics, business, and everyday life. This useful noun came from the verb *deal*. The basic and earlier senses of the verb had to do with dividing, separating, distributing, and sharing, including sharing in a common action, at one time including sex. The verb *deal* came to mean "to transact business with," "to negotiate with," and "to treat someone in a certain way." The central meaning of the noun is "the action of dealing," with the sense varying according to what sort of dealing is going on. *Square deal*, *raw deal*, *new deal*, and *big deal* all seem to have evolved from the business sense of the verb, although some of these uses of *deal* were no doubt colored by other senses of the verb, including the treatment and negotiation senses.

debt   Most users of the word *debt* put the *b* into the spelling of the word without complaining, but some must wonder how it came to be there. The pronunciation of *debt* represents the original pronunciation of the word, which was borrowed from French *dette*. Medieval writers knew that *dette* was derived from Latin *dēbitum*, "debt." In the fifteenth century the spelling *debt*, based on the Latin word *dēbitum*, first appeared. The language reformers of the sixteenth century promoted the spelling *debt* as being more correct. Despite the puzzlement of many schoolchildren, *debt* is now the only acceptable form of the word.

delight   *Delight*, with its connotations of effervescence and brightness of spirit, would seem to have a natural connection with *light*, "not heavy," or *light*, "illumination," but the connection exists in form only. The Old French and Middle English form of the noun *delight* was *delit*, which was derived from the Latin verb *dēlectāre*, "to delight." The spelling *delight* appeared in the sixteenth century, a time when the spelling of English words was still unsettled. Several spellings could represent the same sound, and *delit* was respelled to resemble words that rhymed with it, like *light* and *night.*

Democrat   A Democrat was once a Republican. The political party that elected Thomas Jefferson, James Madison, James Monroe, and John Quincy Adams as president was first called the Republican or Democratic-Republican Party. During the years 1825 to 1828 the party was reorganized. When Andrew Jackson was elected in 1828, the word *Republican* was dropped altogether, and the reconstituted party was renamed the Democratic Party—a name it has kept ever since. A Democrat (with an upper-case *D*) is an adherent of this party, but a democrat (with a lower-case *d*) was simply one who supported democracy, specifically, one of those who during the French Revolution wanted a government by the people. The word *democrat* was borrowed from French to refer to such a person. The French word came from another French word, *démocratie,* "democracy," which goes back to the Greek word *dēmokratia,* derived from *dēmos,* "people, free citizens," and the suffix *–kratia,* "power, rule." In the United States we think of rule by the people as a good thing, but to adherents of the rule of a king or the nobility, a democrat was unpleasant if not frightening. Republicans, of course, often feel that way about Democrats.

dentist   "*Dentist* figures [appears] now in our newpapers, and may do well enough for a French puffer [a writer of puffs or inflated advertisements]; but we fancy Rutter is content with being called a *tooth-drawer.*" In this quotation from the September 15, 1759, issue of the Edinburgh *Chronicle* we see *dentist* in its infancy as an English word, trailing evidence of its French origin. If we had formed a word in English like *dentist,* which comes from the French word *dent,* "tooth," we would have *toothist,* a word that does not exist. But *toothist* and *tooth-drawer* lack the elegance of the

French borrowing *dentist,* an elegance that is shared by other borrowings from French during the past four centuries, such as *ballet, champagne, coquette, coterie,* and *negligee.*

derrick   A grim presence hangs over our oil wells and construction projects, seen only by those who know etymology. Derick, a well-known hangman of around 1600, has been immortalized in the name of contraptions far removed from his fatal business. Credited with a total of more than three thousand executions during his career as a hangman at Tyburn, near what is now Marble Arch in Hyde Park, London, Derick was a natural to have his name come to mean "a hangman; hanging; the gallows." Prior to our modern uses of the term, *derrick,* no doubt humorously, was applied to two types of apparatus used on ships for lifting or moving heavy things. The name, perhaps finally free of gallows humor, was then applied to devices on land as well as sea, such as the large cranes used at construction sites or the tall frameworks on top of oil wells that support boring equipment and that hoist and lower lengths of pipe.

desperado   Contrary to what one might believe, the word *desperado* did not come into English, six-guns blazing, in the American Wild West. In fact, we cannot say definitely how *desperado* got into English. It has generally been thought that *desperado* is a refashioning of the obsolete English noun *desperate* with the Spanish noun suffix *–ado.* A reader of *Webster's II New Riverside University Dictionary* questioned this statement, perhaps with good reason. Historically, but not currently, the form *desperado* has existed in Spanish, although the usual form of the word is *desesperado.* This adjective means "hopeless, desperate."

Formerly it was thought that *desesperado* was not used as a noun; but before the time of the first recorded use of *desperado* in English in 1610, we find *desesperado* used twice as a noun in Spanish. One of these citations comes from a Colombian judicial document treating the misuse of public funds by a local treasurer. The angry treasurer announces that the governor who is prosecuting him is an ideal candidate for stabbing by a *desesperado*. It is not clear whether this is a general threat or whether the treasurer means he might actually stab the governor, but certainly *desesperado* is used here as a noun, as *desperado* could have been as well. The sense here is "a desperate or reckless person," the main sense of *desperado* in English. The possibility exists, then, that *desperado* could have come directly into English from Spanish.

diet *Diet*, "one's usual food," and *diet*, "assembly, conference," are not related words. The first *diet* is ultimately derived from the Greek word *diaita*, meaning "mode of life," especially one prescribed by a physician that includes the regulation of eating habits. In the latter sense *diaita* was borrowed into Latin, whence it passed into French and then into English. The earliest recorded English sense of *diet* is "food, daily provisions," which is still current. The word *diet* meaning "assembly" comes from Medieval Latin *diēta*, derived from Latin *diēs*, "day." The Medieval Latin word had a range of meanings based on the sense "day," such as "a day's journey," "a day's work," and "an assembly or meeting held on an appointed day." All these senses were current for Middle English *diete*, but only the sense "assembly" has survived to modern times. *Diet* is the English name for legislative assemblies in a number of countries, including Sweden, Denmark, and Japan.

disaster A disaster, etymologically speaking, is a calamity brought about by the evil influence of a star or planet. *Disaster* is ultimately derived from Latin *dis–*, a pejorative prefix, and Greek *astron*, "star." Although astrology was very important in ancient and medieval times, the source of the word *disaster* is not

64

Latin but rather Italian, in which the word *disastro* was formed. Neither the French word *désastre* nor the English word *disaster* appeared before the sixteenth century. The meaning "evil celestial influence" did not survive the seventeenth century, and the more general sense has been current since the introduction of *disaster* as an English word.

discover   Christopher Columbus discovered America in 1492, but at that time possibly no speaker of English could use the word *discover* to say that he had. The first recorded use of *discover* meaning "to be the first to learn of" occurred in 1555, appropriately in regard to Columbus. The word *discovery* is first recorded in 1553, again in reference to a voyage. It is probably not coincidental that *discover*, which before had meant such things as "to uncover, expose, disclose," should develop its new sense and also that the word *discovery* should appear in the sixteenth century during the great age of discovery. Both words went on to develop further applications as the exploration of another world—the world of science—progressed. In 1670 we learn of an "alkalisate property" that "was first discovered by preparation and tryals," and in 1676 we read of "discoveries and new inventions."

discus   A *discus* thrower could never throw a *desk*, but he or she could throw a *dish* or a *floppy disk*, though not with the same results. This unlikely statement shows us how far words can travel from their origin, for the three words *desk*, *dish*, and *disk* all come from the Latin word *discus*, a borrowing of the Greek word *diskos*, from *dikein*, "to throw." The Latin word *discus* meant primarily "discus," a flat round object of metal or stone that was thrown in athletic contests. In Late Latin *discus* also meant "dish," and with that sense *discus* was borrowed into Old English as *disc*. *Disc*, though spelled like *disc*, "phonograph record," was pronounced like its descendant, Modern English *dish*, because the spelling *sc* in Old English stood here for the sound (sh). A thousand years later, in the late seventeenth and eighteenth centuries, the word *dis-cus* was borrowed into English with the shortened form *disk* or *disc*, the *sc* now standing for the sound (sk). *Disk* was used especially in scientific writings to indicate various flat round objects and today occupies an important place in the world of computers. During the medieval period Latin *discus* acquired the meaning "table." The Italian descendant of *discus, desco,* preserves this later meaning and is the ancestor of English *desk.*

dismal The adjective *dismal* was originally an assumed Old French noun phrase—*dis mal*—meaning "evil days," from Latin *diēs malī.* In the medieval calendar two days each month were considered unlucky, for example, January 1 and 25 and February 4 and 26. A *dismal day* was one of these unlucky days. By the sixteenth century the phrase *dismal day* had become so common that *dismal* was interpreted as an adjective and came to mean "unlucky" and "causing dread" in general. In more recent times these senses have become obsolete or rare, have lost force, or have become associated with the sense "depressing, gloomy." Today the word does not connote disaster so much as boredom.

dog Although the dog was probably the first domesticated animal, our English word *dog* is relatively new. The Old English ancestor of *dog* appears only once as a translation of the Latin word *canis,* "dog." The usual word for "dog" in Old English was *hund,* the ancestor of our modern English word *hound.* This word is related to the words for "dog" in many other Indo-European languages, including the Latin word *canis,* the Italian word *cane,* and the French word *chien.* During the latter part of the Middle Ages, the Middle English word *dogge,* which came from the Old English word, began to supplant *hound* as the ordinary term for man's best friend. *Hound,* in turn, was more often used specifically with reference to a hunting dog.

The history of *dog* before the single Old English form is unknown, although dogged research might turn up more information. A number of modern languages do have similar words—among them the French term *dogue*, "mastiff"; the Portuguese term *dogue*, "pug"; the Dutch term *dog*, "mastiff"; and the Swedish term *dogg*, "bulldog"—but all of them were borrowed from our own English word *dog*.

dollar "The almighty dollar" is actually mightier than one might think if omnipresence be considered a part of might, for the word *dollar* has been used to indicate several different coins. The German form of *dollar* is *Taler*, which is short for *Joachimstaler*, a silver coin minted in Joachimstal (now Jachymov in northwestern Czechoslovakia) in the sixteenth century. The North German and Dutch form of *taler* was *daler*, the form borrowed into English as *dollar*. From the sixteenth to the eighteenth century the English used *dollar* to refer to the Spanish coin also known as a *piece of eight* or *peso* that was a medium of exchange in Spain and the Spanish-American colonies. This Spanish coin was derived from the Dutch *daler*. Because the North American colonists were familiar with the Spanish coin, Thomas Jefferson proposed that the monetary unit of the newly independent United States be called a *dollar* and resemble the Spanish peso. His proposal was adopted in 1785. A coin similar to the Spanish and American dollar has also been the monetary unit of China, Arabia, and elsewhere.

dollop Although *dollop* seems to be an ordinary enough word, its history before it is first recorded in English in the sixteenth century is mysterious. Its history after that point is documented, but *dollop* developed in ways not totally expected, moving from the field into general discourse, with a slight lapse into bad company, and ending up losing some weight. *Dollop* first had the now obsolete meaning "a patch, tuft, or

clump of something such as grass or weeds in a field."
Only in the early nineteenth century do we find recorded the next sense of *dollop*, "a large quantity of something." This sense is illustrated in a passage written by the nineteenth-century novelist Richard Blackmore: "I sent a great dollop of water into the face of the poor lieutenant." In the early part of the same century *dollop* is recorded in British dialect with the sense "an untidy woman, trollop." An obvious rhyme no doubt suggested itself to a poet writing about such a woman. Over the course of time, besides loitering into dialect, *dollop* has lost quite a bit of weight semantically, for the word now means not only "a large amount" but also "a small amount," as in the statement, "there was not a dollop of truth in the entire story."

doom   The history of the word *doom* illustrates the process of pejoration, the process by which a word with good or neutral connotations acquires evil ones. *Doom* goes back to an Indo-European root that meant "to set, put," and the Germanic word from which it comes has as its meaning "thing set or put down." This could be "a law, statute," or "a judgment," especially in Old English times "an adverse judgment, condemnation, or punishment." *Doomsday*, the day of last judgment in Christian theology, will doubtless be a day of great rejoicing for the just, but the fate of the damned has cast a pall over the connotations of the word.

doublethink   *Doublethink* was coined by George Orwell in his novel *Nineteen Eighty-Four*, which was published in 1949. Orwell wanted to invent a word that meant, as he put it in his book, "the power of holding two contradictory beliefs in one's mind simultaneously, and accepting both of them." Most such inventions are ephemeral, but Orwell's coinage has gained sufficient currency to be included in most general dictionaries of English.

dream "You tell me your dream, I'll tell you mine" becomes an increasingly less desirable proposition as psychoanalysis and psychiatry reach an ever wider public. Airing the skeletons in one's closet, particularly without knowing one is doing so, has little appeal. To a pre-Freudian consciousness, however, dreams originated somewhere else than in the unconscious. In Chaucer's *Troilus and Criseyde* it is written that "priests of the temple say this, That dreams are the revelations of gods, and as well they say . . . that they are infernal illusions; and physicians say that they come from people's constitutions that result from combinations of the four 'humors' or from fasting or from overeating." There is no consensus about the origin of dreams in this passage, and certainly no notion of the unconscious sending forth messages to the ego. Over time, then, although the phenomenon labeled by the word *dream* has remained the same, the word has developed different connotations and associations because of new concepts of what a dream is and where it originates. At least one can still tell one's dreams to psychiatrists, though they will not tell you theirs.

dress A dress is such a common article of modern feminine attire that it is difficult to imagine that the word *dress* at one time did not refer to such a thing. The earliest sense of *dress* was "speech, talk." The relationship of our modern sense to this early sense is explained by the fact that the noun *dress* comes from the verb *dress*, which goes back through Old French *drecier*, "to arrange," and the assumed Vulgar Latin *dīrectīare*, to Latin *dīrectus*, a form of the verb *dīrigere*, "to direct." In accordance with its etymology the verb *dress* had meanings such as "to place," "to arrange," and "to put in order." The sense "to clothe" is related to the notion of putting in order, specifically in regard to clothing. This verb sense then gave rise to the noun sense "personal attire" as well as to the important garment sense, which has made the fortune of many a fashion designer. The earliest noun sense, "speech," comes from a verb sense having to do with addressing or directing words to other people.

dunce The word *dunce* comes from the name of John Duns Scotus, an eminent thirteenth-century scholastic theologian. In the early sixteenth century the humanist scholars of classical Greek and Latin and the religious reformers criticized the *Dunses*, or followers of Scotus, for their resistance to the new learning of the Renaissance and the new theology of the Reformation. By the end of the sixteenth century *dunse* or *dunce* had acquired its current meaning "a stupid person."

E

easel "A painter's ass" is not a phrase that immediately brings to mind an accessory to the artist's profession. But *easel* comes to us from the Dutch word *ezel*, meaning "an ass, one of several hoofed mammals of the genus *Equus*." The Dutch word was eventually extended to mean "an upright frame for displaying or supporting something, such as an artist's canvas," in the same way that the English word *horse* has come to mean "a piece of gymnastic equipment with an upholstered body used especially for vaulting." Developments such as these illustrate the playfulness present in language when its speakers use similarities perceived between two objects in order to name one of them. This kind of naming can involve a dash of wit, as is probably the case with the Dutch word *ezel*. It is certainly the case with the name for a bank of uncovered outdoor seats for spectators. When sitting in the open air in a stadium, one is exposed to the sun just as linens are when they are bleached on a clothesline; thus, *bleachers*.

Eunuch

70

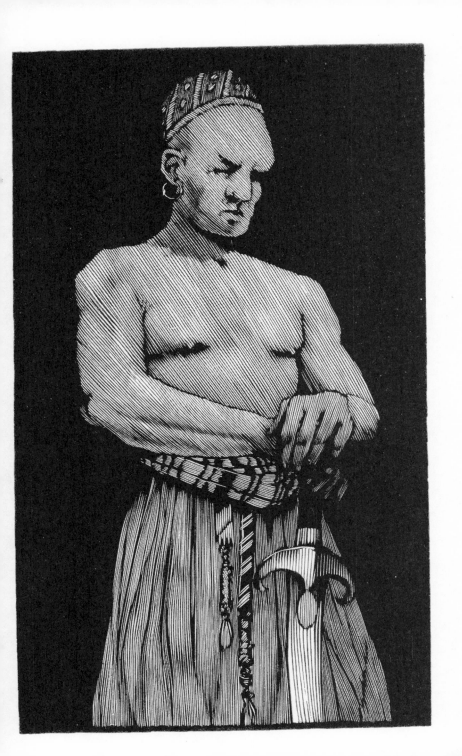

Easter   Although the word *Easter* is the name of a Christian festival, it has a decidedly pagan past. *Ēastre*, the Old English ancestor of our word *Easter*, apparently came from the name of a pre-Christian festival that was celebrated during the spring. This festival was named for a Germanic and Indo-European dawn goddess whose holiday was apparently celebrated at the spring equinox. The Christian missionaries to England helped ease the transition from paganism to Christianity by adopting native words for Christian terms; hence the use of a pagan name for a Christian festival. The word *Easter* is closely related to the Latin word *aurōra* and the Greek word *ēōs*, both meaning "dawn." *Easter* is also derived from the same Indo-European root, *aus-¹*, as *east*, the direction of sunrise. Medieval builders usually placed the altar at the eastern end of their churches, presumably to be nearer to the Holy Land, where Christ rose from the dead on the day we commemorate as Easter.

eavesdropper   One can be an eavesdropper without going near an eavesdrop. The word *eavesdropper* comes from *eavesdrop*, the name for the space of ground close to a building where water drips from the eaves. An eavesdropper was originally someone who stood in the eavesdrop in order to hear private conversations taking place inside. We know that eavesdropping was a crime at least as early as 1487. A record of the English borough of Nottingham states that "juratores . . . dicunt . . . quod Henricus Rowley . . . est communis evys-dropper" (jurors . . . say . . . that Henry Rowley . . . is a common . . . eavesdropper). And a legal glossary of 1641 explains, "Evesdroppers are such as stand under wals or windows . . . to heare news." Of course, eavesdropping is such good sport that it soon moved beyond the confines of the eavesdrop, and the word came to mean listening secretly to others almost anywhere. Sophisticated electronic listening devices have now gotten into the act, but if you eavesdrop without a court order, or without the knowledge of the eavesdroppee, you can still get in trouble with the law.

electricity   The effects of electricity have been observed since ancient times, when it was noticed that amber, when rubbed, attracts small bits of straw, wood, and other light materials. This electromagnetic effect was first studied scientifically in the seventeenth century, and the words *electric* and *electricity* were coined then from the Latin word *ēlectrum,* "amber," which comes from the Greek word *ēlektron.* The English word *electron* does not come directly from the Greek word; it is derived from *electric* and the suffix *–on,* which means "subatomic particle."

eleemosynary   "This is not an eleemosynary institution . . . This is a man concerned about making money." So remarked one "Wall Street trader" in the October 27, 1985, edition of the Boston *Globe,* referring to a large corporation and its controlling stockholder. Eleemosynary corporations exist, of course, and are defined legally as "corporations created for or devoted to charitable purposes or supported by charity." Charity is central to such a corporation and to the word *eleemosynary,* which comes from the same Late Latin word *eleēmosyna,* meaning "alms," as does the word *alms.* *Eleēmosyna* can be traced back to the Greek word *eleos,* "pity," "mercy," qualities not always highly appreciated in some corporate boardrooms.

elephant   Although elephants seem too large to have anything hidden or mysterious about them, the origin of the word *elephant* is mysterious. The mystery lies beyond the Greek word *elephas,* to which *elephant* can be traced. The earliest meaning of the Greek word (as in Mycenaean *e-re-pa*) is "ivory." Other words meaning "ivory" or "elephant" are Latin *ebur,* Sanskrit *ibhas,* and Hittite *lahpas* (Hittite was the language of an ancient people living in Asia Minor about 2000–1200 B.C.). These words can possibly be traced back to the ancient Egyptian word *āb* or *ābu,* "elephant, ivory." The first part of the Greek and Hittite words may go back to the form *eḷu,* "elephant," in Hamitic, the hypothetical source language of other languages such as Egyptian and Berber. This form passed through Egyptian and became Persian *pīl* and Arabic *fīl*, both words meaning "elephant."

eleven The system of counting used by prehistoric Germanic peoples was apparently based on ten. The words *eleven* and *twelve* contain hidden evidence of this in their etymologies. The Germanic ancestor of *eleven* can be reconstructed as *ain-lif-*, a compound of *ainaz*, "one," and *lif-*, a form derived from an Indo-European root meaning "to leave." *Eleven* therefore means "one left over after counting to ten." Similarly, the reconstructed Germanic ancestor of *twelve* is *twa-lif-*, so that *twelve* ultimately means "two left over after counting to ten."

emergency When a submarine experiences an onboard emergency and surfaces as fast as possible, its action reflects the etymology of *emergency*. The word *emergency* comes from *emerge*, which combines the Latin prefix *ex-*, *e-*, "out," and the Latin verb *mergere*, "to sink, dip, immerse." To emerge, then, is to rise as if from immersion. And an emergency is something that comes up and requires immediate attention.

enemy There is no love lost between enemies, but etymologically the loss of love has produced the word *enemy*. *Enemy* goes back by way of the Old French word *enemi* to the Latin word *inimīcus*. *Inimīcus* is, in turn, made up of the Latin negative prefix *in-* and the Latin word *amīcus*. *Amīcus* means "friendly" when used as an adjective and "a personal friend" when used as a noun. Therefore *inimīcus* means "not friendly" or "one who is the opposite of a personal friend; an enemy." We can understand the force of negative prefixes when we contrast the word *enemy* with the words *amiable* and *amicable*. All three go back to *amīcus*.

entrepreneur   "The great violinist [Paganini] has shut himself up in close confinement since his arrival in this country, and refused to receive any one but his *entrepreneur* and his dentist." The sense of *entrepreneur* in this 1871 quotation may not seem apparent since we are accustomed to seeing *entrepreneur* used in contexts such as this one from the November 26, 1959, issue of *The Listener:* "Where their predecessors were flanked by engineers and scientists, the new-style entrepreneurs will be buttressed by sales managers and advertising experts." *Entrepreneur* came into English from French, in which it was derived from *entreprendre*, "to undertake," and meant "someone who undertakes something, including economic undertakings; an agent." In its earliest recorded uses in English, *entrepreneur* meant a person who took a managerial role in the world of music, directing musical institutions and organizing concerts. During the nineteenth century *entrepreneur* in English moved into a realm of larger risks and became "one who undertakes a business venture."

environmental   Environmentalists, en garde! Right Guard® deodorant spray was recently called *environmental* by its advertising agency, illustrating how a word can take on a new meaning because of societal concerns. The word *environmental* gets its meaning from *environment*. The sense of *environment* in the news today is "the combination of external or extrinsic physical conditions that affect and influence the growth and development of organisms"—the sense that *environmental* pertains to in the phrase "environmental pollution." Concerns about the environment and pollution have led not only to the development of deodorants that do not utilize fluorocarbons as propellants but also to the use of *environmental* to describe such deodorants. As recorded by Charles Clay Doyle in the Spring, 1983, issue of *American Speech*, the word *environmental* can now mean "desirable because consistent with or conducive to a clean, safe, and undamaged environment."

epicure Epicurus would not approve of an epicure, either in the present sense of the word, "a person with refined taste, especially in food or wine," or in its archaic sense, "a person devoted to sensuous pleasure and luxurious living." The Athenian philosopher Epicurus (341–270 B.C.), from whose name the word *epicure* is derived, believed that the aim of human life was what he called "pleasure." Pleasure was not associated with profligacy; rather, it was based on the absence of pain and difficulty and the presence of inner peace. Therefore, Epicurus decreed, one should avoid such obvious sources of pain as marriage, children, and public life. The teachings of Epicurus were later completely twisted into a doctrine of sensual hedonism, a fact that explains how the Medieval Latin word *epicūrus*, derived from the philospher's name, and consequently the English word *epicure*, derived from Medieval Latin, came to mean "a sensual hedonist." The current sense of *epicure* is more refined but still not Epicurean.

esquire The form of address Jane Roe, Esq., shows not only the progress of women toward equal rights but also the progress of language over the centuries. *Esquire* goes back to the Latin word *scūtum*, "shield," from which was derived the Latin word *scūtārius*, "shield maker, " which in Late Latin came to mean "a guard armed with a shield." This word then yielded the Old French word *escuier*, "a knight's shield bearer and attendant; a young noble who is not yet a knight." The Old French word came into English in two forms, *esquire* and *squire*, both referring to "a young nobleman who personally attended and carried the shield of a high personage such as a sovereign" or "one ranking under a knight in military service or landed tenure." Since esquires and squires occupied high positions in society, both words came to be considered as desirable titles and were extended to—or perhaps at times appropriated by—people other than the ones who originally had the right to use them. In the United States both titles have been used as honorifics for attorneys, although *esquire* is the only one now so used. Whether male or female, attorneys are always ready to shield their clients.

eunuch The word *eunuch* does not derive, as one might think, from the operation that produced him but rather from one of his functions. *Eunuch* goes back to the Greek word *eunoukhos*, "a castrated person employed to take charge of the women and act as chamberlain." The Greek word is derived from *eunē*, "bed," and *ekhein*, "to keep." A eunuch, of course, was ideally suited to guard the bedchamber of women.

eureka Several towns in the United States owe their name to a discovery made by the great scientist Archimedes (287?–212 B.C.). The story is told that Hiero II, tyrant of Syracuse, asked Archimedes to determine if a certain crown had silver or another cheaper metal mixed in with the gold. Shortly afterward, Archimedes stepped into his bath, which was full of water, and slopped water onto the floor. Therefore, he concluded, a body displaces its own bulk when immersed in water. Archimedes knew that gold is denser than silver; thus a given weight of silver would be bulkier than a given weight of gold and would displace more water. He leapt from his bath crying *"Heurēka,"* which in Greek means "I have found it." Not stopping to clothe himself, Archimedes dashed home to test his conclusion and soon discovered that the crown was not pure gold. Unfortunately, we do not have a report of what the no doubt unhappy Hiero exclaimed when he heard the news.

Recorded evidence shows that Archimedes's exclamation came into English in the seventeenth century, spelled *heureca* when first used but later almost always spelled *eureka*. Since the eighteenth century the word has been used to express delight at finding something. California chose *Eureka!* as its state motto in 1849, although it is not clear whether this was delight at finding gold or delight at finding a golden land of promise. The reason for naming towns Eureka is often similarly vague. Eureka, Colorado, and Eureka, Nevada, are in rich mining areas, but Eureka, Kansas, was supposedly named after the discovery of a spring—water being more precious than gold in that thirsty Plains state.

exchequer The Chancellor of the Exchequer, Great Britain's governmental department corresponding to our Treasury, would never count out the Crown's revenues on a chessboard. But the Exchequer got its name from the checkered cloth resembling a chessboard that covered the counting tables of the Norman and Angevin kings of England. The word *exchequer* is derived from the Old French word *eschequier*, "chessboard." The x in *exchequer* is an etymological phantom. Many Old French words beginning with *es–* came from Latin words beginning with *ex–*, but *eschequer* is derived from the Latin word *scaccārium*, "chessboard." When other English words such as *exchange* (from Old French *eschangier* and Vulgar Latin *excambiāre*) were respelled to reflect their Latin origins, *exchequer* was erroneously altered in the same way.

F

facet It sounds much more impressive to say that a problem has many facets than to say that it has many little faces. However, *facet* comes to us from the French word *facette*, which originally meant "a little face." As one might expect, *facet* is first recorded in English with reference to diamonds; Sir Francis Bacon used it thus in 1625 when he wrote about "diamonds cut with Fascets." *Facet* was later used to refer to other substances, such as metals, that had faces like those

(continued)

Fiend

78

of a gemstone. In 1820 we find the first recorded figurative use of *facet*. The gothic novelist Maria Edgeworth mentions a "facet of the mind which it was the interest or the humour of the moment to turn outward." This is evidence that *facet* had been or was being released from its setting to play a more active role in multifaceted human discourse.

facsimile "Make a facsimile of this page, please," is a bit redundant from an etymological point of view. *Facsimile* comes from the Latin phrase *fac simile*, meaning "to make similar," and was at one time written in English as two words. In its first recorded English use *facsimile* meant "the copying of anything; imitation." This use is found in a statement from the clergyman and historian Thomas Fuller, written before 1661: "He, though a quick Scribe, is but a dull one, who is good only at *fac simile*, to transcribe out of an original." We find *facsimile* recorded soon after in the sense "an exact copy, likeness, counterpart, or representation." *Facsimile* was hence an obvious term to use in the nineteenth and twentieth centuries when referring to various methods, such as telegraphy or radio, of transmitting images or printed matter. *Facsimile* was also used as a verb, but the verb use does not seem to have caught on. It is first recorded in a marvelous use by the otherwise obscure Rosina Bulwer-Lytton, Baroness Lytton, in her 1839 novel *Cheveley:* "Two . . . sofas facsimiled each other at either end of the fireplace."

family The nature of the American family may or may not be in flux, but certainly the word *family* has undergone significant shifts in meaning over time. *Family* comes from the Latin word *familia*, which meant "household; servants; a body of persons closely connected by blood or affinity." One now archaic sense of *family* in English was "the servants of a house," as used by Daniel Defoe in his *Journal of the Plague Year*, published in 1722: "I was a single man . . . but I had a family of servants." A related but still current sense of *family* is "all the people in one house or under one head, including parents and children as well as servants." This sense is reflected in a legal citation from 1631: "His family were himself and his wife and daughters, two mayds, and a man."

Our modern use of *family*, referring to a small kinship group, may not have become dominant until as late as the early nineteenth century. The sense is clearly defined by James Mill in 1829 as "the group which consists of a Father, Mother and Children." This use of *family* for the smaller group reflects major economic and social changes, such as industrialization, that favored a smaller family unit. Although Mill's definition no longer applies to all modern families—especially those including single parents—the earlier sense of "household" still describes the various kinds of groups living together under the same roof.

fan Since some sports fans are disposed to wild acts and excessive partiality, it may not surprise their critics to learn that behind our word *fan* lies a history of lunacy, demonic possession, and religious zeal. *Fan* is short for *fanatic*, which goes back to the Latin word *fānāticus*. *Fānāticus* comes from *fānum*, "temple," and means "belonging to a temple" as well as "inspired by orgiastic rites; enthusiastic; frantic." The earliest recorded English use of the noun *fanatic* refers to a lunatic, while *fanatic* as an adjective is first recorded with reference to behavior of the sort that might result from possession by a god or demon; hence, frantic or furious behavior. In the seventeenth century when religious controversy between Puritans and Royalists ran high in England, the noun and adjective were applied to religious zealots. The noun *fanatic* was used as a hostile epithet for those who refused to accept the doctrine and practices of the Church of England. The noun and adjective *fanatic* are still used to refer to religious zeal but they can also apply to other types of zeal, including, for example, an enthusiasm for baseball, as in "she is a fanatic when it comes to watching the World Series on television."

farm Money and farms are intimately connected, both economically and etymologically. The word *farm* is derived from the Medieval Latin word *firma*, "fixed payment," a derivative of the Latin word *firmus*, "fixed, firm." The earliest sense of the English word *farm* is "a fixed yearly amount payable as a tax or rent," since it was a common practice to lease agricultural lands for a fixed annual rent rather than a percentage of the crop. The word *farm* was also applied to land occupied on such terms. From the sixteenth century on *farm* was used to indicate any cultivated agricultural land, regardless of the circumstances of its tenancy or ownership.

farrow The word *farrow*, "a litter of pigs," and the word *pork*, "the meat of a pig," look very different, but both go back to the same Indo-European form, *porko-*. *Porko-* is the common forebear of both the Old English ancestor of *farrow*, *fearh*, "little pig," and the Latin word *porcus*, "pig," from which our English word *pork* is derived. The development of *fearh* from *porko-* illustrates a linguistic process called Grimm's Law that is peculiar to Germanic languages. This law was formulated by Jakob Grimm, one of the Grimm Brothers who gave us *Grimm's Fairy Tales*. Grimm's Law observes that the consonants originally existing in Indo-European changed in a systematic way in the earliest Germanic speech. In the development of *porko-* to *fearh*, *p* changed to *f* and *k* changed to *h*, which in *fearh* represented not the sound of *h* but rather the sound of *ch* in the Scots word *loch*. The Latin word *porcus*, in which *c* is a spelling of the sound of *k*, preserves most of the features of the Indo-European form *porko-*. Thus the relationship between *farrow and pork*, according to Grimm's Law, is not a fairy tale.

fatal When we read the statement "It is fatal to our author ever to blunder when he talks of Egypt," from a work published in 1713, we are at a loss to know what *fatal* means in that context without having some knowledge of the word's history. The Latin adjective *fātālis*, the source of our English word *fatal*, meant primarily "destined by fate," but in later Latin it also took on the malign senses of the noun *fātum*, "fate," from which it was derived, and meant "deadly, destructive." English adopted *fatal* with its original Latin meaning, which appears in the sentence quoted above, although the pejorative sense "causing ruin or death" has now completely supplanted the more neutral sense "destined."

fate   Human beings seem to find it difficult to keep an open mind about the future: they expect either the best of times or the worst of times. The word *fate* exemplifies this tendency. *Fātum*, the Latin ancestor of *fate*, started out neutrally as the past participle of *fārī*, "to say." It originally meant "an utterance," especially an oracle or a prophecy, but even in classical times *fātum* had already come to mean "calamity" and especially "death."

fawn   The word *fawn*, "young deer," is a fascinating example of how a word can pass through various languages and end up looking very different from the way it began. This word's odyssey is particularly interesting because the descendant of the Latin word from which *fawn* comes also exists in English. If we track *fawn* backward, we find that it comes from the Old French word *feon*, also spelled *foun* and *faon*, meaning "the young of an animal" and "a young deer." This Old French word in turn goes back to a hypothetical Vulgar Latin word spelled *fētō* or, in the form that gave us *fawn*, *fētōn–*, "young of an animal." The big surprise comes now. *Fētō* is derived from Latin *fētus*, "offspring," which is just what a fawn is for a deer.

federal   When in a work of 1673 entitled *A True Notion of the Worship of God* we see the Eucharist called "a Fæderal Banquet," we are struck by a sense of *federal* not at all common nowadays. *Federal*, which goes back to the Latin word *fœdus,* "league, compact," is first recorded in English with a sense relating to a covenant, specifically one between God and humankind. *Federal* also had a more general sense, "of or relating to a covenant, compact, or treaty," dating to at least 1660. Because this sense occurred in phrases such as *federal union,* new senses of *federal* developed. One of these senses became central in describing the government of the United States: "Of or relating to a form of government in which a union of states recognizes the sovereignty of a central authority while retaining certain residual powers of government."

female Those who wonder whether *feperson* should replace *female* can set their minds at rest. The word *female* is originally unrelated to the word *male. Female* is a respelling of *femelle,* which is ultimately from the Latin word *fēmella,* a diminutive of *fēmina,* "woman." After its adoption into English from French in the fifteenth century, *femelle* was used primarily as an adjective. This circumstance led to the respelling of the word as *femal,* with *-al* regarded as the adjectival suffix. The spelling *femal,* as well as the word's obvious correlation with the word *male,* suggested an etymological association with the word *male,* an error preserved in the now standard modern spelling *female.*

fiend Discerning the semantic connection shared by a dope fiend, a crossword puzzle fiend, and a fiend with computers is not too devilishly difficult if one understands the history of *fiend.* It is possible that *fiend* goes back to the Indo-European root *pē(i)-,* meaning "to hurt." From this root comes the Germanic form *fijand-,* meaning "hating, hostile." This Germanic form gave us the Old English word *fēond,* which became our Modern English word *fiend. Fēond* meant "adversary, enemy," "the Devil"—the enemy of humankind—"a devil or evil spirit," and "a malevolent or wicked person or animal." *Fiend* later came to be used for "a person or thing that causes mischief or annoyance." People addicted to or obsessed with things can be extremely annoying to others less fiendishly dedicated. This is probably the semantic connection between the use of *fiend* for an annoying person and its use for those addicted to drugs or obsessed with crossword puzzles. One who is obsessed can become quite good at the activity toward which the obsession is directed; hence *fiend* in the sense "one who is particularly adept at something," as in the phrase *a fiend with computers.*

file   The relationship between a file in which you keep documents and a file of soldiers hangs by a thread. The various senses of the noun *file* are derived from two different French words that ultimately have the same etymology. French *file*, meaning "line of soldiers," is the source of our English word *file* in the senses "line" and "row of squares on a chessboard." The French term *fil*, "thread," is the source of our English word *file* in the sense "a receptacle for papers or documents." This sense developed in English from the practice of keeping papers in order by threading them on string or wire. The word has been extended to various storage systems for information and objects of all kinds. Both French words, *fil* and *file*, are derived from the Latin word *fīlum*, "thread."

filibuster   A *freebooter* and a *filibuster* may not share many attributes, but they do share a common linguistic ancestor: both come from the Dutch word *vrijbuiter*, which is derived from *vrij*, "free," and *buit*, "booty." *Freebooter*, first recorded in the sixteenth century, was a direct borrowing of the Dutch word. *Filibuster*, however, has had a more checkered career. The word is first recorded in English in the eighteenth century with the spelling *flibustier*, which was probably a borrowing of the French form of *vrijbuiter*. The French word *flibustier* was also adopted by the Spanish, and it is the Spanish form *filibustero* that is the immediate source of *filibuster*.

The development of the senses of *filibuster* also reflects its Spanish origins. At first *flibustier* or *filibustero* meant "pirate," but in the nineteenth century the word was used in the United States to denote an adventurer who tried to foment revolution in the Spanish colonies of Central America and the Caribbean. It was also used as a verb to indicate the activities of a filibuster. The obstreperous behavior of such pirates was probably uppermost in the minds of those who first applied the term *filibuster* to the obstreperous course taken by legislators seeking to delay or prevent legislative action.

fit   Are the crowd of amateur marathoners, joggers, weight lifters, swimmers, and other fitness devotees engaged in a Darwinian struggle for survival? Such a possibility is suggested by the development of the word *fit*, which refers to at least some of these athletes in the sense "physically sound, healthy." *Fit* is not recorded in this sense until the nineteenth century, the same century that saw the publication of Charles Darwin's *Origin of the Species* and the use of the phrase "survival of the fittest." It has been suggested that the use of *fit* to mean "physically sound" comes from the use of *fit* in this phrase, where it means "suited for a given circumstance or purpose," in this case, survival. It is possible, however, that *fit* developed the sense "physically sound" simply from the general sense "ready, prepared," as for athletic activity. But it does give a certain coloration to one's perceptions of all this amateur athletic activity to see it in Darwinian terms.

fizzle   If a waiter in a time warp placed a copy of the September 17, 1866, Richmond *Enquirer* on your hotel breakfast tray along with your croissants and coffee and you read about an "enterprise that fizzled out in the most contemptible manner," you would immediately recognize the meaning of *fizzle out*, "to fail or die out, especially after a hopeful beginning." But if you picked up a copy of Philemon Holland's translation of Pliny's *Natural History* from two hundred and sixty-five years earlier and read that if asses eat a certain plant, "they will fall a fizling and farting," you would be confronted with a completely unfamiliar meaning of the term.

Fizzle was first used in English to mean, in the decorous parlance of the *Oxford English Dictionary,* "to break wind without noise." Some scholars believe that *fizzle* probably comes from the Middle English word *fisten,* which the *Middle English Dictionary* defines in an equally decorous fashion: "to break wind."

During the nineteenth century *fizzle* took on a related but more respectable sense, "to hiss, as does a piece of fireworks," illustrated in a quotation from the November 7, 1881, issue of the London *Daily News:* "unambitious rockets which fizzle doggedly downwards." In the same century *fizzle* also took on figurative senses, one of which seems to have been popular at Yale. The *Yale Literary Magazine* for 1849 helpfully defines the word as follows: "*Fizzle,* to rise with modest reluctance, to hesitate often, to decline finally; generally, to misunderstand the question." All waffling aside, we can say with assurance that the figurative sense of *fizzle* that has caught on is the one with which we are most familiar today, "to fail or die out,"
just
    as
        this
            discussion
              is
                  doing
                      now . . .
                          with
                            a fizz,
                              a sizz,
                                a sizzle,
                                  and a
                                    wheeze.

flour   The words *flower* and *flour* have no doubt bedeviled many a young speller, but there is good historical reason for the confusion. The word *flour* is simply a specialized use of the word *flower* in a medieval spelling. The flower of wheat or any other grain is the finest part of the meal that is left after the bran has been sifted out. The distinction in spelling between *flour* and *flower* did not become standard until the nineteenth century. In a 1691 book by Thomas Tryon, entitled *Wisdom's Dictates*, we find reference to "Milk, Water, and Flower," while in Milton's *Paradise Lost* (1667) we find "O flours That never will in other climate grow."

fond   It is a good thing to be fond of someone, but at one time it was not desirable to be fond. *Fond* is a word that has undergone melioration, or a shift in connotation from bad to neutral or good. *Fond* was originally *fonned*, meaning "foolish" and "insipid, tasteless." It later meant "foolishly affectionate, doting," but even the mild reproach conveyed by this sense is no longer present in the minds of many users of this word, and *fond* is probably now most frequently used simply to mean "having a strong liking for." The verb *fon*, "to be foolish," of which *fond* was originally a past participle, may be the source of our English word *fun*.

foot   "From the *foot* of my bed I saw the *foot* of the mountain about a hundred *feet* away, but I couldn't walk there because my *feet* were sore." Like other names for parts of the body, such as *head*, the word *foot* has developed a number of senses involving transfer of meaning. The *foot* of a bed or of a grave is so called because it is where the feet are placed, every night or once and for all. *Foot* is also used metaphorically to denote the lowest part of something, such as a mountain, tree, or staircase or the lower part of a page. And finally, a *foot* is a linear measure originally derived from the length of a human foot, fortunately one that was twelve inches long.

fortune A fortunate person possesses a good fortune, not an evil one. The same lack of equanimity in facing the future that led to the restriction of *fatal* to an evil fate is evident in the development of *fortune* and *fortunate*. The Latin word *fortūna*, the source of *fortune*, meant "chance" or "luck," either good or bad. But *fortūnae*, the plural of *fortūna*, meant "possessions, goods," and the verb *fortūnāre* meant "to prosper, to make happy." *Fortūnātus*, a form of *fortūnāre*, is the ancestor of *fortunate* and meant only "happy, prosperous."

frank It is usually possible to find people who will be frank, but it is no longer possible to find a frank Frank. The word *frank*, "straightforward, open," which originally meant "free, not a serf," goes back to the Late Latin word *Francus*, "Frank," a member of the Germanic people who conquered Gaul around A.D. 500. As the dominant group in the newly conquered territory, only the Franks possessed full freedom and perhaps they were frank about that. The idea of political freedom originally conveyed by the English word *frank* was later extended to include freedom of expression as well.

frontier *The frontiers are not east or west, north or south, but wherever a man fronts a fact.*
—Henry David Thoreau, *A Week on the Concord and Merrimack Rivers*, 1849

In confronting the history of *frontier*, we learn that *frontier* and *front* are both derived from the Latin word *frōns*, "forehead, front, façade." *Frontier* was borrowed into English from French in the fifteenth century with the meaning "borderland," the region of a country that fronts on another country. The use of *frontier* to mean "a region at the edge of a settled area" is a specially American development. During most of American history the edge of the settled country was the place where unlimited amounts of cheap land were available to anyone willing to live the hard but independent life of a pioneer farmer. It has long been recognized that the experience of frontier life had an important part in shaping American society and the national character. This sense of *frontier* has also been extended to other areas of achievement and new challenges to the national will:

The New Frontier . . . is not a set of promises—it is a set of challenges. It sums up not what I intend to offer the American people, but what I intend to ask of them.
  —John Fitzgerald Kennedy, speech accepting the Democratic presidential nomination, July 15, 1960

fun   There was a time when you couldn't have any fun. The word *fun*, meaning "amusement," was probably quite new in the eighteenth century, for Dr. Johnson recorded it with disapproval in his 1775 dictionary, calling it "a low cant word." By this Johnson could have meant that *fun* was not proper to use in elevated discourse and that the people who used the word probably did not engage in such discourse. *Fun* may have come from a dialect form of the word *fon*, which meant "to make a fool of, to be foolish." *Fon* itself had become obsolete in the standard language by the end of the sixteenth century. The past participle of *fon*, originally spelled *fonned*, has become the modern English word *fond*.

funky   When asked which words in the English language are the most difficult to define precisely, the lexicographer's answer would surely include the word *funky*— a term heavy on atmosphere but light on contour. A field trip to Sol's Turf Bar in Dallas might even be required to understand the exact meaning of this popular American word. On July 23, 1985, Molly Ivins, a columnist for the Dallas *Times Herald*, wrote about the death of Solly Solomon, the owner of Sol's Turf Bar. His passing jeopardized "what may be the last authentic bit of funk in downtown Dallas," she lamented. Ivins also said that "there used to be a sizable slice of native Dallas sleaze and funk."

A reader of Ivins's column asked the editors of *The American Heritage Dictionary, Second College Edi-*

tion, what *funk* meant in these contexts. The meaning seemed well captured by Geneva Smitherman in *Talkin and Testifyin: The Language of Black America*, where she defined *funky*, from which *funk* is probably derived. According to Smitherman, *funky* means "[related to] the blue notes or blue mood created in jazz, blues, and soul music generally, down-to-earth soulfully expressed sounds; by extension [related to] the real nitty-gritty or fundamental essence of life, soul to the max." We then suggested to our correspondent that Ivins had found in Sol's Turf Bar "the real nitty-gritty or fundamental essence of life."

Be that as it may, *funky* is first recorded in 1784 in a reference to musty, old, moldy cheese. *Funky* developed the sense "smelling strong or bad," which could be used to describe body odor. But *funky* was applied to jazz, too—a usage explained in 1959 by "F. Newton" in *Jazz Scene:* "Critics are on the search for something a little more like the old, original, passion-laden blues: the trade-name which has been suggested for it is 'funky' (literally: 'smelly,' i.e. symbolising the return from the upper atmosphere to physical, down-to-earth reality)." Although the musical sense of *funk* is probably derived from *funky*, *funky* itself comes from the earlier noun *funk*, which meant "a strong smell or stink." This noun can probably be traced back to the Latin word *fūmus*, "smoke." So the smoke-filled air of a basement bar where jazz musicians perform is really a down-to-earth reflection of the word's history.

funnybone The *funnybone*, *aitchbone*, and *wishbone* appear to be whimsically if not mysteriously named. All three names, however, can be explained with the aid of etymology. *Funnybone* is formed from *funny* in the sense of "peculiar." "Peculiar" describes the sensation felt when one strikes the part of the elbow over which the ulnar nerve passes. *Aitchbone*, "the rump bone in cattle," is a good example of a folk etymology—the refashioning of a word so that it resembles a more familiar but unrelated word. *Aitchbone* comes from Middle English *nachebon*, a compound of *nache*, "buttock," and *bon*, "bone." The incorrect division between the article and the noun in *a nachebon* seems to have resulted in a new noun without the *n* on the first syllable. This syllable was interpreted in various ways, for example, as *each*, *ask*, and *aitch*—all familiar English words. The bone itself has no physical resemblance to the letter H. The *wishbone* of a bird such as a turkey gets its name from the time-honored practice of two people pulling on the bone until it breaks. Tradition has it that the person with the longer, or in some places the shorter, half of the broken wishbone will get whatever wish he or she made just before pulling the bone apart.

G

galore
"Refreshments galore!" The user of this phrase intends to convey the idea of abundance or of great numbers. The abundance denoted by *galore* may tend to whet, if not overwhelm, one's curiosity about the history of the word, which is not an ordinary one. *Galore* is one of a small group of words in the English language that has a Celtic origin. It came into English from the Irish phrase *go leór*, meaning "enough," from *go*, "to," and *leór*, "sufficiency." Although *galore* is first recorded in English in 1675, it was probably popularized by Sir Walter Scott. On April 10, 1826, he wrote in his journal, "Sent off proofs and copy galore before breakfast," which certainly should have made the word popular with his publisher.

gangplank
A gang cannot walk the gangplank, regardless of the wishes of the Blackbeards and the Blighs. Although
(continued)

Gauntlet

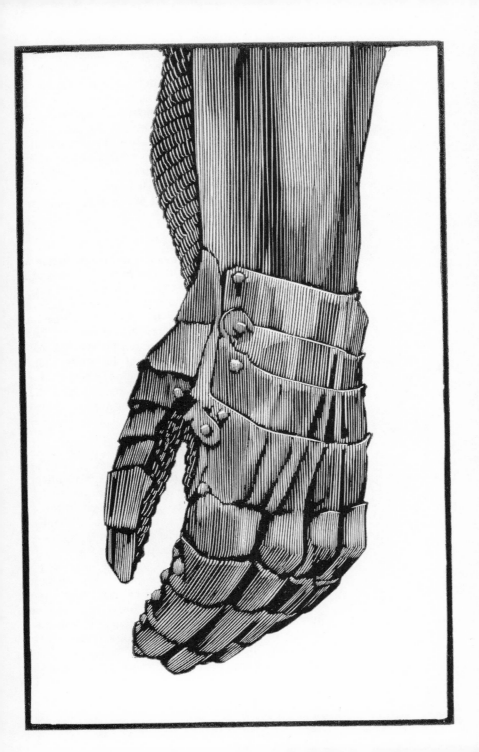

the element *gang-* in *gangplank* and *gangway* is the same as the word *gang*, it preserves an older meaning of that word. In Old and Middle English *gang* denoted the action of walking, with specific applications such as "way, passage," and "journey." A gangplank therefore provides passage between a ship and a landing place, which among pirates was at times a final resting place. *Gangway* denotes a gangplank as well as various other kinds of passageways, such as aisles. *Gang* is related to the Old English verb *gangan*, "to walk, go"; thus a gang is a set of people, animals, or things that go together.

garlic Hidden in the word *garlic* is a figurative reference to its appearance, which we can retrieve by digging at its roots. *Garlic* comes from the Old English word *gārlēac*, which is a compound word made up of *gār*, "spear," and *lēac*, "leek." This compound is based on two resemblances. One reflects the similar smell and taste of garlic and the leek, another plant of the genus *Allium*. The other may reflect the similar shapes of a clove of garlic and a spearhead. The figurative expression originally present in Old English *gārlēac* has lost its point, if not its pungency, in Modern English *garlic*.

gas Benign gases (as well as some not so benign ones) are everywhere around us in the atmosphere. We might be disturbed to think that chaos was also present there. The word *gas* was possibly suggested by the Greek word *khaos* to a seventeenth-century Flemish chemist, Jan Baptista van Helmont. Van Helmont used the term *gas* to describe the purest form of an object. This form consisted of water, of which van Helmont believed everything was ultimately made, but water in a volatile state. Furthermore, that water carried a plan for the form, function, nutrition, reproduction, and perfection of the particular object. According to van Helmont, gas was not very different "from the Chaos of the Auntients [ancients]." In Greek *khaos* meant the first formless state of matter.

94

Van Helmont was also dealing with unformed matter, but his matter was specific to a given object, unlike the Greek *khaos*. We are very familiar with van Helmont's term, but not in the sense in which he used it, a sense last recorded in 1743. *Gas* went on to develop the senses it has today, including the sense referring to the gaseous components of the atmosphere, so we can all breathe easily.

gauntlet   If you throw down the gauntlet, you may end up running the gauntlet, but are you doing two things with any etymological connection? The two English words spelled *gauntlet* are in truth unrelated in origin and meaning; they share only the fate of now being restricted to idiomatic phrases. The first *gauntlet*, "a protective glove," is derived from the Old French word *gantelet*, a diminutive of *gant*, "glove." *To throw down the gauntlet* means "to offer a challenge," which in medieval times was done by throwing down a glove or gauntlet. The second *gauntlet* denotes a type of punishment in which an offender was forced to run between two lines of men who beat him with weapons such as sticks or knotted cords. This word *gauntlet* is an alteration of the earlier English form *gantlope*, which came from the Swedish word *gatlopp*, a compound of *gata*, "lane," and *lopp*, "course." It is not clear exactly why *gantlope* was altered so radically from the original Swedish form, but the change occurred soon after the word was borrowed into English during the seventeenth century.

general   In the profession of arms how general is a general? The Latin adjective *generālis*, from which the English word *general* comes, meant literally "pertaining to the whole genus (kind or class)." The English noun *general*, "a military officer," preserves something of the earlier Latin sense. It designates a general officer, that is, the commander of the general, or entire, army. In the United States several armies make up the Army, and generals are assisted by lieutenant ("holding the place of") generals, major (though in some sense minor) generals, and brigadier (from French *brigade*, "brigade") generals, putting the word *general* into quite general use.

genius Einstein and Beethoven were geniuses, but neither one was a genius in the sense in which we originally borrowed the word from Latin. No mortal could be. In its first recorded English use in 1513 a genius was an attendant spirit, given to one at birth to guide one's fortunes, determine one's character, and lead one out of the world at the time of death. The Latin word *genius* also had other senses that may have contributed to the development of senses in English, inasmuch as Latin was known to many English writers during this period. A few decades after the sense "attendant spirit" appears in English, we find the related sense "characteristic disposition" first recorded. This sense is well illustrated in Samuel Johnson's statement, "Every man has his genius . . . my genius is always in extremes." From this sense it is a short step to "natural talent or inclination," as in this quotation from William Robertson's *History of Scotland*, published in 1759: "His genius was of that kind which ripens slowly." It is also easy enough to understand the development to the senses "native intellectual power of an exalted type" and "one who possesses such power." That development in the meaning of the word was affected by, among other things, the desire of eighteenth-century German writers to distinguish between genius, thought to be original and spontaneous, and talent, seen as a lower order of competence. In a way our geniuses are still our guiding spirits.

gentle The three words *gentile, gentle,* and *genteel* all come from the Latin word *gentīlis*, "belonging to the same nation or clan." This Latin word was used for those belonging to a nation or clan different from one's own; hence, it came to mean a non-Roman and, in Christian writings, a non-Jew or a non-Christian. The Latin word *gentīlis* in this extended sense is the

96

source of our English word *gentile*. The Latin word passed into Old French, as well as into other Romance languages. In these languages the descendants of the Latin word were gentrified, so to speak, and developed the sense "noble, well-born." In the twelfth or thirteenth century the Old French word *gentil* was borrowed into English, in which its earliest recorded sense is "of noble rank or birth, belonging to the gentry, noble." In the sixteenth century the French word was borrowed again as *genteel*, meaning "well-born," although not necessarily "noble."

geranium If you can tell the difference in shape between the bill of a crane and the bill of a stork, you should be able to tell the difference between the plants of the two different but related genera to which the word *geranium* refers. One genus is called *Geranium*, which is ultimately from the Greek word *geranos*, "crane." The genus is so named because the fruits of the plants that belong to it are similar in shape to the bill of a crane. The popular name for these plants is *cranesbill*. The plant commonly called the *geranium* in English belongs to the genus *Pelargonium*, from *pelargos*, the Greek word for "stork." The name for this genus also alludes to the shape of its fruit, which resembles the bill of a stork.

gerrymander "An official statement of the returns of voters for senators give[s] twenty nine friends of peace, and eleven gerrymanders." So reported the May 12, 1813, edition of the *Massachusetts Spy*. A gerrymander sounds like a strange political beast, which in fact it is, considered from a historical perspective. This beast was named by combining the word *salamander*, "a small lizardlike amphibian," with the last name of Elbridge Gerry, governor of Massachusetts—a state noted for its varied, often colorful political fauna. Gerry (whose name, incidentally, was pronounced with a hard g, though *gerrymander* is now commonly pronounced with a soft g) was immortalized in this way because an election district created by members of his party in 1812 looked like a salamander. According to one version of how *gerrymander* was coined, the shape of the district attracted the eye of the painter Gilbert Stuart, who noticed it on a map hanging in a newspaper editor's office. Stuart decorated the map with a head, wings, and claws and then said to the editor, "That will do for a salamander!" "Gerrymander!" came the reply. A new political beast was born then and there.

The word is first recorded in April, 1812, with respect to the creature or its caricature, but it soon came to mean not only "the action of shaping a district to gain political advantage" but also "any representative elected from such a district by that method." Within the same year *gerrymander* was recorded as a verb, too. How did Governor Gerry himself feel about all this? It is thought that he was actually lukewarm about the idea of creating this particular district (which included his home town of Marblehead), although he signed the bill enabling its formation. His linguistic, if not political, fate (he died on November 23, 1814, as vice president to James Madison) teaches a valuable political lesson: if you feel lukewarm, don't sign the bill.

ghost   When the character Aeneas in Chaucer's *Legend of Good Women* says that "this nyght my faderes gost Hath in my slep so sore me tormented" (during this night my father's ghost has distressed me so intensely in my sleep), we know what sort of ghost is meant. This sense of *ghost* is probably the one with the greatest currency in Modern English, although ghosts might reasonably complain of stereotyping, as they are popularly represented as occupying very material sheets. On the basis of this sense, *ghost* has been extended in meaning to refer to things such as a slight trace or bit, as in *a ghost of a chance*, or to one who writes for and gives the credit of authorship to someone else. Traces (or ghosts) of other senses of *ghost*, which were in wider use before it became so specialized in meaning, still survive in the phrase *give up* *the ghost* and the term *Holy Ghost.* In *give up the ghost, ghost* retains the sense "a human soul as the principle of life." In *Holy Ghost* the word refers to the Holy Spirit. This usage harks back to the meaning "a spiritual being."

girl A girl could once be a boy. In Modern English *girl* is the ordinary word denoting a female child. However, in Middle English times from the thirteenth to the fifteenth century *girl* was truly a unisex word: it was used to refer to a child or youth of either sex. Nothing is known of the history of *girl* before its appearance in English, and no clearly related forms exist in any other language.

glamour "The glamour of grammar" is an unlikely combination. The words are related, however, for both are descended from the Greek word *grammatikē* through the Latin word *grammatica*. The Greek word originally meant "pertaining to letters or literature," from *gramma*, "letter, written character." In medieval times the Latin word denoted not just literacy but learning in general, including knowledge of occult sciences such as astrology and magic. The extended sense of the Latin word *grammatica* was preserved by its Old French descendant *gramaire*, which was borrowed into English and became our modern word *grammar*. In the Scots dialect of English the letter *l* seems to have been substituted for the first *r* in *grammar*, which would help explain the form of the Scots word *glamour*, first recorded in the eighteenth century. The Scots word, however, preserved only the sense "magic, magic spell." *Glamour* was introduced into standard English with the meaning "magic spell" by Sir Walter Scott. We also find *glamour* used in this way by Tennyson in 1859 in his *Idylls of the King:* "That maiden in the tale, Whom Gwydion made by glamour out of flowers." The current sense of *glamour*, "alluring charm," developed in English later in the nineteenth century. Such glamour has moved far away from Scottish scenes of enchantment, as we see in a quotation from a February, 1958, woman's magazine: "Kitchen needs glamour badly; looks too antiseptic due to all-over white painted walls." The Usage Panel of *The American Heritage Dictionary, Second College Edition,* would quarrel with the phrase *due to,* favoring *because of* or *on account of* instead; it has expressed no opinions on the subject of glamorous kitchens.

gospel   The ancestor of *gospel* is the Old English compound *goodspel,* literally "good tidings." *Gōdspel* is a loan translation, which means that it literally translates the elements of a word in another language, in this case the Latin word *evangelium. Evangelium* comes from the Greek word *euangelion,* which is derived from *eus,* "good," and *angelos,* "messenger," from which our word *angel* is derived. *Euangelion* in Christian contexts meant "good tidings," specifically the good news of the kingdom of God brought by Jesus. And that is the gospel truth.

gossip   Calling someone a gossip in the Middle Ages was not derogatory at all. *Gossip* was originally a compound of *god,* "God," and *sib,* "blood relation," and meant "godparent." *Sib* is still used but is perhaps better known in the word *sibling* derived from it. At first referring only to the relationship of godparent to godchild, *gossip* was later used to indicate the relationship of godparent to parent or the relationship between the godparents of the same child. *Gossip* thus designated a relationship of peers as much as one between generations, and from such extended senses the meaning "friend, pal," evolved. Knowing our tendency to chat idly about other people with our friends, we should not be surprised that the word came to refer to a person who engages in idle chatter and rumormongering, a sense first recorded in the sixteenth century. Another contemporary sense, "the conversation of a gossip," is recorded for the first time in the nineteenth century, while the verb is first recorded in the sense "to engage in gossip" in the sev-

100

enteenth century. People have been gossiping ever since.

grog When one feels groggy on the morning after the night before, it might be worth noting that the word *grog*, from which *groggy* is derived, is said to have come into existence because of an attempt to curb drunkenness more than two hundred years ago. One version of how *grog* was coined has it that in August, 1749, Admiral Edward Vernon of the Royal Navy, wishing to practice economy and to decrease the number of drunken brawls on his ships as well, ordered that all rations of rum were to be watered down and provided no more than twice a day, six hours apart. The irate but less groggy sailors named this diluted mixture *grog*. *Grog* came from Vernon's nickname, "Old Grog," an appellation he acquired because his boat cloak was made of a coarse fabric called *grogram*. *Grog* and *groggy* are first recorded in English as part of a single statement in the *Gentlemen's Magazine* of 1770, in a glossary of terms for drunkenness: "Groggy; this is a West-Indian Phrase; Rum and Water, without sugar, being called Grogg."

groom A bride would stand beside her *gome* at their wedding, were it not for a linguistic process known as folk etymology. In this process an unfamiliar word element is replaced by, or refashioned to resemble, a more familiar word. The Old English ancestor of *bridegroom* was *brȳdguma*, literally "bride's man," and this Old English word became the Middle English term *bridgome*. *Guma*, related to the Latin word *homo*, "human being, man," was an Old English word for "man" that later became the Middle English and Early Modern English word *gome*, a term that did not survive the sixteenth century. Not long before *gome* disappeared from the language, *groom* came into general use as a word for "man" or "youth," and *gome* in the compound *bridgome* was replaced by the more familiar word *groom*. The modern use of *groom* to mean "bridegroom" results from shortening the compound.

guillotine "At half past 12 the guillotine severed her head from her body." So reads the statement containing the first recorded use of *guillotine* in English, found in the *Annual Register* of 1793. The word occurs in a context clearly illustrating the function of the guillotine, "a machine with a heavy blade that falls freely between upright guides to behead a condemned person." Ironically, the guillotine, which became the most notable symbol of the excesses of the French Revolution, was named for a humanitarian physician, Joseph Ignace Guillotin. Guillotin, a member of the French Constituent Assembly, recommended in a speech to that body on October 10, 1789, that executions be performed by a beheading device rather than by hanging, the method used for commoners, or by the sword, reserved for the nobility. He argued that beheading by machine was quicker and less painful than the work of the rope and the sword.

In 1791 the Assembly did indeed adopt beheading by machine as the state's preferred method of execution. A beheading device designed by Dr. Antoine Louis, secretary of the College of Surgeons, was first used on April 25, 1792, to execute a highwayman named Pelletier or Peletier. The device was called a *louisette* or *louison* after its inventor's name, but because of Guillotin's famous speech, his name became irrevocably associated with the machine. After Guillotin's death in 1814, his children tried unsuccessfully to get the device's name changed. When their efforts failed, they were allowed to change their name instead.

gun Lady Gunilda sounds like the name of a Scandinavian noblewoman—and an aggressive, Wagnerian one at that, given the nature of her name, originally a compound of two Old Norse words meaning "battle," which were also the names of two Old Norse goddesses of battle. However, Lady Gunilda was certainly no lady. Instead, Her Ladyship was a missile-casting "ballista," a siege engine in the form of a huge crossbow. This device was nicknamed Lady Gunilda, in the manner of Krupp's Big Bertha, the powerful artil-

102

lery piece developed nearly six hundred years after we find Lady Gunilda mentioned in a Windsor Castle munitions inventory dated 1330–31. Lady Gunilda seems to have become even more combative over time. The existence of the Middle English word *gonnilde,* which meant "a cannon" and which was also derived from the Old Norse name, makes it seem likely that *gun* goes back to the use of names such as *Gunilda* for siege engines and cannon. (Strictly speaking, *gun* would have come from the normal shortened form, *Gunne,* of the Old Norse name.) During its history in Middle English the word *gun* was used for siege engines and cannon as well as for portable firearms.

guppy   R. J. Lechmere Guppy and his contributions to natural history are for the most part forgotten, but his name is more familiar than that of many a better-known naturalist. Guppy was a clergyman of Trinidad who delighted in ichthyology. In the mid-nineteenth century he sent to the British Museum a collection of New World fishes. Among them was a new species, which was named after him, *Gerardinus guppyi.* The fish was later renamed *Poecilia reticulata* or *Lebistes reticulatus,* but it still bears the common name *guppy.*

guy   "I can't tonight, for I am going to be seduced by a rich old Guy." So appears *guy* in its first recorded use in the sense "a man, fellow," in a work called *Swell's Night Guide,* published in 1847. This use of *guy* may have been influenced by a sense of *guy* that is recorded earlier in English: "a person of odd appearance or dress." Still current chiefly in British English, this sense is first found in Julia Charlotte Maitland's *Letters from Madras during the Years 1836–39 by a Lady:* "The gentlemen are all 'rigged Tropical' . . . grisly Guys some of them turn out!" Even if our original speaker's *guy* was old and odd in appearance, at least he was rich and alive, the latter of which cannot be said for the earliest type of *guy,* "an effigy of Guy Fawkes paraded through the streets of English towns and burned on Guy Fawkes Day."

Guy Fawkes was a leader of the Gunpowder Plot, a scheme to blow up King James I and the Parliament during its ceremonial opening on November 5, 1605. The plot was foiled when Fawkes was arrested on the night of November 4, probably in the cellar of the House of Lords, where the gunpowder was stashed. Fawkes was tortured, signed a confession implicating the other members of the plot in a decidedly shaky hand, and was hanged with his fellow conspirators on January 31, 1606. That same year November 5 became a holiday, Guy Fawkes Day. On that day children wandered through the streets carrying figures dressed in old clothes, which they called *guys* after Guy Fawkes, lit bonfires, and set off fireworks (still a feature of Guy Fawkes Day). Because these figures were dressed in rags and clothes that did not match, *guy* came to mean "a person of odd appearance." This sense in turn gave us the word's use for any guy, including a rich old one.

H

hangnail This article will be of special interest to podiatrists and their patients, who will be fascinated to learn that a corn became a hangnail, in a manner of speaking, through folk etymology. By this process an unfamiliar element in a word is made to resemble a more familiar word—one that is often semantically associated with the word being refashioned. The Old English ancestor of *hangnail* was *angnægl*, a compound of *ang-*, "tight, painful," and *nægl*, "nail, peg." The Old English word originally meant "corn on the foot," the corn being viewed as a painful, hard,

(continued)

Humble Pie

104

rounded excrescence like a nail. Later the descendant of the Old English word had its second element associated with the nails of the fingers or toes and came to mean various kinds of painful conditions in their vicinity. These conditions included what is now called a *hangnail*. Because a hangnail consists of partially detached skin, the unfamiliar element *ang–* was refashioned in modern times as *hang*. A more normal modern development of Old English *angnægl*, and a rare form still current, is *agnail*.

hassock What could be more cosy and domestic than a hassock on which to rest your tired feet? Surprisingly enough, our word *hassock* got its start not in a furniture factory but in a bog. *Hassock*, as well as its ancestor, the Middle English word *hassok*, and probably its earlier ancester, the Old English word *hassuc*, all refer to a dense clump of vegetation, such as coarse grass, found in boggy ground. People at one time removed these clumps, or tussocks, from the bogs and used them as kneeling cushions in churches. (Using these all-natural articles, the good parishioners were not subjected to the annoying ritual of trying to remove unsightly content-certification tags sewn into their hassocks and reading

UNDER PENALTY OF LAW
THIS TAG NOT TO BE REMOVED
EXCEPT BY THE CONSUMER

as is the case today with the objects we call *hassocks*.) At some point, manufactured hassocks based on the idea of the natural ones came into use. *Hassock* then took on the meaning "a thick cushion used as a footstool or for kneeling," first recorded in 1516. Although hassocks continued to be used in churches, they also found a place in the home as a support for the tired feet of people ready to relax after a long day bogged down in that quagmire called The Office.

hearse Today's usual meaning of *hearse*, "a vehicle for transporting the dead," was the latest to develop. The

Latin word *hirpex*, the ancestor of *hearse*, meant "harrow," an agricultural implement that in one of its forms consists of a framework with teeth and is used to break up plowed land. The emergence of the sense "vehicle" occurred through a series of logical steps. The first meaning of the English word *hearse*, recorded in the thirteenth century, was "a framework used for holding candles," which no doubt resembled an agricultural harrow. This framework was used at the Holy Week service of Tenebrae, during which all the candles in church were extinguished in commemoration of Christ's death and descent into Hell. Such hearses also held candles over a coffin at a funeral. Later extensions of the meaning of *hearse* preserved the idea of a framework and the funereal circumstances of its use. In the sixteenth century the word denoted a support for the funeral pall, and in the seventeenth century it indicated the bier or coffin itself. Finally, late in the seventeenth century, *hearse* was used to describe the vehicle that carries the coffin at a funeral.

hector The word *hector*, which is both a noun meaning "a bully" and a verb meaning "to intimidate," is derived from Hector, the Trojan prince killed by Achilles who figures so prominently in the *Iliad*. In the seventeenth century the name of this prince was used generically for a swaggering braggart or bully. In a 1693 work by the annalist Narcissus Luttrel we read that "on Sunday night last 3 hectors came out of a tavern in Holborn, with their swords drawn, and began to break windows." The behavior of such persons is denoted by the verb *hector*, which appeared in English at the same time as the noun.

hedge When we say we need a hedge against inflation, we probably do not stop to think of a leaf-filled hedge bordering an English field, unless the field itself is an investment. The two kinds of hedges are related semantically, however. Hedges have been used in England and elsewhere for hundreds of years as fences to enclose fields and mark the boundaries between them. They also provide shelter for birds and small animals and will, in a pinch, provide the same for human beings. This property of hedges probably gave rise to the sense "a means of protection or defense," which has been current since the fourteenth century. In the seventeenth century that meaning of *hedge* was applied to a financial loss, especially one incurred through investment or gambling. The noun *hedge*, meaning "a protection against financial loss," is derived from the verb.

helicopter The next time you are stuck in a gridlock listening with increasing desperation to the Yeageresque voice of a helicopter pilot confirming your fate on your car radio, you might turn off the bad news. Instead, turn your attention to the name of the vehicle that gives the pilot the freedom of movement to survey your motionless state. The origin of the word *helicopter* is apparent only upon due recognition of its Greek ancestors. *Helicopter* was borrowed from the French word *hélicoptère*, a word constructed from Greek *heliko-* and *pteron*, "wing." *Heliko-* is a form of *helix*, "spiral," that combines with other words and word forms to create new words. The consonant cluster *pt* in *pteron* begins many Greek words but relatively few English words, so English speakers who are unfamiliar with Greek do not think of the word's elements as *helico-pter*. At least some English speakers have analyzed the word into the elements *heli-copter*, as is shown by the clipped form *copter*. This form keeps the wing but loses the spiral. Look out below!

hell The word *hell* has existed since Old English times as the name for an abode of the dead, Christian or pagan. *Hell* is derived from an Indo-European form that probably had the basic sense "hide" or "conceal." *Hell* has many relatives in the Germanic and other Indo-European languages. English words related to *hell* are *helmet*, *hull*, *hole*, *hollow*, and *hall*. The Old Norse word *hel* indicated the abode of the dead (*hel*), like English *hell*, and also denoted the goddess (*Hel*) who ruled it. A Latin relative of *hell* is the verb *occulere*, "to cover over," from which our English word *occult* is derived. A Greek word related to *hell* is the verb *kaluptein*, "to conceal." The name of the goddess Calypso, who hid Odysseus on an island for seven years, is derived from *kaluptein*.

helpmeet   A man should look for a helpmeet who is suitable for him, and he may do this with good etymological justification. The word *helpmeet* owes its existence to a misreading of a passage in the King James Bible. In Genesis 2:18 God promises Adam to "make him an help meet for him," that is, a helper meet or suitable for him. Even in the seventeenth century the words *help meet* were misread as one word, and since the "help" turned out to be Eve, the new compound was interpreted to mean "spouse." *Helpmate*, first recorded in the eighteenth century, is an alteration of *helpmeet* that substituted *mate*, "spouse," for the unintelligible *meet* of *helpmeet*. Although both words are usually used to refer to a spouse, *helpmeet* and *helpmate* are also used for other sorts of helpers or companions. Thomas Pennant in *British Zoology*, published in the mid-eighteenth century, says that "in Minorca the ass and the hog are common helpmates, and are yoked together in order to turn up the land."

hermetic   What do alchemy and an Egyptian god have to do with a hermetic seal? The word *hermetic* is used to refer to an airtight seal because of a roundabout chain of circumstances. *Hermetic* is an adjective derived from the name of the god Hermes, specifically Hermes Trismegistus, the Greek designation for the Egyptian god Thoth, who was regarded as the originator of the science of alchemy. Beginning in the seventeenth century, the adjective *hermetic* meant "pertaining to alchemy" and the occult sciences in general. Alchemy, and later chemistry, was itself known as the hermetic art, philosophy, or science. A hermetic seal was a kind of seal used by alchemists that involved melting closed an opening in a glass vessel. Since the resultant seal was airtight, any similar type of seal has come to be called *hermetic*.

hibernate   An animal hibernating in the Himalayas may escape the rigors of winter biologically, but etymologically winter is very much with it. The English word *hibernate* is ultimately derived from the Latin word *hībernus*, meaning "wintry." *Hīburnus* goes back to the Indo-European root *ghei-²*, from which the Sanskrit form *himā-*, "snow," is also derived. The name *Himalaya* is a Sanskrit compound of *himā-* and *alaya*, "abode, place," and means "the place of snow."

hippocampus   It is part of the human condition to have sea horses on the brain, if not bats in the belfry. The anatomical structure called the *hippocampus*, "one of two ridges along each lateral ventricle of the brain," derives its name from its resemblance to the sea horse, a marine animal belonging to the genus *Hippocampus*. The word *hippocampus*, derived from Greek *hippokampos*, a compound of *hippos*, "horse," and *kampos*, "sea monster," was the name of a creature ridden by Poseidon and other sea gods. According to legend, this beast had a horse's body and a fish's tail.

hobby   Hobbies are generally considered relaxing activities, akin to the play of children, and the history of the word *hobby* seems itself to be involved with play. *Hobby* goes back to *Hobin*, a nickname for *Robin* said to have been used by ploughmen for their horses. *Hobby*, which originally meant "a small horse," became part of the compound *hobbyhorse*, first recorded in 1557 and meaning "a person who performed with the figure of a horse in a morris dance." *Hobbyhorse* is then recorded in other senses, including "a toy horse for children to ride." This last meaning led to the development of the sense "an activity pursued for pleasure" for *hobbyhorse* and hence for *hobby*, which borrowed several senses from *hobbyhorse*, including the sense "pleasurable activity." Thus a grown-up's pleasurable activity was thought to be like a favorite toy horse for a child.

hoggish   The struggles between the *hoggish* and the *dogged* may mean nothing to the *bovine*, but the *feline* and the *foxy* watch closely to see how the outcome may benefit them, while at the same time avoiding being bumped by the *horsy*. This menagerie of adjectives is good linquistic evidence for the close connection between man and beast. Some of the perceived characteristics transferred to man in these zoological adjectives are the selfishness of the hog (*hoggish* from *hog*); the persistence found in certain kinds of dogs (*dogged* from *dog*); the stolidness of the cow (*bovine* from Late Latin *bovīnus*, from Latin *bōs*, "cow"); the slyness of the cat (*feline* from Vulgar Latin *fēlīnus*, from Latin *fēlēs*, "any of several small carnivorous animals, probably including the wildcat"); the craftiness of the fox (*foxy* from *fox*); and perhaps the bulk of a horse in relationship to people in close proximity (*horsy* from *horse*). These adjectives offer proof for the notion that man contains the universe within him.

honcho   *Honcho* sounds like a word out of the American West, keeping company with sheriffs and bandits. But *honcho* actually comes from the Far East, that is, from the Japanese word *hanchō*, "squad leader," a compound of *han*, "squad," and *chō*, "leader." It is said that the word was brought back to the United States by fliers stationed in Japan during both the occupation following World War II and the Korean War. The evidence seems to bear this statement out, for the word is first recorded in James M. Bertram's *Shadow of a War*, published in 1947. Since then, *honcho* has become fully Americanized. We find honchos in all walks of life, from Lawrence Spivak, "retiring honcho of NBC's 'Meet the Press'" (*Variety*, July 16, 1975), to Ray Kroc, "McDonald hamburger honcho"

(*Variety*, June 1, 1977). Then there is John Nemec, the "suspender honcho from San Francisco" (*The New Yorker*, June 19, 1978).

hooker In his *Personal Memoirs* Ulysses S. Grant described Major General Joseph Hooker as "a dangerous man . . . not subordinate to his superiors." Hooker had his faults, of course. He may indeed have been insubordinate; undoubtedly he was an erratic leader. But there is one thing of which he is often accused that "Fighting Joe" Hooker certainly did not do: he did not give his name to prostitutes. According to a popular story, the men under Hooker's command during the Civil War were a particularly wild bunch. When his troops were on leave, we are told, they spent much of their time in brothels. For this reason, as the story goes, prostitutes came to be known as *hookers*. It is not difficult to understand how such a theory might have originated. The major general's name differs from the word *hooker* only in the capital letter that begins it. And it is true that Hooker's men were at times ill-disciplined (although it seems that liquor, not women, was the main source of their difficulties with the provost marshal).

However attractive this theory may be, it cannot be true. The word *hooker*, with the sense "prostitute," is in fact older than the Civil War. It appeared in the second edition (though not in the first) of John Russell Bartlett's *Dictionary of Americanisms*, published in 1859. Bartlett defined *hooker* as "a strumpet, a sailor's trull." He also said that the word was derived from Corlear's Hook, a district in New York City, but this was only a guess. There is no evidence that the term originated in New York. Norman Ellsworth Eliason has traced this use of *hooker* back to 1845 in North Carolina. He reported the usage in *Tarheel Talk; an Historical Study of the English Language in North Carolina to 1860*, published in 1956. The fact that we have no earlier written evidence does not mean that *hooker* was never used to mean "prostitute" before 1845. The history of *hooker* is, quite simply, murky; we do not know when or where it was first used, but we can be very certain that it did not begin with Joseph Hooker. Also, we have no firm evidence that it came from Corlear's Hook.

Scholarly evidence or lack thereof notwithstanding, the late Bruce Catton, the Civil War historian, did not go so far as to exonerate completely the Union general. Although "the term 'hooker' did not originate during the Civil War," wrote Catton, "it certainly became popular then. During these war years, Washington developed a large [district] somewhere south of Constitution Avenue. This became known as Hooker's Division in tribute to the proclivities of General Joseph Hooker and the name has stuck ever since."

If the term *hooker* was derived neither from Joseph Hooker nor from Corlears's Hook, what is its derivation? It is most likely that this *hooker* is, etymologically, simply "one who hooks." The term portrays a prostitute as a person who hooks, or snares, clients.

hopscotch The Scots, many of whom do not like the use of the word *Scotch* except for their whisky (not whiskey, if you please), have no cause to take offense at the word *hopscotch*. *Scotch* in this compound refers to a line marked on the ground in the game. *Scotch*, which first meant "an incision, cut, or gash," comes from the verb *scotch*, of unknown origin, meaning "to make an incision or cut in." The compound *hopscotch* simply refers to hopping a marked line or lines, as is done in the game. As a matter of fact, in seventeenth-century references to the game children played *Scotch-hoppers*. In the eighteenth century the form *hop-scot* made its appearance. Finally, in the early nineteenth century, the short-lived form *hop-score* emerged, along with the still hopping *hop-scotch*.

hostage Although the word *hostage* has appeared in the press frequently during recent years, part of its original meaning never emerges in modern usage. *Hostage,* which goes back through several stages to the Latin word *obses,* "hostage," meant, among other things, "a person given or held as security for the fulfillment of an agreement or as a guarantee of one's good faith." This general sense of *hostage* is still central and current, but in light of the hostage-taking incidents of today, the word *given* in this definition must strike us as incongruous, unless we recall that in earlier years persons sometimes offered themselves or were offered as hostages against the fulfillment of a promise or accomplishment of a deed. The word *held* in the definition is certainly applicable to many recent incidents, as are the Middle English phrases *nimen hostages* and *taken hostages,* both meaning "to take hostages."

humble pie   Every now and then we have to dismount from our high horses, put our pride in our pockets, and sit down to a meal of crow—or humble pie, as the case may be. But eating humble pie at one time required a taste for viscera. *Humble pie* has no etymological connection with humility, although the spelling of the phrase has probably been influenced by the adjective *humble. Humble pie* originally meant a dish made of an animal's *numbles,* that is, its entrails and other internal organs—a gastroenterological delight that would no doubt appeal to those who like haggis. *Numbles,* the original form of the first part of this compound, was borrowed from French in the fourteenth century. In the fifteenth century the variant form *umbles* appeared and existed alongside *numbles* through the eighteenth century, especially in the compound *umble pie.*

The idiom *to eat humble pie* very possibly arose in a dialect in which the *h* at the beginning of words was not pronounced. In such a dialect *umble* and the adjective *humble* would be pronounced alike, and the semantic confusion, or the pun, involved in the idiom would be possible. *Humble pie* is first recorded before 1648 with reference to the actual dish and in 1830 as part of the idiomatic phrase. The idiom is perhaps best preserved in the words of Charles Dickens's mean, crafty, malicious Uriah Heep, who says, in his *h*-dropping dialect, "When I was quite a young boy . . . I got to know what umbleness did, and I took to it. I ate umble pie with an appetite."

humor   The Latin word *ūmōr* or *hūmōr*, from which English *humor* is derived, meant "a liquid, fluid, moisture." The word first appeared in English during the Middle Ages with that meaning. *Humor* came to denote mental qualities and disposition through its use in medieval physiology. A *humor* was therein defined as one of the four principal fluids of the body (blood, bile, phlegm, and black bile). The preponderance of one or another humor in a given person imparted a characteristic temperament or disposition, also called a *humor*. The word then came to indicate changing moods or states of mind, particularly whimsical and capricious fancies that, when revealed in action, afford amusement to others. *Humor* at last came to mean the ability both to amuse others and to appreciate those things that are amusing.

hussy   *Hussy* and *housewife* were originally synonyms, both meaning "mistress of a household." The word *hussy*, "a saucy or mischievous girl; an immoral woman," illustrates a normal phonetic development of the Middle English compound *huswif*, which is also the ancestor of our Modern English word *housewife*. The development of *huswif* into *hussy*, completed by the seventeenth century, included the loss of *w* and later the loss of *f*. *Housewife* is much closer in spelling than *hussy* is to their common Middle English ancestor, *huswif*, but today we do not pronounce the vowels in *housewife* as they were pronounced in Middle English *huswif*. The *u and i* in *huswif*, pronounced (ōō) and (ē) in Middle English, are now pronounced (ou) and (ī). As *hussy* acquired its pejorative semantic baggage, *housewife* became restricted in meaning to the original sense of the word.

iceberg To go below the tip of the word *iceberg* etymologically and semantically is to find that *iceberg* is probably a borrowing of the Danish or Norwegian word
isberg, although it is also possible that the word came
from the Dutch word *ijsberg.* These words are all
compounds formed from a word meaning "ice," such
as Danish *is,* and a word meaning "mountain, hill,"
such as Danish *berg. Iceberg* in English is first recorded with the meaning "an Arctic glacier that
comes close to the coast and is seen from the sea as a
hill or protruberance." About fifty years later the
word is recorded in the sense "a massive floating
body of ice broken away from a glacier," the only
current sense having to do with ice. *Iceberg* then developed figurative senses, one of which is "a cold or
aloof person."

Another figurative development reflects the fact that
only about one ninth of an iceberg's total mass appears above the water. At first *iceberg* alone was used
figuratively, as a statement in the July 26, 1964, edition of *The Observer* indicates: "This . . . situation is
illustrated by what is . . . called the iceberg of disease.
Above the surface is the illness we know about." The

Iris

expression *tip of the iceberg* is first recorded in 1969 in Michael Gilbert's *Etruscan Net,* although the quotation makes it clear that the expression is not new: "I believe that Broke's been made the victim of an elaborate frame-up. I think, to employ a well-known metaphor, that all we can see at the moment is the tip of the iceberg, and that there is depth beyond depth below it."

idiom   "I'm going to pack it up, take a powder, and make the scene somewhere else." This sentence would undoubtedly be the despair of anyone unfamiliar with English because it is constructed almost entirely of idioms. An idiom is a speech form or expression that is peculiar to itelf grammatically or that cannot be understood from the individual meanings of its elements. *Pack it up,* for example, does not mean "to pack something up" but rather "to stop doing, finish." The word *idiom,* like *idiot,* is derived ultimately from Greek *idios,* "private." The Greek word *idiōma* meant basically any peculiarity or unique feature, and especially a peculiarity of language or literary style. In English the word *idiom* was first used to mean "language in general," then "dialect," and finally "a peculiarity of expression, phrase, or grammatical construction," as in the phrase with which we leave the gentle reader, *so long.*

idiot   *"If the law supposes that," said Mr. Bumble . . . "the law is a ass—a idiot."*
              —Charles Dickens, *Oliver Twist,* 1837–38

The law is made by public officials, but the Greek word *idiōtēs,* the source of our word *idiot,* is derived from *idios,* "private," and originally meant a private citizen in contrast to a public official. The use of *idiōtēs* was extended to the private element of other pairs of opposites, such as *layman/professional, layman/priest, common person/distinguished person,* and *unskilled worker/craftsman.* In general, a person of no special status, knowledge, or skill was *idiōtēs,* and the term thus became one of abuse.

118

ignoramus   In the early seventeenth century the word *ignoramus* referred to an ignorant, arrogant attorney. The word has undergone several changes in meaning since its initial migration from Latin into English, however. In Latin *ignōrāmus* means "we do not know." It is the first person plural form of the verb *ignōrāre*, "to have no knowledge." *Ignoramus* appeared before the bar in English prior to 1577 and was used up to 1827 as a legal term meaning "we take no notice of it." The term was used as a grand jury's endorsement upon a bill of indictment when the evidence was deemed insufficient to send the case to a trial jury. *Ignoramus* also took on a general sense, "an answer that admits ignorance of the point in question," and a figurative sense, "a statement of ignorance."

Perhaps because of these senses, the Latin one, and the original legal meaning, a 1615 play "written to expose the ignorance and arrogance of the common lawyers" was entitled *Ignoramus* and featured a lawyer so named. From this use or similar uses of *ignoramus* as a proper name, the word was generalized to mean "an ignorant person." We find the word first recorded in this sense in a poem written about the same time by Francis Beaumont. The poem is entitled *Vertue of Sack* (with *sack* being a general name of a variety of white wines imported to England in the sixteenth and seventeenth centuries from Spain and the Canary Islands) and states: "Give blockheads beere, And silly *Ignoramus*, such as think There's powder-treason in all Spanish drink." *Powder-treason* here refers to the Gunpowder Plot, a scheme to blow up King James I and the Parliament during its ceremonial opening on November 5, 1605, a plot in which Spain was thought to have been involved. The quotation seems to imply that imbibing a Spanish product bordered on the treasonous, which is an ignorant notion indeed.

illth   Newly coined words rarely gain widespread acceptance, even when they have impeccable credentials, as did *illth*, a word fashioned according to an established pattern of word formation by a major British author, John Ruskin. Ruskin made it clear what he was up to in *Unto this Last*, published in 1860, when he referred to his lexical creation as "a corresponding term" for *wealth*. He used *wealth* in a special way to mean "useful things in the right hands." *Illth* was the opposite, that is, "useful things in the wrong hands." *Illth* was formed, as was *wealth*, by adding the suffix –*th* to *weal* or *well* in the case of *wealth* and to *ill* in the case of *illth*. Three other instances of *illth* are recorded after Ruskin's coinage of it, including one by another major author, George Bernard Shaw. Shaw used *illth* as the heading of a section in *Fabian Essays in Socialism*, published in 1889. He pointed out that "an elegant rosewood and silver coffin, upholstered in pink satin" and handcrafted for a dead dog, cannot be considered wealth when "meanwhile a live child is prowling barefooted and hunger-stunted in the frozen gutter outside. . . . Luxuries are not social wealth." They were, to Shaw, illth. Despite the support of Ruskin and Shaw, the word *illth* is found no more, until now. If you can, use *illth* in good health.

imp An imp in your garden at one time would not have been tearing up the shrubbery and trampling the peonies. Rather, it might have been a plant shoot. Since ancient times gardeners have practiced the art of grafting, that is, joining a shoot to an established plant, which nourishes and supports it like a parent. Anglo-Saxon gardeners called the grafted sprig or shoot an *impa*, a noun derived from the Old English verb *impian*, "to graft." In time *impa* became *imp*, and the word came to mean "a child or offspring," as well as "a grafted shoot." By the late sixteenth century it was often used specifically for a demon, a child or "imp" of the Devil or of Hell. Not surprisingly, the word *imp* eventually lost the neutral meaning "a child or offspring." If a child is called an *imp* today, it is because that child is mischievous and behaves like a little devil, in or out of the garden.

inch A child would be much happier to grow an inch rather than an ounce, while a dieter would be much less upset to grow by an ounce rather than by an inch in certain areas. The two units of measure are clearly not interchangeable despite the fact that both words go back to the Latin word *uncia*. The differences in meaning and form are explained by their histories. The Latin word *uncia*, meaning "a twelfth part," was in fact borrowed into English twice. *Uncia* came into Old English as *ynce*, denoting a linear measure of one twelfth of a foot. The word remains in Modern English as *inch*. *Uncia* also developed into Old French *unce* as a unit of weight equal to one twelfth of a pound. This word was borrowed into Middle English and survives in Modern English as *ounce*. The system of troy weight still used for precious metals is based on a twelve-ounce pound. The more common avoirdupois system contains a sixteen-ounce pound.

incunabula   In a Gutenberg Bible we find the story of the infant Jesus wrapped in swaddling clothes and laid in a manger. The connection between a Gutenberg Bible and swaddling clothes does not stop there, however. These Bibles are known as *incunabula*, as are any books printed before 1500. *Incunabula* comes from the Latin word *incūnābula* (from the prefix *in*– and the word *cūnābula*, "cradle"), which means "the apparatus of a cradle, including the bands or straps used to hold a baby in." The word also meant "this apparatus regarded as the symbol of infancy or one's earliest years." In 1861 in John M. Neale's *Notes, Ecclesiological and Picturesque, on Dalmatia*, we find the first recorded English use of *incunabula* as a term for books produced in the infancy of printing: "What are incunabula? you ask. It is the name that Germans give to books printed before 1500."

inflammable   Should you be extremely careful to avoid hitting that tanker truck in front of you if it is labeled *inflammable?* Yes, you should (as you should in any case), because *inflammable* is derived ultimately from the Latin prefix *in*–, "in," and the noun *flamma*, "flame." There is, however, another prefix *in*–, meaning "not," which English also borrowed from Latin, and the word *inflammable* can be misconstrued as meaning "not capable of burning." In order to eliminate possibly dangerous confusion about the combustibility of various materials, safety officials in the twentieth century have adopted the term *flammable*, which had a brief life in the early nineteenth century, to mean "able to burn." Materials that do not burn are unambiguously labeled *nonflammable*.

influenza The term *influenza season* does not have a familiar ring to it, but *flu season* is all too well known. *Flu*, shortened from *influenza*, is first recorded in English in 1839 in an utterance eliciting our profound compassion for its author, the poet Robert Southey, who says in a letter, "I've had a pretty fair share of the Flue." To find out where the word *influenza* originated, we must look to Italian, from which we borrowed it. The Italian word *influenza* came from Medieval Latin *influentia*, meaning "inflowing" and, probably, "flowing from the stars of a fluid that affected human existence and earthly things." *Influenza* developed the sense "outbreak of any epidemic disease," apparently from the belief that some astrological or occult influence was involved in epidemics. The word appeared in phrases such as *influenza di febbre scarlattina*, "scarlet fever outbreak," and hence also meant "an epidemic." In 1743 *influenza* was specifically used for the outbreak of a highly contagious disease in Italy. This illness spread throughout Europe and then to England, carrying its name with it. *Influenza* and its shortened form *flu* remain in use for epidemic diseases like the Hong Kong flu or the Asian flu (known, it is said, in the People's Republic of China as the Australian flu), but they have also been used as general terms for less serious illnesses, such as deep colds. For a time *influenza* was even used figuratively, as in this statement from the June 29, 1891, edition of the London *Daily News:* "Some months ago the markets were said to be suffering from financial influenza."

intrapreneur

INTRAPRENEUR: *These corporate risk takers are very much like entrepreneurs. They take personal risks to make new ideas happen. The difference is that they work within large organizations instead of outside them. I call them "intrapreneurs"—my shorthand for intracorporate entrepreneur. . . . In the fall of 1978 . . . I . . . coined the word "intrepreneur."*

> —Gifford Pinchot III, management consultant, in his book *Intrapreneuring*, 1985

. . . But wait!

However, it seems only fair to draw attention to the fact that the word intrapreneur was originated by Norman Macrae, deputy editor of The Economist. It is a very useful word and deserves wider recognition on this side of the Atlantic, but credit should be given where credit is due.

> —Ralph Landau, "The Origins of the Intrapreneur," *Business Week*, August 22, 1983 (Nexis, quoted in *The Barnhart Dictionary Companion*, Winter 1984, Volume III, Number 4)

. . . But hold the phone! . . . Three transatlantic calls later . . .

It wasn't me; it was Gifford Pinchot.

> —Norman Macrae, Deputy Editor, *The Economist*, April 4, 1986

Entrepreneur, the extracorporate opposite number of *intrapreneur*, is more than 150 years old, having come into English from French in 1828. *Intrapreneur*, which may be defined as "a person within a large corporation who takes direct responsibility for turning an idea into a profitable finished product through assertive risk-taking and innovation," is no more than eight years old. Yet *intrapreneur*, a very new coinage, has gained currency quite fast. It has also spun off various derivational forms such as the gerund *intrapreneuring* (the title, of course, of Gifford Pinchot's book), the noun *intrapreneurship* (also used in the book by Pinchot but found in other contexts, such as this one taken from a September 30, 1985, interview with Stephen Jobs in *Newsweek*: "The Macintosh team was what is commonly known as intrapreneurship—only a few years before the term was coined—a group of people going in essence back to the garage, but in a large company"), the adjective *intrapreneurial* ("the new intrapreneurial spirit," as used in Pinchot's book), and another noun, *intrapreneurialism* (" . . . what has become known as intrapreneurialism, where people within the corporation acquire more adventurous small business outlooks," by Ian Hamilton-Fazy, "An uneasy co-existence," *The Financial Times*, October 23, 1984, as quoted from Nexis in *The Barnhart Dictionary Companion*, Winter 1984, Volume III, Number 4). Broad use of a word and the development of numerous derivational forms are strong signals of potential staying power within the language over the long term.

Intrapreneur and its spinoffs are of particular interest to etymologists and lexicographers because the words illustrate the steady, ongoing changes occurring in English. It is also good that we were able to verify the facts behind this coinage, since the people variously credited with it are among the living. After all, it is pretty difficult, even with telecommunications satellites and transatlantic trunk lines, to call Chaucer for an insight.

iris Flowers in the garden and a membrane in the eye share the name of a Greek goddess. Iris was the goddess of the rainbow, a messenger of the gods who passed between earth and sky, just as the rainbow appears to do. In Greek the word *iris* was used for any bright-colored circle surrounding another body, including the iris of the eye. It was also the name for various species of the botanical genus now known as *Iris*. The Roman author Pliny the Elder says in his *Natural History* that "Iris . . . blooms with multicolored appearance, as does the rainbow, whence its name." Our word *iris*, which came into English from Greek through Latin, still has these senses that the Greek word *iris* had, even though Iris herself has pretty much vanished from sight.

iron curtain   "From Stettin in the Baltic to Trieste in the Adriatic an iron curtain has descended across the Continent." In this sentence from his address of March 5, 1946, at Westminster College in Fulton, Missouri, Winston Churchill introduced the modern world to the phrase that has characterized the social, political, and military barrier existing between the Soviet bloc and the West. Churchill, however, was not using this phrase for the first time in his speech, nor was he the first to use it. The phrase is initially found in English in a world far removed from that of international politics. In the March 13, 1794, edition of the London *Times* appears the information that "an iron curtain has been contrived, which, on such occasion of [fire], would compleatly prevent all communication between the audience and stage."

Figurative uses of the phrase soon developed, the first one occurring in 1819 in the Earl of Munster's account of his travels in India: "On the 19th November we crossed the river Betwah, and as if an iron curtain had dropt between us and the avenging angel, the deaths diminished." In another account of a journey, that of Ethel Annakin Snowden through Bolshevik Russia, published in 1920, we find the first recorded use of the phrase referring to the geographic entity that is Soviet Russia: "We were behind the 'iron curtain' at last!" And Churchill himself used the phrase some ten months before his famous Missouri speech in a May 12, 1945, top-secret telegram to President Harry S Truman: "An iron curtain is drawn down upon their front. We do not know what is going on behind."

island   If you were marooned on a deserted island or isle, you might kill at least a little time by considering the relationship between the words *island* and *isle*. These words are synonymous but unrelated, in spite of their apparent similarities in pronunciation and spelling. The word *isle* is derived from Latin *insula*, which developed into Old French *ile*, the form originally borrowed into English. The word *island* is a native English word whose earliest form was *īgland*. Until the seventeenth century the ordinary form of the word was *iland*, which was the spelling used in the King James Bible and Milton's *Paradise Lost*. In the fifteenth century the French respelled *ile* as *isle*, inserting an etymologically "more correct" *s* from Latin *insula*. The English adopted this spelling for *ile* and respelled *iland* as *isle-land* and *island*, probably from a mistaken notion that the native word was a compound of French *ile* and English *land*. As for me, I'll take Manhattan.

J

jackanapes　How the word *jackanapes* originated and came to mean "ape," "conceited person," and "mischievous child" is only partly understood. *Jackanapes*, first recorded in a political poem written about 1450, was used as a nickname for William de la Pole, 1st Duke of Suffolk. (As a principal adviser to Henry VI, the duke, like anyone else in such a powerful position, had his enemies—powerful enemies who managed to have him beheaded in 1450.) The nickname appears in the poem as *Jack Napis*. The first part, *Jack*, is the man's name used familiarly, or in this case contemptuously, for a person. The second element, *Napis*, may be a reference to the city of Naples.

The duke's emblem was a chain and clog, the weight attached to the leg of an animal, such as a tame ape, to hinder its movement. By association, perhaps, *jackanapes* became a name for a tame ape or monkey. The word could then be used figuratively for those who behaved like monkeys, including conceited people and mischievous children.

Jungle

jaunty "See how finely bred he is, how juntee [jaunty] and complaisant," says a character in John Crowne's 1675 play *The Country Wit*. To understand the use of *jaunty* in this speech, we must know that *jaunty*, like *gentle* and *genteel*, is a borrowing of the French word *gentil*, "noble." *Jaunty* at one time did commonly mean "genteel" or "well-bred," but it is also found early on with other senses, including "elegant" and "sprightly." Characteristics such as sprightliness and ease of manner were thought to be typical of those who attempted to behave as if they were well-bred, whether they actually were or not.

jazz *If the truth were known about the origin of the word "Jazz" it would never be mentioned in polite society.*
—Clay Smith, "Where is *Jazz* Leading America?" *Etude,*
September, 1924

The origin of *jazz*, the central meaning of which is "music characterized by a strong but flexible rhythmic understructure with solo and ensemble improvisations on basic themes and chord patterns," is still one of the most controversial word mysteries in American English. H. L. Mencken has described as "bitter" the etymological wars raging around this word. To characterize the situation in any other way would be mere jive.

The one thing we can say with assurance about jazz is that it is truly American music, most likely developed by small, informal groups of black and Creole performers playing in New Orleans and its environs before 1900. The rhythmic patterns of jazz are said to be based on a potpourri of African melodies, old field chants sung by slaves, work chants sung by prisoners and laborers, and French and Spanish tunes with which the Creoles were familiar.

If jazz has a mixed, mysterious ethnocultural flavor, so too does the body of theories surrounding the word itself. At the risk of being accused of going on an etymological toot, we recount here some of the explanations offered for the origin of the word. For

128

many years, efforts were made to establish the eponymous heritage of *jazz*—that is, to prove derivation of
the word from the names of various black performers,
such as Charles (*Chas*) Alexander or Washington, a
ragtime drummer from Vicksburg, Mississippi, who
flourished around 1895; Jasper (perhaps also called
Jass or *Jazz*), a dancer who lived on a plantation near
New Orleans; and Jasbo (*Jas*) Brown, a Chicago musi-
cian. Others have attempted to establish that *jazz* is
derived from a Louisiana Creole verb, *jaser,* meaning
"to speed up" or "to chatter and make fun." Still others have tried to prove that the word is African in
origin. None of these efforts has been successful. In
fact, the approximate date at which the word was
first used in English has never been established. Nor
can we be absolutely certain whether the noun or the
verb is the older form.

Cloaking the entire matter in a blue haze is the theory that *jazz* is ultimately derived from an American
dialect word meaning "to engage in sexual relations,"
and as Mencken says, "it is so defined by many lexicographers." Mencken observes that the application
of the sexual sense of the word *jazz* "to the kind of
music it now designates was perhaps not unnatural,"
but the specifics of the application, "when, where,
and by whom that extension was made, [are] not yet
known." One hypothesis, however, is that of Clay
Smith, whose words are cited at the beginning of this
entry. Smith believes that the extension originated in
Western mining honky-tonks during the 1890's. Com-
menting on the word during the mid-1920's, he
claims that "the vulgar word 'Jazz' was in general currency in those dance halls thirty years or more ago."
Similarly, Godfrey Irwin, in his book *American
Tramp and Underworld Slang,* suggests that "jazz music was so named originally because it was first played
in the low dance halls and brothels where sex excita-
tion was the prime purpose."

Amid all this confusion about *jazz*, we might turn for
the last word to Louis Armstrong, who when asked
what jazz was replied, "Man, if you gotta ask, you'll
never know."

jeans   The Jordache® look began in Genoa, etymologically
speaking. Jeans are made of a twilled cotton cloth
that was probably originally called *Gene fustian*.
Gene is the Middle English form of *Genoa*; *fustian* is
"a kind of cloth made from cotton, flax, or wool." It
is thought that the shortened form, which in Modern
English is *jean*, came to refer to the cloth. The plural
form *jeans* then came to designate garments made of
this material. Robert Smith Surtees gave us the first
recorded use of the term in his novel *Handley Cross*,
published in 1843: "Septimus arrived flourishin' his
cambric, with his white jeans strapped under his
chammy leather opera boots." Jordache, move over.

Jehovah   The name *Jehovah* for God, which came into being
because of an error in reading Hebrew, did not exist
as a Hebrew word. It is actually a combination of two
Hebrew forms that was caused by a peculiarity of the
Hebrew writing system. The Hebrew alphabet consists
only of characters for consonants; vowels are indicated as dots or points written in characteristic positions above or below the consonants. The Hebrew
name for God, whose consonants are transliterated
YHWH, was considered so sacred that it was never
pronounced, and its proper vowel points were never
written. In some texts the vowel points for a completely different word, *Adōnāi*, "lord," were written
with *YHWH* to indicate that the word *Adōnāi* was to
be spoken whenever the reader encountered the word
YHWH. *YHWH* was never intended to be pronounced with the vowels of *Adōnāi*, but Christian
scholars of the Renaissance made exactly that mistake. The forms *Iehovah*—using the classical Latin
equivalents, including *I*, pronounced (y), of the Hebrew letters—and *Jehovah*—substituting in English *J*,
pronounced (j), the consonant sound that the letter *i*
represented at that time—came into common use.

jeopardy   The word *jeopardy* illustrates the human tendency to
anticipate the worst in an uncertain situation. Its Old
French source, *iu parti*, "divided game," originally de-

noted a problem in chess and then came to mean a position in any game for which the chances of winning or losing were even. In English *jeopardy* retained the senses of the French word but extended them to mean "an uncertain or undecided situation." By Chaucer's time, the late fourteenth century, *jeopardy* had acquired its modern sense of "peril, danger."

journeyman   A *journeyman*, "a skilled craftsman," is not an itinerant worker. *Journeyman* preserves an older sense of the word *journey* that reveals the origins of *journey*. A journeyman was originally a daily worker, that is, one who worked for another for daily wages. He was distinguished from an apprentice, who was learning the trade, and a master artisan, who was in business for himself. *Journey* is derived from the Old French word *journee*, which meant "day" and "a day's work." *Journee* also meant "a day's travel" and then "trip," whether the travel took a day or not.

jovial   "Be bright and jovial among your guests tonight" was Lady Macbeth's charge to her husband before the banquet at which Banquo's ghost spoiled any hope of joviality for Macbeth. By this point in the action true joviality was beyond Macbeth anyway, even if he had been given the astrological help characterized by the word *jovial*. The ultimate source of *jovial* is Latin *joviālis*, an adjective derived from *Jovis*, another name for the Roman god Jupiter. The meaning "jolly, convivial," for *jovial* can be traced to astrological notions about the planets and other celestial objects. Astrologers believed that the planets had specific influences on persons and events. The planet Jupiter in a person's horoscope had a very favorable influence and was regarded as a source of happiness. A jovial person was literally one influenced astrologically by the planet Jupiter and displaying mirth and conviviality.

jungle   Tarzan might be suprised to learn that the word *jungle* is not African in origin nor does it come from a word that only meant "land densely overgrown with tropical vegetation and trees." *Jungle* goes back to the Sanskrit word *jangala* or *jāngala*, meaning "an arid, uncultivated region" and also "any kind of uncultivated area, such as heavily forested land." The Sanskrit word *jangala* passed into various Indian languages and from one or more of these languages into English. *Jungle* in English was used for land overgrown with vegetation, for the vegetation itself, and for such land outside India, including Tarzan's home. *Jungle* was also extended figuratively in various ways. We have, for example, asphalt jungles, concrete jungles, blackboard jungles, academic jungles, corporate jungles, and, in a February, 1972, issue of *The Guardian*, the government official who "lit up some lurid corners of the taxation jungle."

junket   A good congressional junket could include lots of food and maybe a picnic, two things that are involved in the semantic development of the word *junket*. The ultimate source of *junket* is the Latin word *juncus*, "rush." *Junket* was once the name of a kind of food served on rushes. The word now means "a custardlike food," "a party, picnic, or outing," or "a trip." The transitional stage between the meanings "a food" and "a trip" is found in the meaning "picnic." The sense "a trip taken by a public official at public expense" developed in the United States. In his *Political Dictionary* William Safire makes the point that "an overseas tour by a congressman or candidate is described by him as a *fact-finding trip*, and as a *junket* by his opponents, who usually add 'at the taxpayers' expense.' " *Junket* has obviously acquired negative connotations.

junta   If you join a junta at an important juncture, you do something that is at least etymologically well connected. *Join*, *juncture*, and *junta* are all derived ultimately from Latin *jungere*, "to join," *join* coming into English by way of French. *Junta*, which came into our language through Spanish or Portuguese, first

132

referred in English to a deliberative or administrative council or committee in either Spain or Italy. The juntas most familiar to us today are probably the ones consisting of a small group holding power in a country after a coup d'état, hardly a group the average person might want to join: what goes up must come down.

kale   The word *kale*, "a variety of cabbage," exhibits one
of the most important features distinguishing the
Scots dialect from standard English: the use of long *a*
where the standard language has long *o*. With regard
to this feature Scots is more conservative. The Old
English form of *kale* is *cāl*, from Latin *caulis*, "cabbage." In the twelfth and thirteenth centuries most
dialects of Middle English had changed all Old English long *a*'s to long *o*'s, but the northern dialects, of
which Scots is the most important modern representative, did not. The word *kale* has the same Old English ancestor as the word *cole*, which can refer to
cabbage and other plants of the genus *Brassica*. *Cole*
represents the standard development of the Old English word *cāl*. Other pairs of words that exhibit the
two different developments of Old English long *a* are
kame/comb, *laird/lord*, and *hale/whole*.

kangaroo   Does *kangaroo* mean "I don't understand," the reply
of an indigenous inhabitant of Australia when asked
the name of this marsupial? This charming suggestion
is highly speculative, but then, the true origin of *kangaroo* has not been determined either. Captain James

Kangaroo

Cook, the English explorer who claimed part of Australia for Great Britain, gives us in 1770 the first recorded instance of the word, which he says was the original inhabitants' name for the animal (*Kangooroo* or *Kanguru*). Other writers later claimed that *kangaroo* was obsolete in Australian languages, was only a local word, or was a mispronunciation of an aboriginal word. The information from Cook is probably trustworthy, however, and at least in the part of Australia that he visited, *kangaroo* or something like it was indeed the name for this animal. One wonders if *kangaroo* could be related to the aboriginal words *kanggandi*, "to lead, conduct; accompany; bear a child," *kanggarendi*, "to bring forth," or *kanggariburka*, "a woman who bears many children." Certainly the kangaroo displays its young prominently.

kibitz The lapwing, the green plover, or the pewit never sits down at a card table but is often present nevertheless. In German the word for lapwing is *Kiebitz*. Perhaps because of its inquisitive appearance while searching for food or because of its shrill cries that frighten game away from hunters, the *Kiebitz* had its name transferred to a busybody who looks on at cards, giving us the German verb *kiebitzen*, "to look on." Borrowed into Yiddish as *kibitsen*, the word then came into English as *kibitz*, meaning "to look on and offer unwanted and usually meddlesome advice to others."

kind Can thunder be kind? To find out we must look at the history of the word *kind*. *Kind* is a word that has undergone melioration. By this process a word with neutral connotations develops favorable ones. *Gecynde*, the Old English ancestor of *kind*, meant "natural, inborn, inherent," and was used of such fearsome things as death and thunder. In the thirteenth century, however, *kind* was used to mean "well-born" and "of a good nature." These senses have passed out of standard English, but the derived sense "possessing all the (good) qualities usually attributed to those of good birth" underlies the modern meanings of *kind*.

kudos　No one would ever receive a single kudo were it not for a misunderstanding. The word *kudos* is etymologically a singular form, a modern borrowing of Greek *kudos*, "glory, renown." In very recent times, however, *kudos* has been reanalyzed as a plural form, because it looks like one, and consequently the new singular *kudo* sometimes occurs in writing. Certain features of *kudos* predispose it to this kind of treatment. In the first place, it is an unfamiliar word to many people unversed in the classics, for it is drawn from the vocabulary of Homer. Secondly, it did not often occur as the subject of a sentence, where the verb could provide a clue to whether *kudos* was singular or plural. And finally, *kudos* has no recorded plural in English. A person unfamiliar with Homeric Greek who saw the form *kudos* in English would be likely to interpret it as the regular plural of a noun ending in *o*, like *typos* for *typo* and *altos* for *alto*. Once *kudos* was treated as a plural, the linguistic pressure to supply a singular was very strong.

Although the form *kudo* has not achieved general acceptance and the construction *kudos are* is considered incorrect, the linguistic processes in the development of *kudo/kudos* as the singular and plural forms of an English noun are highly productive, as linguists would say, and have been going on in English and other languages since prehistoric times. The development of the singular *pea* from the earlier singular form *pease* is an example of the same process.

lacuna   A tropical *lagoon* in the South Pacific and a *lacuna*, or textual gap, in a Middle English manuscript would seem to have little in common. But the relationship between the meanings of these two words can be found in the notion of something hollow or empty that underlies them both. The Latin word *lacūna*, the immediate source of our English word *lacuna* and the ultimate source of *lagoon*, meant basically "a hollow." In Latin the word also denoted a hollow where water collected and meant "pond, sea." Latin *lacūna* developed into Italian *laguna*, a term used for the bodies of water characteristic of the area around Venice. This word was borrowed into English as *lagoon* and was later extended to similar bodies of water formed by coral reefs. The English word *lacuna* is a direct borrowing of Latin *lacuna* in the sense "gap." It was first used in English to mean "a gap in a manuscript or inscription," and this sense is still current. The anatomical sense, "a cavity or depression," is probably a scientific reborrowing of the same Latin word.

Learned

lady Ladies as well as lords might be interested to learn that the word *lady* was not originally an honorific title, even though it designated a woman of social standing, at least within her own household. The Old English form of *lady, hlǣfdīge,* denoted the mistress of a household, especially one who had authority over servants and other dependents. The word is ultimately a compound of *hlāf,* "bread," and *dīg-,* a form meaning basically "to build, knead," which is related to the words *dough* and *dairy.* As the "bread kneader" of the household, a lady was in a position of some authority, a circumstance reflected in the later development of the word, notwithstanding the fact that most ladies of the nobility would probably have little to do with kneading bread.

lame duck Readers of the *Wall Street Journal* can answer most of Horace Walpole's question, asked in 1781: "Do you know what a Bull, and a Bear, and a Lame Duck are?" Bulls and bears still inhabit Wall Street, but the lame ducks have long since waddled off to the smoke-filled rooms of politics. *Lame duck* was originally British stock exchange slang for "one who cannot meet his financial obligations and must therefore default"; in short, an insolvent. It later came to refer to another species, specifically a defeated American politician serving out the balance of his term of office. The December 8, 1910, issue of the New York *Evening Post,* for example, refers to "Lame Duck Alley," which is "a screened-off corridor . . . where statesmen who went down in the recent electoral combat may meet." The term still refers to any elected officeholder or group that, having failed to win an election, has yet to migrate to friendlier climes, away from dark horses, stalking-horses, barnacles, boll weevils, gypsy moths, killer bees, and of course, new brooms.

lampoon The editors of the *National Lampoon* and its parent, the *Harvard Lampoon,* will probably not be surprised, although others may be, to learn the origin of the

word *lampoon*. *Lampoon*, meaning "a broad satirical
piece that uses ridicule to attack a person, group, or
institution," comes from the archaic French word
lampon, "a drinking song." *Lampoon* is thought to be
derived from *lampons*, "let us drink," which is said
to have been a common refrain of seventeenth-
century French satirical poems. *Lampons* is a form of
lamper, "to swig, toss off, or gulp down drink." *À
votre santé*, lampoonists!

laser   A laser was first a maser, not, however, because it was
an "amazer." A laser is "a device that converts incident electromagnetic radiation of mixed frequencies
to one or more discrete frequencies of highly ampli-
fied and coherent visible radiation." Its name is an
acronym, a word formed by combining the initial letters of a name or the initial letters or parts of a series
of words. In the case of *laser* the words involved are
"*l*ight *a*mplification by the *s*timulated *e*mission of *r*a-
diation." *Laser* was first the name of a particular type
of maser, a laser that originally emitted microwaves,
which explains the *m* rather than the *l*. *Maser* was
extended as the name for devices that emit radiation
in other parts of the spectrum besides the microwave
range, but then *laser* came into existence as an acronym for devices that emitted radiation in the visible
light range. *Laser* in turn was generalized for all such
devices independently of emission range. The acro-
nymic tendency seems to have stopped here, unless
one can turn up a *uvaser* (ultraviolet) or an *xraser*.

last-ditch   Consider carefully before making your next last-ditch
effort. You just might end up in the trenches. The adjective *last-ditch* did, in fact, originate in the world
of trench warfare. It came from the phrase *last ditch*,
whose first recorded use is found in Bishop Gilbert
Burnet's *History of My Own Time*, written sometime
before 1715: "There was a sure way never to see it
[Holland] lost, and that was to die in the last ditch."
The expression literally means "to die while defend-
ing the last ditch of an entrenchment," even though

it is used figuratively here to mean "to fight to the end." In 1798 a statement was published by the citizens of Westmoreland, Virginia, saying that they knew "but one additional Obligation, To die in the Last Ditch or uphold our Nation." And in 1821 Thomas Jefferson refers to "a government . . . driven to the last ditch by the universal call for liberty." The adjectival use of the term is found in the twentieth century, as in Marshall McLuhan's *Mechanical Bride*, in which he refers to "a last-ditch stand of denuded minds."

latchkey child   It would appear that the latchkey child is a phenomenon of recent times. But the use of the term *latchkey child* goes back farther than we might think. Heloise the hinter, in discussing a column written for such children, describes them as "the kids with divorced parents or both parents working who have to let themselves in the house when they come home" (*New York Times*, December 2, 1982). The notion of letting themselves in, of course, explains the use of *latchkey* in this compound. We actually find the term used as early as 1944 in the title of an NBC radio program, "Latchkey Children," part of a series called *Here's to Youth*. In 1945 the phrase *latch-key kids* was transported to Australia by American soldiers and used to mean children who had to stay home alone because their mothers were working in war industries.

lawn   At one time you never had to mow the lawn. The word *lawn*, which now denotes a carefully kept, ornamental plot of closely mown grass, originated as a variant spelling of *laund*, an obsolete word that meant "a woodland glade." *Laund* was borrowed from the Old French word *lande*, which entered Old French from a Celtic source. *Lande* looks like our word *land* and the two words are distant kinfolk. *Land* goes back to the Germanic word *landam*, which is related to the Celtic source of the Old French word *lande*.

leap year Does a leap year jump? It is thought that this term for a 366-day year originated because adding an extra day to the year caused a "leap" in the Church calendar of festivals. In normal 365-day years a fixed festival that in one year fell on a weekday, such as Tuesday, would fall on Wednesday the next year, but in a leap year—after the extra day had fallen—the festival would occur on Thursday, having leaped, or leapt, right over Wednesday.

learned We would not say "What did your professor learn you today?" but we would call a professor "learned." The word *learned*—pronounced (lûr′nĭd)—is historically the past participle of the verb *learn* and now functions independently as an adjective. Since Old English times *learn* has always meant "to gain knowledge." In Middle English it also meant "to teach," although this sense is no longer current in Modern English. In Middle English *learned* could have the sense "taught," as in the statement "His sones . . . were lerned to ride" from John Capgrave's *Chronicle of England* (published circa 1464). The word *learned* has survived as an adjective, especially with senses such as "scholarly" and "erudite."

legend A legend calls to mind heros and heroines rather than the reading we do to find out about them. The word *legend*, however, is derived from the Latin word *legenda*, a form of the verb *legere*, "to read." In Medieval Latin *legenda* was used to mean "something to be read," particularly the narrative of a saint's life. These biographies were considered important as historical records and moral examples. In the fourteenth century the word was borrowed into English as *legend*. It is likely that the utterly incredible exploits and events recounted in some legends led to the development of the sense "unverified story, myth."

lemur A lemur, with its large eyes, soft fur, and foxlike muzzle, strikes some people as cute, although clearly this is not a universal reaction, since its name conjures up the spirits of the dead. The word *lemur* comes from the Latin genus classification *Lemur* given to the animal by the Swedish eighteenth-century botanist Linnaeus, who chose the name because of the ghostly appearance of its face, which is pallid with dark eyes and nose. Linnaeus associated lemurs with *lemures*, which in ancient Rome were "the malevolent spirits of the dead considered as frightening specters."

Lent Spring partially overlaps in time with Lent, the forty weekdays from Ash Wednesday until Holy Saturday observed by Christians as a season of fasting and penitence, an important fact for the the development of the present meaning of the word. *Lent* is derived from the Old English word *lencten*, which meant both the season of spring and the ecclesiastical season of Lent. *Lencten* is ultimately derived from the same root as the adjective *long*. The meaning "spring" probably arose because spring is the time of year when the days grow longer. The ecclesiastical sense developed from the fact that Lent partly coincides with spring.

lewd A thousand years ago it was no disgrace to be a lewd person. The word *lewd*, from Old English *lǣwede*, originally meant "lay, not belonging to the clergy." As time passed and new senses of the word developed, each subsequent sense of *lewd* took on a worse connotation than the one before. Such a pattern of sense development is called pejoration. During Middle English times the word *lewd* ran the gamut of senses from "lay" through "unlearned," "low-class," "ignorant, ill-mannered," and "wicked" to "lascivious." The last sense is the only one that survives in Modern English.

liberal The Latin adjective *līberālis*, from which *liberal* is derived, is formed from the adjective *līber*, which meant "free," especially in the sense "freeborn, not a slave." Many senses of *līberālis*, and therefore of *liberal*, reflect this derivation. The sense "generous" denotes an attribute thought to be characteristic of a freeman, who had a relatively high social status. The Latin word *līberālis* was then extended to mean "noble, gentlemanly." Although this sense is not recorded for our English word *liberal*, it survives in the phrase *liberal arts*, which originally designated those branches of learning that were suitable for persons of high social rank.

limousine *In the generous luxury [of] a . . . limousine . . . long-distance travelling is limousine-smooth.*
                                —*Country Life*, September 13, 1973

The word *limousine* probably came to mean a type of automobile for one or both of the following reasons. The first suggestion is that the automobile originally known as a limousine had windows only in the back, while the front was open except for a windshield. The automobile, by a considerable stretch of the imagination, was thought to resemble a cloak worn by shepherds from the French province of Limousin. The second suggestion is that the inventor of this type of automobile, Charles Jeantaud, was from the city of Limoges in Limousin, and in honor of his province he named the automobile a *limousine*. In any event, the term, borrowed from French into English, is now used for a luxurious automobile driven by a chauffeur who sits in a section divided by a partition from the passenger compartment—a rather elegant cloak.

litmus Although litmus paper is familiar material to anyone who has spent time in a chemistry lab, the origin of the word *litmus* is probably not. This paper is treated with litmus, a blue powder derived from certain lichens that changes to red in acid solutions and becomes blue again in alkaline solutions. The word *litmus* goes back to the Old Norse word *litmosi*, meaning "herbs used in dying." The compound *lit-mosi* was formed from the words *litr*, "color," or *lita*, "to color," and *mosi*, "moss, lichen."

lord A wealthy lord may have a lot of bread, but at one time a lord watched out for the real thing. The actual as well as the symbolic importance of bread as a basic foodstuff is exhibited by the word *lord*, which is derived from a compound formed in very early Old English times from the words *hlāf*, "bread," and *weard*, "ward, guardian." *Lord*, therefore, literally means "guardian of the bread." Since such a position was the dominant one in a household, *lord* came to mean a man of authority and rank in society at large.

Low German To those hearing them for the first time, the terms *Low German* and *High German* might seem based on a size difference or a social one. The differences involved, however, are linguistic and topographical. The name *Low German* for the northern German dialects is a translation of German *Plattdeutsch*, literally "flat German." The term refers to the topography of the area where these dialects are spoken: northern Germany, bounded by the North and Baltic seas, in flat, low-lying country. Toward the south the terrain becomes progressively more mountainous until it reaches the Alps. The dialects of the more elevated region are consequently called *High German*.

lust In Old English times you could take lust or leave it. *Lust* originally was a word of neutral connotations, meaning simply "pleasure." The word is related to the now archaic verb *list*, meaning "to wish to, be inclined to." In theological usage Old English *lust* referred to pleasures and desires that were considered sinful, especially sexual desire. In this context *lust* was a term of opprobrium. The implication of reproach has carried over to the sense "an overwhelming desire or craving." The meaning "pleasure" is now obsolete.

lynch   *Whereas, many of the inhabitants of Pittsylvania . . . have*
sustained great and intolerable losses by a set of lawless
men . . . that . . . have hitherto escaped the civil power
with impunity . . . we, the subscribers, being determined to
put a stop to the iniquitous practices of those unlawful and
abandoned wretches, do enter into the following
association . . . upon hearing or having sufficient reason to
believe, that any . . . species of villany [has] been
committed within our neighborhood, we will
forthwith . . . repair immediately to the person or persons
suspected . . . and if they will not desist from their evil
practices, we will inflict such corporeal punishment on him
or them, as to us shall seem adequate to the crime
committed or the damage sustained. . . . In witness whereof
we have hereunto set our hands, this 22nd day of September
1780.

These are the words of a compact drawn up by Captain William Lynch and a group of his neighbors. At the time, Pittsylvania County, Virginia, was troubled by its "set of lawless men." The courts were too distant to deal with them, so it was agreed to punish criminals without due process of law. Both the practice and the punishment came to be called *lynch law* after Captain Lynch. Although lynch law and lynching are mainly associated with hanging, other punishments, including ones not ending in death, were used.

When Lynch's group resorted to hanging, they did so in a manner calculated to ease their consciences. Lynch described it to a friend in 1811: "The person who it was supposed ought to suffer death was placed on a horse with his hands tied behind him and a rope about his neck which was fastened to the limb of a tree over his head. In this situation the person was left and when the horse in pursuit of food or any other cause moved from the position the unfortunate person was left suspended by the neck—this was called 'aiding the civil authority.' "

William Lynch died in 1820, and the inscription on his grave notes that "he followed virtue as his truest guide." Thus the good captain, who certainly hadn't invented vigilante justice, but had tried to justify it, was sentenced to the disgrace of having given his name to the terrible practice of lynching.

macaronic Is macaroni the stuff of poetry? Perhaps not, but the word *macaronic*, which describes a kind of poetry, is derived from the Italian dialect word *macarone* or *maccarone*, "dumpling," which is also the source of the English noun *macaroni*. *Macaronic* compositions are written in a mixture of Latin and the vernacular language, usually with a comic or satirical effect. The word first appears in the work of Tisi degli Odassi, a fifteenth-century Italian poet. In the early sixteenth century the poet Teofilo Folengo, describing his own verses, explained that such compositions could be compared with macaroni. Both were simple mixtures of various ingredients, macaroni being "a gross, rude, and rustic dish composed of flour, cheese, and butter." A hearty meal indeed, and certainly not one associated with worms, as is *vermicelli*, another word discussed herein.

magazine The word *magazine* was borrowed from the Old French word *magazin*, "storehouse." It is ultimately derived from the Arabic word *makhzan*, which comes from the verb *khazana*, "to store." The use of *magazine* to mean "a periodical publication" is a specialized development of the original, more general

Misericord

sense "storehouse." *Magazine* was at one time used in book titles to mean a storehouse of information on a special topic, equivalent to the use of *encyclopedia* today. The word was also used in the titles of periodical publications that contained a storehouse of miscellaneous literary works, articles on various topics, and other features. From the latter use the word *magazine* became a general term for all such publications.

mail   The search for the history of the word *mail* is in the bag. *Mail*, "material handled by the post office," is a survivor of the days when the few letters and dispatches that were exchanged were carried by horsemen in their traveling bags. In Middle English times the word *mail*, borrowed from the Old French term *male*, simply meant "bag," especially one carried by a traveler for provisions. Such bags were also used to carry letters, and the word *mail* eventually came to designate the contents rather than the container. Before *mail* had added this sense, the compound *mailbag* would not have been something full of letters but rather something full of redundancy.

malaria   Etymologically, it would be impossible to contract malaria in Buenos Aires, a city whose name means "good air." Within the word *malaria* is a reference to an outmoded notion of how such an illness was caused. *Malaria* comes from the Italian word *mal'aria*, which is derived from *mala*, "bad," and *aria*, "air." It was thought that the illness called *malaria* was caused by the unwholesome state of the air in marshy districts. When it was discovered in the late 1800's that the anopheles mosquito carried the disease, *malaria* was medically redefined with greater precision, but the original name of the malady remained.

margarine   After studying the history of the word *margarine*, would one be justified in saying that serving it to those who don't like it is like casting pearls before swine? Margarine is a relatively new substance, the product of modern chemistry. Both the substance and its name originated in France during the nineteenth century. The substance was originally made from a combination of animal fats, one of which was called *margaric acid* (*acide margarique* in French). The adjective *margaric* or *margarique* is derived from the Greek word *margaron*, "pearl," and was applied to the compound in question because its crystals had a pearly sheen. Margarine is naturally white; it is colored yellow in imitation of the natural yellow color of butter.

Martian The phrase *Martian invasion* probably means something to fans of H. G. Wells and Orson Welles, although most people never expect to witness such an influx. These fans might be surprised to learn the other ways in which the adjective *Martian* has been used, because *Martian* may be unfamiliar to them in these three contexts: "The judges . . . Into the Martian field adowne descended"; "Martian-month"; and "My heart [temperament] is Martian." To understand these uses of *Martian* we need to be reminded that Mars was the Roman god of war and that the planet Mars was named after him, just as the month of March was. Furthermore, according to astrology, the planet Mars influenced one's temperament in certain ways, perhaps by making a person self-willed or stubborn. Hence the field is Martian martially, the month calendrically, and the heart astrologically.

martinet Attention! Martinets will be pleased to learn that the term for them has an impeccable ancestry. *Martinet* is from the name of Jean Martinet, inspector general of infantry for Louis XIV in the seventeenth century. Martinet's strict drills, designed to mold the infantry into a focused fighting unit, were imitated elsewhere in Europe. In fact, the first recorded use of *martinet* in English, in William Wycherley's 1676 play *The Plain Dealer*, recalls the system of drill invented by

151

Martinet: "What, d'ye find fault with Martinet? . . .
'tis the best exercise in the world." The next recorded
use of *martinet*, in John Moore's 1779 *View of Society and Manners in France, Switzerland, and Germany*, shows which way the wind was blowing with
this word. Moore, who has been watching regiments
of German and French troops, comments that German soldiers are defeated "upon every slight occasion," while French troops are never outdone. The
Germans nonetheless do not perform any better than
the French troops "and any difference would, in my
opinion, be dearly purchased at the price of treating
one soldier like a spaniel. . . . let our Martinets say
what they please, there is surely some difference between men and dogs." *Martinet* here means "a military officer who is a stickler for discipline." The word
now refers to any rigid disciplinarian as well as to
anyone who demands absolute adherence to rules.
Martinets may not be pleased to learn that Jean Martinet was killed by his own troops, supposedly by accident.

maudlin   If it had not been for Mary Magdalene, a person
could not be maudlin. The word *maudlin* is an English development of the second name of Mary Magdalene, a woman mentioned in the gospels. She has also
been identified with certain anonymous women in
the New Testament, especially the sinful woman who
washed Jesus's feet with her tears (Luke 7). From
these and other fragments of Scripture evolved the
popular legend of Mary Magdalene as a reformed
prostitute who became one of Jesus's most devoted
and favored female disciples. She was frequently depicted in art as weeping copiously for her sins, and it
is this attribute of hers that gave rise to the current
sense of the adjective *maudlin*, "effusively or tear-
fully sentimental."

mayday   "Mayday, mayday!" comes the international distress
signal over the radio, and nobody stops to ask why

the first of May is being mentioned at this time of crisis. *Mayday* in fact has nothing to do with the first of May. Instead, it is a spelling that represents the pronunciation of French *m'aider*, "help me," or the latter part of the phrase *venez m'aider*, "come help me," either of which are quite appropriate at such a critical juncture.

meal At one time you ate food during a meal, but a meal was not food. The usual current sense of *meal*, "food served and eaten at one sitting," has existed since the thirteenth century, but it was actually an extension of the Old English meaning "fixed time for eating." The Old English word *mǣl* meant not only "fixed time" but also "measure" and "mark." *Meal*, descended from an Indo-European root that meant basically "measure," is related to the Latin word *metīrī*, "to measure," and the Greek word *metron*, "measure, poetic meter."

meat Meat just isn't what it used to be. The word *meat* is an example of a word whose meaning has become narrower in the course of its development. In Old English the word denoted food of any kind, but chiefly solid food in contrast to liquids. This is the sense of meat in compounds such as *sweetmeat*, "a piece of candy," and *nutmeat*, "the edible part of a nut." In later medieval times *meat* came to signify animal flesh in contrast to fish, and at times in contrast to poultry as well. In very recent times *meat* has occasionally been restricted to a particular kind of animal flesh, such as pork.

mesmerize When the members of an audience sit mesmerized by a speaker, their reactions do not take the form of dancing, sleeping, or falling into convulsions. But if Franz Anton Mesmer were addressing the audience, such behavior could be expected. Mesmer, a visionary eighteenth-century physician, believed cures could be

153

effected by having patients do things such as sit with their feet in a fountain of magnetized water while holding cables attached to magnetized trees. Mesmer then came to believe that magnetic powers resided in himself, and during highly fashionable curative sessions in Paris he caused his patients to have reactions ranging from dancing or sleeping to convulsions. These reactions were actually brought about by hypnotic powers that Mesmer was unaware he possessed. One of his pupils, named Puységur, first used the term *Mesmerism* for Mesmer's practices. The related word *mesmerize*, having shed its reference to the hypnotic doctor, lives on in the sense "to enthrall."

mess   The word *mess* was not a mess for a long time. *Mess* has been in the English language since the fourteenth century, but its meanings "a disorderly jumble" and "an untidy condition" did not develop until as late as the nineteenth century. *Mess* (derived from the Latin word *missus*, "course of a meal," from the verb *mittere*, "to place") originally meant "a quantity of food" or simply "food." The word was used without disparagement, as it still is, for example, in the phrase "a mess of peas." In the nineteenth century *mess* was also used to refer to an unpalatable mixture of food, and it is likely that this usage gave rise to the modern meanings, which have been extended beyond references to food. In addition to "a portion of food," *mess* in medieval times also meant "a group of persons who usually eat together." This sense has been preserved in expressions such as *mess hall* and *officers' mess*.

methinks   Methinks that *methinks* may seem ungrammatical to users of Modern English. Strictly speaking, the archaic form *methinks* is not one word but two: the pronoun *me* and the obsolete verb *think*, meaning "to seem." This obsolete verb is related to but is not the same as the current verb *think*, meaning "to have in mind." *Methinks* is an impersonal construction;

that is, one without an expressed subject. In *me-thinks*, *me* is the indirect object of *think* and *thinks* is the third person singular form of the verb. The construction *methinks* means "it seems to me," not "I think."

migraine   Those afflicted with migraine headaches will not be surprised to learn that the word *migraine* goes back to a Greek word, *hēmikrania*, that is derived from *hēmi-*, "half," and *kranion*, "upper part of the head, skull." While suffering a migraine, of course, one feels that at least half of one's head is splitting in pain. Actually, the term in Greek meant "pain on one side of the head or face," as *migraine* usually does today.

miniature   The idea of smallness was not originally part of the meaning of *miniature*. The word is derived from Latin *minium*, "red lead," a compound of lead used as a pigment. In medieval times chapter headings and other important divisions of a text were distinguished by being written in red, while the rest of the book was written in black (a color scheme that we too have adopted). The Latin verb *miniāre*, derived from *minium*, meant "to color red." *Miniātūra*, the future participle, described the process of writing in red. Sections of a manuscript were also marked off with large ornate initial capital letters, which were often decorated with small paintings. *Miniātūra* was used to denote these paintings as well. Since the paintings were necessarily very tiny, *miniātūra* came to mean "a small painting or object of any kind."

minute   How minute is a minute? The noun *minute* and the adjective *minute* are both descended from the Latin word *minūtus*, "small" (derived from the verb *minuere*, "to lessen"). The adjective is a direct borrowing of the Latin word. But the noun has a more complex history. The noun *minute* is derived from *minūta* in the Latin phrase *pars minūta prima,* "first little part," in which *minūta* is the feminine singular form of the adjective *minūtus.* In Medieval Latin *minūta* and *minūtum,* the neuter singular form of *minūtus,* were used to mean "one sixtieth of a unit." Units such as the degrees of the circle or the hour were, and still are, of course, divided into sixty parts.

misericord A dagger, a support for someone who is standing, and a special monastic apartment are all called by the same name because, strangely enough, they are all examples of mercy. The word *misericord* goes back to Latin *misericordia,* "mercy," derived from *misericors,* "merciful," in turn derived from *miserērī,* "to pity," and *cor,* "heart." In Medieval Latin *misericordia* was used to denote various merciful things, and these senses were borrowed into English. *Misericordia* referred to an apartment in a monastery where certain relaxations of the monastic rule were permitted, especially those involving food and drink. The word also designated a projection on the underside of a hinged seat in a choir stall against which a standing person could lean, no doubt a merciful thing during long services. Finally, *misericordia* was used for a dagger with which the death stroke was administered to a seriously wounded knight.

mob Every age has its linguistic fads and ephemeral coinages; occasionally some of them survive and become part of the standard vocabulary. In the seventeenth and eighteenth centuries the abbreviation of long words or phrases to one or two syllables had a vogue that was much deplored by the self-appointed literary watchdogs of the day. *Mob* is one such abbreviation that caught on. It is short for *mobile,* which was used in the early seventeenth century to mean "the masses." In this usage *mobile* was itself a shortening of the Latin phrase *mōbile vulgus,* "the excitable populace." The note of contempt originally inherent in the English word *mob* was also found in the Latin phrase.

156

money *The love of money is the root of all evil.*
—I Timothy 6:7

Money may be the root of all evil, but the root of the word *money* is a divinely mysterious epithet. One of the titles of the Roman goddess Juno was *Monēta*, a name whose exact meaning is not known. *Monēta* is probably derived from the same root as the verb *monēre*, "to bring to mind, remind." The temple of Juno Moneta was the place where money was coined, and the name *Monēta* became a word meaning "the mint" and by extension "coined money." *Monēta* developed into the Old French word *moneie* with the sense "coined money," which was borrowed into English in the fourteenth century. The Latin term *monēta* meaning "mint, a place where money is coined," was borrowed into the Germanic languages before Old English times and descended into Old English as *mynet*, whose modern form is *mint*.

mouse Of mice, muscles, and men. The word *muscle* goes back to the Latin word *mūsculus*, which is derived from Latin *mūs*, "mouse." *Mūsculus* meant "mouse" and also "muscle," probably because some muscles suggest mice in their rippling motion and appearance.

moving picture "I went afterwards to see a famous moving Picture, & I never saw any thing so pretty," wrote Jonathan Swift in 1713 in his *Journal to Stella*. Did the cinema already exist in the eighteenth century? Of course not. What Swift had seen in fact was a device that represented objects in various stages of motion and so displayed these representations as to create the effect of motion itself. Such pictures were of various types, including so-called flip books, which were known in antiquity. The term *moving picture* was then transferred to the type of moving pictures with which we are familiar. Its first recorded use in this sense was by Queen Victoria in 1896: "We were all photographed . . . by the new cinematograph process, which makes moving pictures by winding off a reel of films."

music   The history of the word *music* is music to the minds of artists and classicists. *Music* goes back to the Greek word *mousikē*, which is derived from *Mousa*, "Muse," any of the nine daughters of Zeus and Mnemosyne, the goddess of memory. *Mousikē* was originally an adjective that meant "pertaining to the Muses," referring to any of the arts over which the Muses presided, including poetry, drama, and dance, as well as song and instrumental music. Music was so important to the Greeks, however, that *mousikē* was used to refer especially to that branch of the arts. The Romans borrowed the Greek word, and by medieval times the Latin term *mūsica* referred only to the musical art.

muumuu   *Mumus were designed by the well-intentioned missionary ladies . . . as a covering for the Hawaiian women, in the early days when a few flowers sufficed for a garment.*
                                          —Don Blanding, *Hula Moons,* 1930

Muumuu is a borrowing of a Hawaiian word that means literally "cut off." The dress was so named because, having no yoke at first, it looked cut off at the neck. As Blanding states, this shapeless dress was associated with missionaries who were attempting to hide feminine nudity. These missionaries provided Hawaiian women with Mother Hubbard dresses, from which the muumuu was locally adapted. The well-meaning cover-uppers had no notion that the muumuu would become typical Hawaiian dress, that it would become stylish outside Hawaii, or that someday it would be referred to in passages like this one, from *Enemies of Bride* by Osmington Mills, published in 1966: "It was Madeleine, tousle haired, in a short mu-mu with . . . Ella in a still shorter mu-mu."

mystery   Could Nero Wolfe or Ellery Queen have penetrated the mysteries to which the Greek word *mustērion*, the ultimate source of our word *mystery*, referred? These mysteries were secret religious ceremonies in which only the initiated could participate. In Greek *mustērion* also meant "a secret, mystery," a sense that has passed down to its English descendant, *mystery*. From this sense, which in English can be more fully defined as "something that is not fully understood or that baffles or eludes the understanding," has come the familiar sense, "a fictional work dealing with a puzzling crime." There is not necessarily anything religious about these crimes, but only the initiated, such as Miss Marple and company, can solve them.

namby-pamby   We are being very literary when we call someone a *namby-pamby*. This word is derived from the name of Ambrose Philips, a little-known poet who wrote verse that incurred the sharp ridicule of two other eighteenth-century poets, Alexander Pope and his friend Henry Carey. Their ridicule, inspired by political differences and literary rivalry, actually had little to do with the quality of Philips's poetry. In poking fun at some children's verse written by Philips, Carey used the nickname *Namby Pamby*: "So the Nurses get by Heart Namby Pamby's Little Rhimes." Pope then used the name in the 1733 edition of his satirical epic *The Dunciad*. The first part of Carey's coinage came from Amby, or Ambrose. *Pamby* repeated the sound and form, but added the initial of Philips's name. Such a process of repetition is called reduplication. After being popularized by Pope, *namby-pamby* went on to be used generally for people or things that are insipid, sentimental, or weak.

Naugahyde   The Naugahyde seats of a sporty convertible might look and feel like leather although they are not. However, the name *Naugahyde*, a trademark for fabrics

Namby-pamby

coated with vinyl, tries to make up for this, as does
the product's appearance. The *Nauga–* part of the
trademark comes from *Naugatuck*, the name of a
town in Connecticut where the product was first
made. The last part of the word, *-hyde*, is a modified
form of *hide*, "an animal skin," such as one that may
be made into leather.

nausea Nausea is so unpleasant that one hardly wants to read
about it, but it might help to know that etymologically the word *nausea* originated as it ought to, with
a ship. *Nausea* goes back to the Greek word *nausia*,
ultimately derived from *naus*, "ship." *Nausia* meant
"seasickness" and generally "stomach disturbances
characterized by the need to vomit." Although *nausea* begins with a ship, it is pure coincidence that the
last three letters of the word spell *sea*.

neat To: All Chief Executive Officers

Would you like your liquor or your money neat? The
adjective *neat* is derived from the Old French word
net, which had several meanings. A basic sense of the
French word was "free from dirt, clean." Liquor that
contained no impurities was called *neat*, a sense that
survives in the meaning "undiluted." An amount of
money that was not liable to any reduction was also
considered *neat*. Another form of the Old French
word *net* had the same spelling and meanings but a
different pronunciation. It survives in the English
word *net*, meaning "remaining after all deductions
have been made." Thus, *neat* profit and a *net* profit
are exactly the same in meaning and in origin. Tell
that to your stockholders at the next annual meeting.
They'll think it's neat.

nice Since its adoption from Old French in the thirteenth
century the word *nice* has developed from a term of
abuse into a term of praise, a process called meliora-

162

tion. *Nice* is derived from the Latin word *nescius*, "ignorant," and was used in Middle English, as in Old French, to mean "foolish; without sense." By the fifteenth century *nice* had acquired the sense "elegant" in conduct and dress, but not in a complimentary way: *nice* meant "overrefined, overdelicate." This sense survives in the meanings "fastidious" and "precise, subtle." To the extent that delicacy, refinement, and precision have favorable connotations, *nice* developed corresponding senses.

nickel Is the metal nickel demonic? Copper has been known and worked since ancient times, but nickel was isolated and identified only in the eighteenth century. Nickel is found in an ore that resembles copper ore; the German name for the ore is *Kupfernickel*, literally "copper demon." The ore was so named because it produces no copper but can be mistaken for copper ore, just as fool's gold looks deceptively like gold. Baron Axel Frederic Cronstedt, the mineralogist who first isolated nickel in 1751, took its name from the second element of the word *Kupfernickel*.

nickname What's in a nickname? It's literally an additional name. The Middle English form of the word *nickname* was originally *ekename*, from *eke*, "addition" (related to the verb *eke*), and *name*, "name." *Ekename* acquired an initial *n* from the indefinite article *an* that frequently preceded it; *an ekename* came to be spelled and pronounced as if it were *a nekename*. In modern times the syllable *neke-*, which was not recognizable as an English word, was respelled *nick-*, and the spelling *nickname* has been the usual form ever since.

nicotine Jean Nicot could have been the sixteenth-century Marlboro Man. While serving as French ambassador to Portugal in the late 1550's, Nicot cultivated plants from tobacco seeds that Portuguese explorers had brought back from the New World. Nicot first introduced tobacco to the French nobility and then grew a crop that he sold for a profit in Paris. Nicot has been remembered in several ways for his enterprise. For one thing, the Swedish botanist Linnaeus named the genus that includes the common tobacco plant *Nicotiana* in his honor. But we are most familiar with another word containing Nicot's name, *nicotine*, which was formed in French after *Nicotiana*. This new word was the name given to the oily substance found in tobacco leaves when it was first isolated in 1818.

nightmare   If you have ever had a nightmare in which you thought you were suffocating, read on. In Old and Middle English *mare* was a word denoting an evil spirit. Although the spirit was imagined to be female, the word *mare* is unrelated to the modern word *mare*, "female horse." *Nightmare* is a compound of *night* and the old word *mare;* it designated an evil spirit thought to afflict sleeping persons by sitting on them and causing a feeling of suffocation. *Nightmare* was also used to mean both the feeling itself and the dream that produced it.

-nik   *Sputnik*, the high-flying Russian satellite of the fifties, and *beatniks*, the dropouts of the fifties, share only one thing, the suffix *–nik*. This suffix, which came into English from Russian and Yiddish, means "one involved in or associated with a specified thing or quality." A *beatnik* is a person associated with the *beat generation*, a counterculture movement originating in San Francisco that stressed unconventional behavior as a means of social criticism and self-expression. *Beat* in this expression probably meant "overcome with hard work or difficulty," perhaps influenced by *beat*, "the rhythm of music with a beat, such as jazz." *Sputnik*, Russian for "fellow traveler (of earth)," literally means "one associated with a path" or "one who takes the same path as another." The name of this satellite as well as the word *beatnik* helped popularize the suffix, which was used in words like *Muttnik*, for a satellite carrying a dog, and *draft-nik*, *protestnik*, and *computernik*. The addition of *-nik* often creates a word that is humorous or disapproving, such as the recent self-explanatory coinage *successnik*.

Although popularized in the fifties and sixties, the suffix had appeared previously in English; for example, in *Narodnik*, "a type of Russian agrarian socialist," and *nudnik*, "a pest, bore." Recently the Russian word *otkaznik*, derived from *otkazat'*, "to refuse," has been partially translated as *refusenik*, referring to a Soviet citizen who has been refused the right to emigrate from the U.S.S.R.

niobium Chemistry is a serious science, but it has its fanciful moments, which are revealed, for example, in the names of some of the elements. The word *niobium* is derived from *Niobe*, the personification of grief in Greek mythology. She was the daughter of the god Tantalus, who gave his name to the mineral ore tantalite. Because the element *niobium* is extracted from tantalite, it was named after Tantalus's offspring, Niobe.

noisome One can be noisome without making the least bit of noise. Neither in meaning nor in origin does *noisome* have any connection with the word *noise*; the similarities are purely coincidental. *Noisome*, meaning "offensive to the point of arousing disgust; harmful, dangerous," is a compound formed in Middle English from *noy*, an obsolete word meaning "harm" or "annoyance," and the suffix *-some*, which is still current in Modern English, where it is used to form adjectives with the general sense "characterized by some quality." *Noy* is related to the modern verb *annoy*, whose source is the Latin phrase *in odium*, "harmful, odious."

O

obvious It may not be immediately obvious, but the word *obvious* is derived ultimately from the Latin phrase *ob viam*, literally "in the way." Metaphorical senses of the Latin phrase and of the Latin adjective *obvius* derived from it were "at hand" and "exposed." The English word *obvious*, a borrowing from Latin, preserved these senses at first, but they are now obsolete. The current sense, "easily perceived," is a development of the English word.

October Demand a recount on your calendar. The Roman year originally began in March. Consequently, October was the eighth month, as its name suggests, for the word *October* is derived from Latin *octō*, "eight." The names of other months are also derived from the Latin names of numbers. *September*, the seventh month of the Roman calendar, is from *septem*, "seven"; *November*, the ninth month, is from *novem*, "nine"; and *December*, the tenth month, is from *decem*, "ten." The months now known as July and August were originally named, respectively, *Quintīlis*, "fifth month," and *Sextīlis*, "sixth month." They were later renamed to honor Julius Caesar and the emperor Augustus.

Opium

oil   *. . . the stink of oil hung heavy in the Texas air. It*
penetrated the houses the gardens the motorcars the trains
passing through towns and cities. It hung over the plains
the desert the range . . . Giant rigs straddled the Gulf of
Mexico waters. Platoons of metal and wood marched like
Martians down the coast across the plateaus through the
brush country. Only when you were soaring in an airplane
fifteen thousand feet above the oil-soaked earth were your
nostrils free of it.

—Edna Ferber, *Giant,* 1950

When the word *oil* is mentioned, images of multimillionaires and their wells pumping black gold come immediately to mind: the fictional Bick Benedicts, the Jett Rinks, the J. R. Ewings, and the real oilmen— the Hunts, the Gettys, the Rockefellers. The word *oil,* however, is related to a substance with a pleasant smell that would not make the fortune of J. R. Ewing. The word goes back to the Latin word *oleum* (notice that this is part of *petroleum,* derived from *petra,* "rock," and *oleum,* "oil"). *Oleum* comes from the Greek word *elaion,* both words meaning "olive oil" or "another oily substance." *Elaion,* in turn, derives from *elaia,* "olive tree, olive." The word *oil* is first recorded in English in the early thirteenth century. We find no clear uses of the word for any oil besides olive oil (and a miracle-working oil obtained from saints' bones) until the fourteenth century. It is difficult to say when *oil* came to mean "petroleum," but this is clearly an important meaning of the word today. J. Paul Getty himself said, "Without oil, there would be—there could be—no civilization as we know it." Whether or not that is an oleaginous statement we leave to the reader to determine.

opium   *Some men . . . maken slepinge medecines that the kittinge*
[surgery] be noght [not] felede [felt], as is opium.

—*The Cyrurgie of Guy de Chauliac,* circa 1425

Lady Stafford used to say to her sister, "Well, child, I have
come without my wit to-day"; that is, she had not taken
her opium.

—Horace Walpole, *Letters,* 1751

168

The origin of the word *opium* is innocent enough. It is derived from the Greek word *opion*, meaning "poppy juice, opium," from the Greek word *opos*, "juice, specifically vegetable juice, the milky juice drawn from a plant by tapping it." The drug opium is obtained from the juice of unripe pods of the opium poppy. This plant and its derivatives were not discovered by the ancient Greeks, however. Since prehistoric times people have known the effects of opium, and the plant was used medically in Egypt before the Greeks started to use it. And although we associate opium with the Far East, opium smoking did not become a serious problem there until about the mid-seventeenth century.

The two quotations at the head of this article reflect the double-edged nature of opium. Its derivatives, codeine, heroin, and morphine, are better known today as our friends and foes than is opium itself. The figurative use of the word *opium* reflects its role as an agent that numbs or stupefies. The most famous example of such a use is in Karl Marx's 1844 phrase, *das Opium des Volks*, "the opium of the people." In using *opium* to refer to religion, Marx was anticipated in English by Bishop Thomas Morton, who in *A Preamble unto an Encounter with P. R.*, published in 1608, denounced those who were "stupefied with that Opium of implicit faith and blind devotion."

otorhino-
laryngology

Otorhinolaryngology is the type of medical specialty that drives the layperson to despair, both of pronouncing the word properly (ō'tō-rī'nō-lăr'ĭng-gŏl'ə-jē) and of having any notion of what it means. The words *ear, nose,* and *throat* are quite clear, however, and that is what is meant by *oto-, rhino-,* and *laryngo-,* which are combining forms, or word elements that combine with other word forms to create compounds. *Oto-* is derived from Greek *ous*, "ear," *rhino-* from Greek *rhis*, "nose," and *laryngo-* from Greek *larunx*, "larynx or upper part of the windpipe."

Ouija　Prince Charles quashed the rumor that he was using Ouija boards to make contact with his deceased uncle Lord Mountbatten by saying, "I don't even know what they are." For the prince's information, *Ouija* is a trademark for a board with the alphabet and other symbols on it and a planchette, or small triangular board with a pointer supported by two casters and a vertical pencil, which is said to spell out telepathic and spiritualistic messages on the board when the operator's fingers are placed lightly upon it. In case the prince wonders whether positive results can be obtained by using such a device, he should be told that this trademark is made up of the French word *oui*, "yes," and the German word *ja*, "yes."

ounce　Although a lynx and an ounce are two different animals, their names share a common source upon which good etymologists can pounce. The word *ounce* is currently a name for the snow leopard, a large Asian mountain cat, but in earlier times it was used for other large cats, especially the lynx. The source shared by *ounce* and *lynx* is the Greek word *lunx*. The Greek word was borrowed into Latin as *lynx;* English adopted the Latin form directly. The form *ounce* comes from Old French. The normal development of Latin *lynx* in Old French was *lonce*. The initial *l* in this word, however, was interpreted as the definite article *la*, whose vowel would be dropped before a word beginning with a vowel. The Old French form *once* arose from this mistake. English borrowed the French form *once*, which by a regular change in English became the modern form *ounce*.

oxygen　One of the most important substances on earth is misnamed. The word *oxygen* was coined in French by the chemist Antoine Laurent Lavoisier in the eighteenth century, soon after the element was isolated. The French word *oxygène* was intended to mean "acid-producing," from the Greek word *oxus*, "sharp," used in the sense "acid," and the Greek suffix *–genēs,* "born," misinterpreted as "producing." At that time oxygen was thought to be an essential component of an acid. Although this is not the case, the name *oxygen* has persisted for the element. Perhaps this information will be a breath of fresh air to anyone who has ever made a mistake.

pal   "That old pal of mine. My buddy, my chum." *Pal*,
like *buddy* and *chum*, has an informal, thoroughly
"American" ring to it. One might think that *pal* had
been a fixture in the English language forever. In fact,
pal is a fairly recent acquisition from a rather exotic
source—the language of the Gypsies. First recorded in
English in the seventeenth century, *pal* was borrowed
from Romany, the Indic language of the Gypsies, specifically from a word meaning "brother, comrade,"
which occurs as *phal* in the Romany spoken in England and as *phral* in the Romany spoken in Europe.
Gypsies speak an Indic language because they originally migrated to Europe from the border region between Iran and India. In other Indic languages we
find related words meaning "brother," such as Hindu-
stani *bhāi*; Prakrit *bhāda, bhāyā*; and Sanskrit *bhrātṛ*.
All these terms trace their ancestry to the same Indo-
European word as does our word *brother*.

palace   All roads lead to Rome; so, in a way, do all palaces.
Our word *palace* goes back to the name of the most
important of the seven hills of Rome, the Palatine
Hill, known in Latin as *Palātium*. From at least 330
B.C. the hill was the site of many grand houses,
among them the residence of the emperor Augustus.
Subsequent emperors, including Tiberius and Nero,

Periwig

also built houses on the Palatine Hill, and as a result *Palātium* came to mean "one of the imperial residences on the Palatine." The word then began to denote other royal residences. *Palātium* passed into various languages, coming into English by way of Old French, as well as from the Latin word *Palātium*.

palm　A palm reader who also reads tea leaves might consider reading tree leaves, specifically the leaves of the palm tree. *Palm* meaning "palm of the hand" and *palm* meaning "palm tree" are both descended from the same Latin word, even though they are considered separate words in Modern English because of the different routes by which they entered the language. The Latin word *palma*, meaning "palm of the hand," denoted the palm tree because the leaves of that tree resemble an outspread hand. Old English borrowed *palma* to mean "palm tree." But English already had another word, *folm*, for "palm of the hand." And *folm* itself goes back to the same Indo-European form *pl̥mā*, "flat or palm of the hand," as does Latin *pálma*. However, in Middle English times *paume*, the French descendant of *palma*, was borrowed for "palm of the hand" and supplanted *folm*. The letter *l* was added to *paume* to reflect the spelling of the Latin word, and the word was eventually transformed into our Modern English *palm*.

pander　Pandering to the low tastes of the great gray masses may seem even less desirable when we consider the origin of the word *pander*. It comes ultimately from the character of Pandaro in Boccaccio's circa 1340 poem *Il Filostrato*, the primary source for Chaucer's *Troilus and Criseyde*, probably written about 1380. This character—the cousin of Criseida in *Il Filostrato* and Criseyde's uncle in Chaucer's poem—acts as the successful go-between for the two lovers in both works. Our word *pander* comes directly to us from *Pandare*, the name Chaucer used in *Troilus and Criseyde*. This word was first a noun, an early sense of which was "a go-between in sexual intrigues, procurer," first recorded in 1530. Around 1600 Shakespeare played an anachronistic game with this sense in his *Troilus and Cressida*. Shakespeare's Pandarus, supposedly speaking to the lovers during the Trojan War, says, "If ever you prove false one to another, since I have taken such pains to bring you together, let all pitiful goers-between be called to the world's end after my name; call them all Panders." *Pander* went on to develop the sense "one who caters to the low tastes and desires of others."

pan out   *But Dr. Brett cautioned that what sounds exciting from the Moon does not always pan out in the laboratory.*
—London *Daily Telegraph*, December 14, 1972

If Dr. Brett had been talking about hunting for gold on the moon, there would be a solid connection between his use of the expression *pan out* and its original use in gold mining. *Pan out*, like the verb *pan* itself, comes from the noun *pan* in the sense "a shallow circular metal vessel used in washing gold from gravel." The expression *pan out* was used in a variety of senses, including "to wash gold-bearing earth in a pan"; "to obtain gold by washing ore in a miner's pan"; and, with reference to a mine or mineral-bearing soil, "to produce gold or minerals." From such literal usages *pan out* was transferred to other situations. In Frederick Whymper's *Travel and Adventure in the Territory of Alaska*, published in 1868, we are told that "it panned out well" means that "it gave good returns." All these uses occurred first in American English, making the expression a true Americanism.

paparazzo   *Annoyed at first by the swarming* paparazzi, *[Margaret Trudeau] turned the situation into absurdist theater by snapping pictures of fellow lensmen snapping her picture.*
—*Newsweek*, May 2, 1977

The paparazzis' *flashbulbs . . . light up like fireflies.*
—*Newsweek*, March 22, 1976

Paparazzi resemble insects as they swarm around a celebrity like bees around a queen or pop their flashbulbs like so many fireflies. Paparazzi are reporters or photographers, especially free-lancers, who doggedly search for sensational stories about celebrities or take candid pictures of them for magazines and newspapers. We have borrowed the singular form *paparazzo* and its plural *paparazzi* from Italian. The word *paparazzo* comes from the name of a character, Signor Paparazzo, a photographer in Federico Fellini's 1960 film *La Dolce Vita*. The shutterbug's name in turn derives from the Italian dialect word *paparazzo*, "a kind of buzzing insect."

Fellini himself explained his inspiration for the character's name to Ron Galella (noted for his photographic pursuit of, among others, Jacqueline Kennedy Onassis). In a letter quoted in Galella's 1974 book *Jacqueline*, Fellini said: "When I was a schoolboy in Rimini . . . I shared a desk with a very restless boy who was always squirming, who was always talking so fast that his words came out stuck together in an endless buzzing. A teacher baptized him 'Paparazzo,' which in my part of the country is an insect, a sort of mosquito that's always emitting a buzz. While I was writing the script for *La Dolce Vita* that nickname came to mind, and so I named one of the photo-reporters Paparazzo."

parachute   Free-falling through the sky with an unopened parachute, a skydiver might be gratified to learn the etymology of the word for this useful device, if, of course, he or she is not preoccupied with other, more weighty matters. The second element of the word is *chute*, which, in the French word *parachute* that we have borrowed, means "fall." Obviously, skydivers hope that the *para–* part of the word will be more helpful. French *parachute* is modeled on the French words *parapluie*, "rain umbrella" (*pluie* meaning "rain") and *parasol*, "a sunshade." French *parasol* comes from the Italian word *parasole*, "sunshade," the ultimate model for words like these, in which *sole* means "sun" and *para–* comes from the verb *parare*, "to prepare, ward off." Now you can pull that ripcord.

particular   What is the bill of particulars regarding *particular?*
The word *particular* is derived from Latin *particula,*
"a little part." The Latin adjective *particulāris,* derived from *particula,* originally meant "pertaining to
one part, partial." The word was frequently used in
contrast to *universālis,* "universal," and in this way
came to refer to a single specific person or thing.

pasty   A meal at which you were served pasties, pasta, pâté,
and meat patties would not only be filling, it would
be etymologically incestuous. The noun *pasty,* "a
meat pie," was borrowed in the fourteenth century
from the Old French word *pasté. Pasté* is derived
from the Medieval Latin word *pastāta,* "a meat dish
wrapped in dough." Medieval Latin *pastāta* in turn
goes back to the Latin word *pasta,* "dough paste," the
source of Italian *pasta. Pâté* is the modern French
form of *pasté.* Borrowed into English in the eighteenth century as a synonym for *pasty, pâté* now usually means a meat paste or *très élégant* meat loaf
without a pastry crust. *Patty* comes from English or
French *pâté* by association with *pasty.*

patter   Comedians would hardly believe that their patter has
anything to do with prayer. But the word *patter* goes
back to *pater,* a shortened form of *paternoster,* the
Latin designation for the Lord's Prayer, from *pater,*
"father," and *noster,* "our," the first two words of
that prayer. In the medieval church Christian prayers
were learned and recited in Latin. Sometimes the
prayers were recited rapidly, with little apparent regard for the actual sense of the words. From this practice arose the Middle English verb *pateren* with the
senses "to say the paternoster," "pray," and "mutter
prayers rapidly and insincerely." In "We, harke, he
jangelis [chatters] like a jay . . . Me thynke [It seems
to me] he patris [patters] like a py [magpie]," from
the *York Mystery Plays* of circa 1450, *patter* has
taken on the sense "to chatter," from which developed our Modern English noun *patter.*

pawn　Pawns are the peons of chess and with good reason. The words *pawn,* "one of the pieces used in chess," and *peon,* "unskilled laborer," are both derived from the Medieval Latin word *pedō,* "something that goes on foot; foot soldier." *Pawn* can be traced back to *pedō* by way of Old French *peon* or *paon* and Anglo-Norman *poun,* "foot soldier; pawn in chess." And *peon* goes back to *pedō* by way of words in various languages, such as the same Old French *peon* in the sense "soldier or domestic on foot" and Spanish *peón* and Portuguese *peão,* both meaning "pedestrian, pawn in chess, foot soldier, or day laborer."

pea　*Pease-porridge hot,*
Pease-porridge cold,
Pease-porridge in the pot,
Nine days old.

The need for contrast between singular and plural forms of nouns is so important in English that very few nouns now have identical singular and plural forms. Those that do tend to be long-term survivors rather than borrowings or new formations: *sheep* and *deer* are as old as English itself. Many words originally having identical forms for the singular and plural eventually developed new plurals ending with the regular English plural suffix *-s:* the word *daughter,* for instance, now has the plural *daughters,* although it once had the plural *dohtor,* which was the same as the singular in Old English. Still other words developed new singular forms, and the word *pea* is an example of this reverse process. The regular plural of the Old English ancestor of *pea* had the ending *-an.* In Middle English the descendant of this Old English word developed plural forms, such as *pese* and *pease,* that were identical with singular forms; hence you could request one pease or two pease. Around the beginning of the seventeenth century people began to interpret the sound represented by *s* as a plural ending, and a new singular, spelled *pea* in Modern English, was developed to conform to the usual pattern of English nouns. If *pease-porridge* were named today, it would be called *pea-porridge.*

peculiar There was once nothing peculiar about the word *peculiar*, because the sense "odd" developed well after the word was borrowed into English. *Peculiar* is derived from the Latin word *pecūliāris*, which originally meant "pertaining to private property" and was itself derived from *pecū*, "cattle," since livestock was once the quintessence of private property. *Pecūliāris* went on to develop the extended sense "belonging to oneself alone." The English word *peculiar* was used with the senses of the Latin word *pecūliāris*, but it eventually came to mean "exclusive, unique," and then "unique" in the sense "singular, unusual, odd."

pedigree The symbol ⅄ is important to blue bloods and owners of blue-blooded animals, at least according to the accepted hypothesis for the origin of the word *pedigree*. The Old French name for this symbol was *pied de grue*, meaning literally "foot of a crane," because that is what it looked like. This Old French word arrived in English by way of Anglo-Norman *pe de grue* and has given us our word *pedigree*. The word for the symbol, which was used in genealogical charts to indicate succession, took on the broader meaning "a genealogical chart, genealogical relationship; genealogy." So if you have a good pedigree, you can always put your best foot forward.

pen Is the feather mightier than the sword? The English word *pen*, "a writing implement," is derived from the Latin word *penna*, which originally meant only "feather." The Latin word for a writing implement was *stilus*, which meant "a stake." Since the ancient Romans wrote on wax tablets, any pointed instrument would do and ink was unnecessary. However, the subsequent use of paper or parchment required ink, which was applied with the shaft of a large feather sharpened and split for that purpose. In later Latin times *penna* acquired the meaning "a feather used to write with; pen." *Penna* descended into Old French as *penne*, which English borrowed with both senses, "feather" and "pen," the former of which is now obsolete.

penicillin   *In the rest of this article allusion will constantly be made to experiments with filtrates of a broth culture of this mould, so for convenience and to avoid the repetition of the rather cumbersome phrase "Mould broth filtrate," the name "penicillin" will be used. This will denote the filtrate of a broth culture of the particular penicillium with which we are concerned.*

—Alexander Fleming, *The British Journal of Experimental Pathology,* 1929

In this quotation from the writings of the discoverer of penicillin we view the word *penicillin* almost at it moment of birth. Fleming derived the name *penicillin* from the genus name of the mold *Penicillium notatum,* from which he originally obtained the antibiotic. The name has since been applied to other antibiotics obtained naturally from other molds or made synthetically from them.

The genus name *Penicillium* comes from the Latin word *pēnicillus,* "paintbrush," to which our word *pencil* can also be traced. *Penicillium* was so named because of its brushlike sporangia, or spore-bearing structures. The Latin word *pēnicillus* in turn can be traced back to the Latin word *pēnis,* "tail, male organ," which we have also borrowed.

peninsula   Floridians may be interested to learn more about the origin of the word describing the geomorphological configuration of their great state. The word *peninsula* is borrowed from the Latin word *paeninsula,* which in turn is derived from *paene insula,* meaning literally "almost an island." *Peninsula* refers not only to land that is almost surrounded by water but also to a piece of land whose boundary is mostly coastline, as is the case with Florida.

periwig   For more than a century—from about 1660 to 1780—decorative false hair crowned the heads of fashionable men and woman in Europe. The English called such headdresses *perukes* or *periwigs,* both of which words are derived from the Old Italian word *perrucca,* which originally meant "bushy head of hair."

180

Perrucca was borrowed into Old French as *perruque,* which developed the sense "wig." English speakers rendered the Old French word in various ways, which explains the existence in Modern English of the synonymous words *peruke* and *periwig. Periwig* was then shortened to *wig,* the form now in common use.

pest   An investigation into the etymological, if not the entomological, life cycle of the word *pest* illustrates the interesting transformations in meaning that a word can undergo over a considerable period of time. The earliest sense of *pest* in English, first recorded in the sixteenth century, is far removed from its more common meanings today. Four centuries ago the word meant "a deadly epidemic disease, specifically the bubonic plague." *Pest* in this sense came to us from the French word *peste* or its source, the Latin word *pestis,* both meaning "plague, pestilence." The English and the French words then came to mean "someone or something that is destructive, harmful, or troublesome," a sense first recorded in English during the seventeenth century. David Livingstone, the British explorer and missionary, used the term in a way familiar to many modern-day apartment dwellers. In his 1865 *Narrative of an Expedition to the Zambesi* he called cockroaches "those destructive pests." Over the years *pest* finally broadened in meaning, adding the sense "any nuisance."

petrel   Petrels are noted for flying so close to the water that they appear to be walking on it. Their name may have come from this behavior, although the origin of the word is not known for certain. In Part I of his *Voyage to New Holland,* published in 1703, the English explorer and pirate William Dampier, a stormy petrel himself, gave the first recorded version of that explanation: "As they fly . . . they pat the Water alternately with their Feet, as if they walkt upon it; tho' still upon the Wing. And from hence the Seamen give them the name of Petrels, in allusion to St. Peter's walking upon the [Sea of Galilee]."

philodendron Does that philodendron in your living room seem to be growing toward the maple in your front yard? The name *philodendron*, derived from Greek *philos*, "loving," and *dendron*, "tree," literally means "fond of trees." The name was given to this genus of climbing plants because in their tropical American habitat they twine about trees.

piano As the loudest passages of Rachmaninoff, Liszt, or Brahms pour forth from a piano, those in the audience who know that *piano* means "soft" in Italian might be puzzled at this counterpoint. *Piano*, however, is also a shortened form of *pianoforte*. Both words have been borrowed into English, although *piano* is much more common. *Pianoforte* comes from the full name of the instrument, *clavicembalo con il piano e il forte*, "harpsichord with soft and loud." This name, given to the instrument around 1709 by its inventor, Bartolommeo Cristofori, expressed the fact that, unlike a harpsichord, a piano could produce sounds that varied in loudness and duration.

picnic Finding the ultimate origin of the word *picnic* is certainly no picnic. The word comes from the French word *pique-nique*, whose origin is not known with absolute certainty. It seems most likely that it was formed from the French verb *piquer*, "to pick." The word *pique-nique* may have originated in the seventeenth century, when it referred to a meal for which each guest contributed a dish to be served, a sort of seventeenth-century potluck. English *picnic*, in this sense, is first recorded in the mid-eighteenth century. At some point it became common to hold such parties outdoors, and by the nineteenth century *picnic* referred to any open-air meal.

pioneer *Come my tan-faced children,*
Follow well in order, get your weapons ready,
Have you your pistols? have you your sharp-edged axes?
Pioneers! O Pioneers!
    —Walt Whitman, *Pioneers! O Pioneers!* 1865

The Old French word *pionnier* that is the source of
our word *pioneer* is derived from another Old French
word, *pion*, "foot soldier," a derivational connection
apparent in the quotation above. *Pion* goes back to
the Medieval Latin word *pedō*, "something that goes
on foot; foot soldier," as do our English words *pawn*
and *peon*. *Pionnier* and *pioneer* originally referred to
a soldier whose task was to prepare the way, as by
digging ditches and building earthworks and roads,
for the main body of troops marching to a new area.
From this use the word was applied in English, as in
French, to anyone who ventures into an unknown region and opens the way for others to follow.

pompadour   *Reagan looks good at the rostrum: a tall figure with ruddy
cheeks, his reddish-brown hair swept back in a slight
pompadour.*
                              —*The New Yorker*, May 24, 1976

The *pompadour* hair style of a 1950's rock 'n' roll star
can be traced in name to a mistress of Louis XV in
the mid-eighteenth century. Madame de Pompadour,
who may have been raised from an early age to fill
such a post, occupied it well. She was pleasant to the
king's wife, pleasing to the king, and in later years
politically indispensable to him. Because she was the
arbiter of fashion at that time, the word *pompadour*
derived from her name has been used for such things
as a type of cloak, a fabric pattern covered with sprigs
of flowers, a pink or crimson color, a South American
bird with crimson-purple plumage, and several hair
styles, including the one worn by early rock 'n' roll
stars, in which the hair was brushed up and back
from the forehead.

poodle   When it rains cats and dogs, the dogs ought to be
poodles. The word *poodle* comes from the German
word *Pudel*, short for *Pudelhund*, both meaning "poodle." *Pudel* comes from Low German *pudeln*, "to
splash in water." *Pudeln* in turn is derived from *pū-
del*, "puddle," a term related to our word *puddle*. *Pudel* is part of the name of the *Pudelhund* because the
dog was once used as a waterfowl retriever.

posh "Oh yes, Mater, we had a posh time of it down there." So in *Punch* for September 25, 1918, do we find the first recorded instance of that mysterious word *posh*, meaning "smart and fashionable," although in a 1903 book by P. G. Wodehouse, *Tales of St. Austin's*, there is a mention of a waistcoat that was "push." The latter may be a different word, but in either case the dates of occurrence are important because they are part of the objection to deriving *posh* from the initials of "Port Out, Starboard Home." This was the cooler, and thus more expensive, side of ships traveling between England and India in the mid-nineteenth century, and the acronym *POSH* was supposedly stamped on the tickets of first-class passengers traveling on that side of ships owned by the Peninsular and Oriental Steam Navigation Company. No evidence whatever exists for this theory, however.

The *Oxford English Dictionary Supplement* may have found a possible source or sources for *posh*. Another word *posh* was nineteenth- and early twentieth-century British slang for "money," specifically "a halfpenny, cash of small value." This word is borrowed from the common Romany word *påsh*, "half," which was used in combinations such as *påshera*, "halfpenny." *Posh*, also meaning "a dandy," is recorded in two dictionaries of slang published in 1890 and 1902, although this particular *posh* may be still another word. This word or these words, however, are much more likely to be the source of *posh* than "Port Out, Starboard Home," although the latter certainly caught the public's etymological fancy and has endured to this day.

post The meaning "mail" of the word *post*, ultimately derived from Latin *pōnere*, "to place, put in position," was the result of an old method of delivering mail. In the sixteenth century mounted couriers called "posts," stationed at designated places along certain highways and byways, rode in relays with royal dispatches and other papers. As the system of mail delivery expanded during the next two centuries, *post* was applied to a delivery of mail and to the organization responsible for the entire system of mail delivery.

pound The word *pound* has several unlikely abbreviations. As a unit of weight it is abbreviated *lb.*, and as a unit of British currency, it is signified by a stylized *L* or *£*. But how can the word *pound* be shortened to letters it does not contain? The etymologist has the answer. The word *pound*, meaning both "a measure of weight" and "an amount of money" (originally "a pound weight of silver"), is descended from the Old English word *pund*, which goes back to the Latin word *pondo*. In Latin *pondo* was a part of the phrase *libra pondo*, in which *libra*, familiar to us from astrology as "the scales," meant "a unit of (weight) measurement" and *pondo* meant "by weight." The Romans often shortened the phrase to *pondo*, the element that has come down to us, but the abbreviations *lb.* and *L* or *£* continue in use, preserving a vestige of the initial word of the phrase.

prestige Lest we be bamboozled into believing that the word *prestige* always connoted eminent, influential status, let us examine its early history. Strangely enough, *prestige* first meant "an illusion, conjuring trick, deception, imposture." English borrowed it from French, with the French term *prestige* going back to Latin *praestīgiae*, "a trick, deceit." In French *prestige* developed a sense referring to influence achieved through such things as success, renown, or wealth, which was borrowed into English and first recorded in 1829. John Stuart Mill, writing in 1838, uses this sense of *prestige* while seeming to keep in mind its earlier sense. As he observed, "the *prestige* with which [Napoleon] overawed the world is . . . the effect of stage-trick."

priest When John Milton in his sonnet "On the New Forcers of Conscience under the Long Parliament" denounced the elders, or presbyters, of the Presbyterian

Church by saying "*New Presbyter* is but *Old Priest* writ large," he was aware of the etymological relationship between the two words. *Priest* and *presbyter* are both descended from the Greek word *presbuteros*, which literally meant "elder," the comparative form of *presbus*, "old man." The Greek word was used in early Christian writing to denote one of the orders of ministers. *Presbuteros* was borrowed into Latin and from there into the Germanic languages, appearing in Old English as *prēost*, which became our modern word *priest*. Because Old English *prēost* and its descendants referred not only to Christian ministers but also to Jewish and pagan priests, *presbuteros* was reborrowed as *presbyter* during the sixteenth-century Reformation to apply only to officials of the Christian church. Milton thus made an inspired pun, for *presbyter* was a longer word than *priest*, yet had the same etymological source.

private   The military rank *private* may be a misnomer, since a private seems not to have much of a private life, at least during basic training. The English adjective *private* comes from the Latin word *prīvātus*, "not in public life," a derivative of *prīvus*, "individual." The noun *private*, meaning "a soldier of the lowest rank," developed from the adjective *private* in the sense "not holding an official or public position." Just as a private citizen holds no public office, so a private soldier has neither special responsibilities nor the rank that goes with them.

prize   The Price is Right or the Prize is Right? *Prize* was at one time the same word as *price*. *Price* came from the Old French word *pris*, which derives from Latin *pretium*, "value, price, reward." *Pris* had a range of senses, including "money paid for something," "prize," and "esteem." Our word *price*, which came into English from French, is commonly used today
(continued)

only in the sense "sum of money, cost." *Price* also meant in Middle English, as it had in Old French, "reward, prize." During the past four hundred years this sense and related senses have broken off from *price*, becoming thought of as a separate word. From the sixteenth to the eighteenth century *prize*, our spelling for this word, was simply one of a number of possible spellings for *price*. Now come on down!

procrastination

No idleness, no laziness, no procrastination; never put off till tomorrow what you can do today.
—Lord Chesterfield, *Letters*, December 26, 1749

procrastination is the art of keeping up with yesterday.
—Don Marquis, *certain maxims of archy*, 1927

Procrastination is intimately connected with tomorrow rather than yesterday, etymologically (and practically) speaking. *Procrastination* goes back to the Latin verb *prōcrastināre*, "to postpone, delay," which is derived from the prefix *prō-*, meaning "forward in time," and the adjective *crastinus*, "relating to tomorrow," from the noun *crās*, "tomorrow." Keeping this in mind, you will always know approximately when you will get something done if you procrastinate: tomorrow, and tomorrow, and tomorrow!

procrustean

We can easily see how the word *procrustean* came to mean "producing or designed to produce conformity by ruthless or arbitrary means" and "having merciless disregard for individual differences or special circumstances" if we look into the ancestry of the term. *Procrustean* is derived from the name of the legendary Greek robber Procrustes, who dwelt in Eleusis and was later killed by Theseus. According to one version of the legend, Procrustes would force strangers to lie down in one of his two beds—one bed being short; the other, long. If the unfortunate victim was longer than the short bed, Procrustes would cut the victim to fit. Victims shorter than the long bed were stretched out with weights in an early version of the rack. This legend also led to the use of the phrase *bed of Procrustes* to refer to great inflexibility.

propaganda   *Congregatio de propaganda fide:* if the third word in this Latin phrase looks familiar, it should. Our word *propaganda* goes back to this title, which means "Congregation for Propagating the Faith," *propaganda* being a form of the Latin verb *propāgāre*, which originally meant "to reproduce a plant by layers or slips" and then came to mean "to disseminate religious faith." *Propaganda* in English first referred to the Roman Catholic committee of cardinals in charge of foreign missions. The word is recorded in 1718 in the title "The Congregation of the Propaganda" and in 1819 by itself. *Propaganda* then came to mean "any association, systematic scheme, or concerted movement for the propagation of a particular doctrine or practice." This general sense was used in a 1790 letter by James Macpherson in which he discusses the French Revolution: "All Kings have . . . a new race of Pretenders to contend with, the disciples of the propaganda at Paris or, as they call themselves, Les Ambassadeurs de genre humain." Finally, in 1908, *propaganda* is recorded in the sense most familiar to us, "the systematic propagation of information or ideas by an interested party," again with reference to the Church: "The Church . . . soon felt a need of new methods of propaganda and government" (Lilley and Tyrell, translators, *Programme of Modernism*). The word went on to denote material disseminated in such a way, as well as the means of such dissemination. William Safire has said that this word is "one of the few that mean the same to both Communists and anti-Communists."

protean   Someone who writes poetry, runs the mile, designs clothing, and plays the cello is truly protean in abilities. But to be like Proteus, from whose name the word *protean*, meaning "variable; versatile," comes, would defy the powers of even a Renaissance person.

189

Proteus was a Greek sea god who had the power to change his shape. Proteus also had the gift of prophecy, but those who wished to consult him had to bind him securely first. He would then change into various shapes, such as a wild boar, a tiger, a rush of water, or a raging fire. A questioner who could keep Proteus restrained until he returned to his original shape would receive an answer, although one must wonder if by then the inquirer could still remember the question.

prune   The words *prune* and *plum* came into English by separate routes from the Latin word *prūnum,* "a plum." *Prūnum* was borrowed into the West Germanic languages at a very early date with the letter *l* instead of the letter *r.* The Old English form was *plūme,* which became *plum* in Modern English. In Old French the Latin word *prūnum* became *prune.* English then borrowed *prune* from French with the specialized meaning "dried plum."

pundit   The next time you meet a pundit ask whether he or she knows anything about Sanskrit. *Pundit* comes from the Hindi word *paṇḍit,* meaning "learned man," from Sanskrit *paṇḍita-,* "learned, skilled; learned man, scholar." First recorded in English in the seventeenth century, *pundit* came into our language referring specifically to a learned man of India who had a knowledge of Sanskrit and the philosophy, religion, and jurisprudence of his country. In the nineteenth century *pundit* is found in the sense "a learned expert or teacher," a colloquial or humorous usage. The *Saturday Review* of March 15, 1862, mentions "a point upon which the doctors of etiquette and the pundits of refinement will differ." In modern usage *pundit* seems mostly to refer to an authority or critic or to one who makes statements in an authoritative way. William Safire points out that "the term is widely applied to almost any member of the newspaper and radio-television fraternity encompassed in Eisenhower's 'sensation seeking columnists and commentators.' " Any Sanskrit spoken by those media commentators?

pupil   The pupil of the eye is so called because of the tiny image reflected in it. Our word *pupil* goes back to the Latin word *pūpilla*, meaning "a girl under the care of a guardian," "a little doll," and "the pupil of the eye." *Pūpilla* in turn is derived from *pūpa*, "a girl, doll." This use in Latin of *pūpilla* for a doll and the pupil of the eye is probably based on or parallel to the senses of the Greek word *korē*, which means "girl; puppet, doll; pupil of the eye." *Pupil* in the sense "a student" goes back to Latin *pūpilla*, too, and also to another word, *pūpillus*, "a minor under the care of a guardian," which is derived from *pūpus*, "a boy, child."

Quaalude   The trademark *Quaalude* for the sedative and hypnotic agent methaqualone is an example of how a
product name is carefully chosen for a positive public
response. Methaqualone was developed in the 1960's
by William H. Rorer, Inc. At that time, the company's best-known product was Maalox, a digestive aid
that derived its name from its ingredients, *magne*-
sium and *al*uminum hydroxides. To enhance the
product recognition of their new sedative drug, the
company incorporated the *aa* of *Maalox* into the
name *Quaalude*. The other elements of the name are
presumed to be a contraction of the phrase *quiet in-
terlude*, a soothing, even poetic description of the
drug's effect. *Quaalude* is now a trademark of the
Lemmon Pharmacal Company.

quahog   Quahogs and geoducks have nothing to do with mammals and birds in spite of the apparent similarity of
their final elements—*hog* and *duck*—to the words
hog and *duck*. *Quahog* and *geoduck* were borrowed
into English from Native American languages. *Quahog*, the name of an edible clam with a hard,

Queen

rounded shell, found abundantly from the Gulf of St. Lawrence to the Gulf of Mexico, comes from Narraganset *poquaûhock*, "quahog." Narraganset is a language spoken by a tribe that inhabited the area of Rhode Island. *Geoduck*, improbably pronounced (gōo'ē-dŭk'), is the name of a big clam weighing up to twelve pounds and found in coastal waters from British Columbia to southern California and especially in Puget Sound. Its name comes from the Puget Salish word *g*ʷ*idaq*, meaning "geoduck."

quaint   The adjective *quaint* is ultimately, but not directly, derived from the Latin word *cognitus*, "known," the past participle of *cognoscere*, "to know, learn." English did not borrow the Latin word but did borrow its Old French descendant *cointe* or *queinte*, which had developed senses of its own that were far removed from the meaning of the Latin word. The Old French term *queinte* basically meant "wise," "skilled," and "clever." From these senses *queinte* developed other meanings, such as "cleverly or ingeniously made or done" and "strange, curious." The usual modern sense of our English word *quaint*, "charmingly old-fashioned," is probably not a direct outgrowth of the now obsolete senses borrowed into English from French; rather, it stems from an artificial revival of *quaint* by writers of the romantic period. Many of these writers were interested in medieval customs, traditions, and literature, and they occasionally used obsolete and charmingly old-fashioned words—not always correctly—when writing about medieval topics.

queen   A queen and her gynecologist are related etymologically, as this investigation proves. The word *queen* is a native English word; its Old English form was *cwēn*. *Queen* is related to Greek *gunē*, "woman," both of which words go back to the Indo-European root *g*ʷ*en-*, "woman." Greek *gunē* is the source of our English prefix *gyneco-*, also meaning "woman," which has combined with the forms *-logy* and *-ist* to give us the word *gynecologist*.

194

quibble *These lawiers have ... such quibs and quiddits [quibbles] that beggering their clients they purchase to themselves whole lordships.*
—Robert Greene, *A Quip for an Upstart Courtier,* 1592

Quibblers may take comfort in knowing that their carping is part of a long tradition of fine points, small details, and subtle distinctions, out of which tradition the word *quibble* itself comes. *Quibble* probably goes back to the Latin word *quibus,* a form of the Latin pronoun and adjective *quī,* meaning "who, which." *Quibus,* the plural form used to express the dative and ablative cases, meant such things as "to whom" and "from whom." This syntactic form appeared frequently in Latin legal documents; hence the word became associated with petty details and fine distinctions. From *quibus* we may have acquired the English word *quib,* meaning "an evasion of the point or a petty distinction," and thence probably the noun and verb *quibble.*

quiche Quiche may seem to be a quintessentially French dish, but the word *quiche* is actually a Gallicized German word. *Quiche* was originally a specialty of Lorraine, a region in northeastern France bordering on Germany. Both French and German are spoken in Lorraine, which (along with Alsace) was claimed as territory by both countries at various times throughout history. The word *quiche* was borrowed into French from Alsatian German *Küche,* a diminutive of the German word *Kuchen,* "cake."

quickie *Motion pictures which are ground out wholesale by the studios at the rate of one a week are called* quickies.
—*American Mercury,* December, 1926

It takes but a short time to explain that *quickie* is a noun formed from the adjective *quick* and the suffix *–ie* or *–y,* a suffix that means "one having to do with or characterized by." The quotation heading this article illustrates the fact that *quickie,* although it can now mean a number of things, first referred to cheap,

quickly made motion pictures. The word is encountered often in our fast-paced life, with two of its
senses shown in these quotations:

Here's a quicky for you when you get a blank spot about
what to make for that summertime snack.
— Petticoat, July 17, 1971

I could do with a quicky.
— Bruce Marshall, *Red Danube*, 1947

In the first context above the word means an easily
prepared recipe; in the second, a rapidly quaffed alcoholic drink. It is worth mentioning that the suffix in
use here is very productive in word formation: other
words formed like *quickie* include *fatty, biggie,*
smarty or *smartie, cutie, longies,* and *toughie.* So far,
however, there is no *slowie.*

quicksilver How is it that quicksilver is quick? The name *quick-*
silver for the element mercury is a translation of the
Latin phrase *argentum vivum*, literally "living silver."
Mercury was given this name because it is a silvery-
colored metal that is liquid at ordinary temperatures.
In *quicksilver* the word *quick* preserves its original
but now archaic sense "living, alive." We are familiar
with this sense of *quick* in the phrase *the quick and*
the dead, where *the quick* means "the living."

quisling *A vile race of quislings—to use the new word which will*
carry the scorn of mankind down the centuries.
— Winston Churchill, speech at St. James's Palace,
London, June 12, 1941

Entry of the word *quisling* in the thesaurus of opprobrium is a prime instance of how, in Mark Anthony's
words, "the evil that men do lives after them," a
thought eloquently restated by Churchill in 1941.
Major Vidkun Abraham Lauritz Jonsson Quisling, a
Norwegian appointed by Hitler as the "minister president," or resident cat's-paw, of the Nazi puppet government in Norway, had been little more than a very
bad joke to his countrymen before the Nazi takeover

196

of their country on April 9, 1940. (Quisling, who had been the minister of defense from 1931 to 1933, resigned to form his own Norwegian fascist party, but managed to attract only a tiny following. At the time, many people thought he was mentally ill.) During the Nazi occupation the real power over Norway rested with the Reichskommissar; however, Quisling was invested with sufficient authority to send almost a thousand Jews to their death in concentration camps and to attempt wholesale Nazification of the Norwegian churches, schools, and young people. He even managed to have his portrait displayed on his country's stamps. When Norway was finally liberated, Quisling's regime was cancelled: he was arrested, charged with treason and murder, found guilty, and executed on October 24, 1945. His name, which became a synonym for any traitor-collaborator, was first recorded in English in this sense on April 15, 1940, just six days after his treachery paved the way for the Nazi invasion of his country. In an article discussing the threatened Nazi takeover of yet another country, Sweden, the London *Times* noted that "Comment in the press urges that there should be unremitting vigilance also against possible 'Quislings' inside the country." At that moment in history *quisling* took its place alongside other names for traitors, notably *Judas, Brutus,* and *Benedict Arnold.*

quixotic   Humming "The Impossible Dream" in the shower does not necessarily mean that one is quixotic, but it may be a symptom of the quality referred to by this word. *Quixotic,* meaning "idealistic without regard to practicality," comes from the noun *quixote,* which is, of course, derived from the name of the hero of the romance by Miguel de Cervantes about a knight with high but impractical ideals. The novel about the father of quixotism and quixotry also has given us the phrase "to tilt at windmills." Don Quixote, thinking windmills were giants, fought with them; we do the same sort of thing when we battle people or things that are not our enemies. Reference to these windmills is first found in 1644 in a work by John Cleve-

land, *The character of a London diurnall*: "The
Quixotes of this Age fight with the Wind-mills of
their owne Heads."

quorum   *Quōrum vos . . . unum esse volumus.*

An of whom must be present to decide on the proposal.

In the apparently meaningless English translation
above we see the original sense of the Latin word that
is the source of our word *quorum*, which, if substituted for "of whom," makes the sentence meaningful.
Quorum, "the minimum number of officers and
members of a committee or organization who must
be present for the valid transaction of business," was
originally a form of the Latin pronoun and adjective
quī, "who," which expressed a plural number in the
genitive case, the case that typically marks possession
or source. *Quōrum*, meaning "of whom," was used in
commissions to designate certain persons as members
of a body. The Latin wording was as follows: *"quōrum* [of whom] *vos* [you] . . . *unum* [one] (*duos*,
etc. [two, etc.]) *esse* [be] *volumus* [we will]," or "of
whom we will that you be one (two, etc.)." *Quōrum*
was then used in Middle English in a new sense (first
recorded in 1426) referring to justices of the peace,
usually ones known for their learning or ability, who
had to be present to constitute the court. Then the
familiar sense of our English word *quorum* developed
from the notion of those having to be present. Members of Congress hastening to respond to a quorum
bell might well ask, *"Of whom* does this bell toll?"

quoth   *"Take thy beak from out my heart, and take thy form
from off my door!"
Quoth the Raven, "Nevermore."*
                    —Edgar Allan Poe, "The Raven," 1845

The archaic verb *quoth*, which persists in English in
large part because of Poe's encounter with the raven,
is unrelated to the modern verb *quote* in spite of the
similarity of sound and spelling. *Quoth* means "said"

198

and is derived from Old English *cwǣð*, a form of
cweðan, "to say, speak." The verb *quote* is derived ultimately from Latin *quot,* "how many." In medieval
times sections of books were marked with numbers,
as chapters are today, for easy reference. The Medieval Latin verb *quotāre,* derived from *quot,* meant "to
mark with numbers," referring especially to the marking of books. Our word *quote,* which comes both
from *quotāre* and its Old French descendant *coter,*
with the same sense, developed more general senses.
The English verb was used to mean "to give a number
as a reference" and "to cite, refer to." Finally *quote*
came to mean "to repeat a passage word for word"
rather than "to refer to a passage obliquely, by numbers or other shorthand."

racket   In handball you do not use a racket, or do you? The word *racket* comes to us from the Old French term *raquette*, which meant "palm of the hand, sole of the foot," as well as "racket." This mixture of senses can be explained by the history of racket games. The game of tennis, for example, was originally played with the hands; in French it is still called *le jeu de paume*. The transition in meaning of the word *raquette* from "palm" to "racket" was a natural one, especially since the physical transition in the way the game was played was gradual, moving first from hand to glove, then to a glove with a binding of cords on its palm, then to boards, then to a short-handled paddle, and finally to a long-handled racket. The Old French word *raquette* is ultimately derived from Arabic *rāḥat*, a form of *rāḥa*, "palm." Let's give our court game players a big hand.

raid   The members of an army traveling on a particular *road* to carry out a *raid* probably would not draw a connection between the two words. However, *raid* and *road* descend from the same Old English word

River

rād. The *ai* in *raid* represents the standard development in the northern dialects of Old English long *a,* while the *oa* in *road* represents the standard development of Old English long *a* in the rest of the English dialects. Old English *rād* meant "the act of riding" and "the act of riding with a hostile intent; that is, a raid," senses that no longer exist for our word *road.* It was left to Sir Walter Scott to revive the Scots form *raid* with the sense "a military expedition on horseback." The Scots weren't making all the raids, however. Others seem to have returned the favor, for we find these words in the Middle English *Coventry Leet Book:* "Aftur a Rode . . . made uppon the Scottes at thende of this last somer." The "Rode" was led by the non-Scottish Duke of Gloucester, who was later crowned as Richard III, and Henry Percy, Duke of Northumberland.

raise You can raise or rear a child. The word *raise* comes from the Old Norse term *reisa,* and *rear* is a native English word, but both are descended from the same Germanic ancestor, *raizjan.* Under certain conditions the Germanic *z* became *r* in the West Germanic languages, of which English is one. However, the original consonant (spelled *s*) remained in the other Germanic languages, including Old Norse. Both *raise* and *rear* are related to *rise.* No words related to these three verbs have been found outside of Germanic.

ramble To ramble on is fine as long as one has plenty of time or a patient audience. But an explanation of the word's origin would certainly hold the attention of almost any audience. *Ramble* probably comes from the assumed Middle Dutch word *rammelen,* used of animals such as cats and rabbits and meaning "to be excited by sexual desire and wander about." *Rammelen* in turn comes from the Middle Dutch word *rammen,* meaning "to copulate with, cover." Having looked into *ramble,* perhaps we should now study *wanderlust,* another lusty subject of investigation in this book.

rare   Before modern times the adjective *rare,* meaning "lightly cooked," referred only to eggs. Although its application to other foods, especially meat, occurs in some English dialects, this use of the term *rare* was considered an Americanism until very recently, when it was adopted into standard British usage. *Rare,* "lightly cooked," is descended from Old English *hrēr.* It is not related to another adjective *rare,* "uncommon," the source of which is Latin *rārus,* "scattered, uncommon."

raven   The raven that quoth "nevermore" might have said a lot more had it been so inclined, specifically about the ancestry of its name. *Raven* goes back to an Indo-European root, *ker–²,* that has contributed to English a number of terms that denote the making of sounds or the names of birds. Words expressing the idea of noise and going back to this root are *ring, retch* (from Old English *hrǣcan,* "to clear the throat"), *screak, screech,* and *shriek.* English bird names that come from this root are *rook* (from Germanic *hrō-kaz,* "crow," literally "croaking bird"), *shrike,* and *raven. Cricket,* the insect, also goes back to the same root.

rectangle   For anyone who has difficulty remembering that a rectangle is a parallelogram with a right angle, the etymology of the word *rectangle* could prove helpful. Our English term is composed of the Latin elements found in, for example, the Late Latin word *rectiangulum,* "a right-angled triangle," used in the writings of Isidore of Seville, an early medieval Spanish bishop who compiled an encyclopedia. His word can be traced back to Latin *rectus,* "straight, vertical, right," and *angulus,* "angle." So, now, what's a rectangle?

redline   *Redline* is a verb that can be used on the ground, in the air, or at sea, depending on one's intentions. The use of a red line is, of course, a common way of drawing immediate attention to something; however, when one redlines a person or thing—be it a name on a roster, an aircraft, a map, or a neighborhood—the intent and the results are decidedly negative. The earliest recorded use of *redline*, dated 1942, has to do with military troops. To *redline* a soldier was "to cross his name off the payroll for a particular month because of an irregularity, such as an improper signature." This sense of *redline* was then generalized, for an article in the December 4, 1966, edition of the London *Sunday Times* gives *red-lined* as G.I. jargon, meaning "canceled or classified unserviceable," which has been used specifically with regard to aircraft since World War II. The Summer, 1979, issue of *Verbatim* records this usage and tells us that "to redline an aircraft . . . is 'to ground' it."

A third sense of *redline* is recorded in the 1960's. This sense, "to mark a given area on a map as a warning, as to motorists," is reflected in a quotation from the January 18, 1961, edition of the Richmond, Virginia, *Times-Dispatch:* "the American Automobile Association may 'red-line' Prince George county because of its policy toward traffic violators."

A fourth, very common real-estate sense of *redline* is first recorded in 1967. This sense, relating to financial embargoes of decaying neighborhoods, is "to discriminate against an area or neighborhood deemed a poor financial risk by refusing to grant loans, mortgages, or insurance to." It probably stems from the practice of marking those areas in red on maps.

A fifth sense of *redline* comes from a different kind of red line, that is, not a pencil or ink line but rather a line on a gauge that marks the safe limit, as of engine speed, for the operation of something, such as a racing car. The verb *redline* has developed two senses relating to this kind of line. One is "to indicate the highest safe speed;" the other, referring to a device, is "to be in the condition of having an indicator at the red line on a gauge." This sense is illustrated in a passage from the 1985 book by Tom Clancey *The Hunt for Red October:* "The [power] plant [on the Soviet submarine] achieved its high power not with a

sodium-cooled system . . . but by running at a far
higher pressure than any reactor system afloat . . . the
price of this was a reactor that at full power was *red-
lined* on every monitor gauge—and in this case the
red lines were not mere symbolism. They signified
genuine danger."

redress The meanings of *dress* and *redress* have diverged so
far in Modern English that it is difficult to see that
they were once more closely related. Both *dress* and
redress were borrowed from Old French, in which the
verb *drecier* meant "to arrange." In Modern English
dress has narrowed its meaning primarily to "clothe,"
although it still has the sense "to prepare or arrange";
you *dress ship*, for example. The Old French word
redrecier, the source of our word *redress*, meant "to
rearrange"; thus, as we can see, *redrecier* was closely
related to the Old French word *drecier*. But *redrecier*
also meant "to rectify," and it is along this semantic
line that our borrowed word *redress* has developed,
becoming denuded of its semantic relationship to
dress.

regatta What does a fashionable Newport regatta have to do
with hucksters? We must look into the history of the
word to find out. In English *regatta* first referred specifically to certain boat races held on the Grand Ca-
nal in Venice. The name of these races is derived
from the northern Italian dialect word *rigattare*,
which meant, among other things, "to wrangle, sell
by retail as hucksters do, to contend, to cope [join
battle, encounter], or fight," according to a sixteenth-
century Italian-English dictionary. It is clear that
hucksters have an etymological right to be present at
regattas, just as the crews of the sailboats who contend with one another for victory do.

remacadamize To understand how the form *remacadamizing* was
put together, we must cover a fair amount of etymo-

logical ground. This form is an extreme case of how a single English word can be made up of elements from more than one language—in this case, from five different languages: Latin, Old Irish, Hebrew, Greek, and Old English. *Remacadamizing* means "making or repairing a road again according to a system devised by the British inventor John L. McAdam in the early 1800's," that is, by putting down successive layers of stone that has been broken into pieces of nearly uniform size. The first element of the word is *re-*, a prefix that comes to us from Latin and in this case means "again." The second element is *mac-*, a common prefix in Scottish and Irish surnames, which means "son of" and goes back to the Old Irish word *macc*, meaning "son." Next we have *Adam*, a common surname, from the Hebrew name of the first man on earth. The Hebrew word means "man" and is related to other Hebrew adjectives meaning "red, especially of earth." The Hebrew word was probably used as the name of the first man because the Bible says he was made from earth. Then comes the suffix *–ize*, which goes back to the Greek verbal suffix *–izein, –ize*, meaning in this instance "to treat according to the process of McAdam." Finally comes the suffix *–ing*, derived from the Old English suffix *–ung* or *–ing*. Our suffix *–ing* makes the verb into a verbal noun.

republic The word *republic* is derived from the Latin term *rēs pūblica*, "public affairs, the state," which comes from *rēs*, "thing, affairs, business," and *pūblica*, "public, common." The Romans' idea of the state is summed up by the phrase *rēs pūblica*, for they regarded government as the concern of all the people (*pūblica* is derived from *populus*, "the people"). Although the Roman state was never truly democratic, like some of the Greek city-states, the Romans strongly believed that it was everyone's duty to serve the common good. After lasting almost 500 years the Roman republic was replaced by imperial rule, but the republican idea has survived long enough to be influential in modern European and American history.

Republican

Urge them to forget previous political names and organizations, and to band together under the name I suggested to you at Lovejoy's Hotel in 1852, I mean the name "Republican."

So wrote A. E. Bovay to Horace Greeley in 1854. In that same year the new antislavery party chose the name *Republican*, running John C. Frémont as its first candidate. Although the name had not been in recent use, at an earlier time the party of Jefferson, Madison, Monroe, and John Quincy Adams—the ancestor of our present Democratic Party—had been called the Republican, or Democratic-Republican, Party. Their opposition was called the National Republican Party. Clearly, *Republican* was viewed as a positive word, perhaps inevitable in a republic, wherein supreme power rests with the people who govern through their elected representatives.

This sense of *republic* and the sense of *republican* meaning "one who supports a republican form of government" are recorded slightly later than the senses of *republic* and *republican* relating to the state or the public good. These two different sense groups, one having to do with the state and the other with a specific form of government, can be traced back to the Latin phrase *rēs pūblica*, from which the English words *republic* and *republican* are ultimately derived. *Rēs pūblica* meant such things as "affairs of state," "the state," "the public good," and also "a state in which all citizens participate." *Rēs pūblica* became the French word *république*, from which was derived *républicain*, an altered form of which is our word *republican*. Both of the early noun senses of *republican*, "a supporter of the state" and "a supporter of a republic," can be traced to the division of sense in *rēs pūblica*.

Moving back now to the proper noun *Republican*, eighty years after the fact it is interesting to see how the *Oxford English Dictionary* defined the Republican Party when the section of the dictionary containing *republican* was published: "A party . . . which favours liberal interpretation of the constitution, extension of the central power, and a protective tariff."

revamp The word *revamp* has to do with shoes, not seductive
women. *Revamp* is formed from the English prefix
re-, "again," and the verb *vamp*, "to refurbish." The
verb *vamp* is derived from the noun *vamp*, from Old
French *avantpie*, a compound of *avant*, "before," and
pie, "foot." A *vamp* is the part of a shoe or boot covering the instep and sometimes extending over the
toe. The verb originally meant "to provide a shoe
with a new vamp" and was used figuratively to refer
to any kind of restoration and refurbishing. Although
the prefix *re-* in *revamp* means "again," it functions
primarily as an intensifier. As for *vamp*, "an unscru-
pulous woman who seduces or exploits men with her
charms," it is simply a shortening of the English word
vampire.

rich The close connection between wealth and power can
be seen in the semantics of the word *rich*. The word
rīce, the Old English ancestor of *rich*, basically meant
"powerful," although it also meant "wealthy" and "of
high rank." In Old English times it was likely that a
person would possess either all three attributes or
none. In Middle English the sense "wealthy" pre-
dominated because Old French *riche*, which meant
"wealthy," influenced the development of the native
word. The French word and the English word share a
common Germanic ancestor, which was borrowed
from a Celtic relative of Latin *rēx*, "king." Many English words are related to *rich*, among them, *rajah*,
realm, *regime*, and *reign*.

right The political sense of *right*, meaning "conservative"
or "reactionary," goes back to the French Revolution.
In the French National Assembly of 1789 the nobles
sat on the president's right and the commoners sat on
the left. The nobility as a group tended to be politically more conservative than the commoners. In later
assemblies and parliaments seating continued to be
assigned on the basis of political views as established
in the first assembly.

ritzy Although the Ritz hotels may seem exclusive territory to many of us, language has made them a public domain. Founded by the Swiss entrepreneur César Ritz (1850–1918), the establishments have long captured the imagination as symbols of grandeur and elegance. Particularly in the 1920's the name became synonymous with the flashy style and arrogance of wealth. Incorporated into the title of a short story by one of the era's favorite authors ("The Diamond as Big as the Ritz," by F. Scott Fitzgerald) and into the lyrics of a song by one of our greatest songwriters ("Puttin' on the Ritz," by Irving Berlin), the name evokes the glittery opulence of the age. Today we apply the adjective *ritzy* to anything lavishly splendid, from clothing to entertainment. So the Ritz is a part of our lives, even if we've never dallied behind a potted palm.

river The Latin word *rīpa*, to which our English term *river* can be traced, meant "riverbank" and not the water flowing between the banks. The shift in meaning took place in an intermediate stage between Latin *rīpa* and English *river*, that is, in Old French and Anglo-Norman, where the Old French word *riviere* and the Anglo-Norman word *rivere* meant "river" as well as "riverbank."

robot Coinages rarely take hold, but the word *robot* is an exception. This term was coined by the Czech author Karel Čapek in his play *R.U.R.*, the title of which stands for "Rossum's Universal Robots." Čapek, a playwright, novelist, and essayist, revealed in *R.U.R.* and *The Insect Play* the problems of a machine-dominated society. *R.U.R.*, written in 1920 and translated into English a few years later, was highly successful. Shortly thereafter, the word *robot*, derived from the Czech term *robota*, "forced labor, drudgery," gained widespread currency in English. From it, several other words developed through normal patterns of suffixation: *robotization* and *robotize* in the 1920's and *robotics*—a popular term today—in the 1940's.

Thus, *robot* has withstood the lexicographer's test of time. Not only that, it has spawned at least three descendants. Not bad at all for a machine.

rocket　Sophisticated rockets soaring into space have a rather prosaic origin, at least from an etymological standpoint. The etymological contrails of *rocket* lead us back to Italian, specifically to the Italian word *rocchetta*, which is a diminutive of *rocca*, meaning "rock." This particular *rock*, however, is not quite as down to earth as it sounds, for it means "distaff, a staff used in spinning to hold unspun material, such as wool." The cylindrical shape of the *rocca* led to the use of its diminutive *rocchetta* to mean "an apparatus consisting of a cylindrical case containing an inflammable mixture, which when ignited propels the apparatus."

Such devices, the invention of which is ascribed to the Chinese as early as A.D. 1000, were used as military weapons or as fireworks. In *The Generall Historie of Virginia, New-England and the Summer Isles*, published in 1624, Captain John Smith said that "in the evening we fired a few rackets, which flying in the ayre . . . terrified the poore Salvages." Although modern rockets propelled by powerful engines can carry much heavier payloads to more distant targets, they are called rockets because they operate on the same basic principle that Captain Smith's projectiles did. The engine provides thrust by the ejection of gases produced when substances inside the device are burned. The word *rocket*, first recorded for the modern device in 1919, was used in this context by the American pioneer of rocketry Robert H. Goddard.

romance　Most users of the word *romance*, with its hints of passion and exotic climes, do not realize that it goes back to Rome, the great wellspring of organization and law. From the Latin name *Rōma*, "Rome," is derived Latin *Rōmānus*, "of Rome and its people," and from this word comes *Rōmānicus*, "of the Roman

210

type or people." The Vulgar Latin word *Rōmānice,*
"in the Roman tongue," is hypothesized to be the
next development, and from this comes Old French
romans, "the French language," descended from Latin
(the tongue of the Romans) but not Latin. Old
French *romans* also meant "a work composed in
French." The word *romans* first referred to any sort
of work, but it narrowed in scope and came to mean
a particular type of vernacular composition—a chival-
ric tale in verse, a sense that we borrowed from
French along with the word *romance.* Later, in the
sixteenth and seventeenth centuries, *romance* meant
"a long prose work in which the events were remote
from everyday life." (The romance fiction of today,
though somewhat changed from these earlier types,
remains a lively genre, filled with heroes and heroines
who no longer chase or flee dragons but rather each
other.)

The sixteenth- and seventeenth-century sense of *romance* was influenced by the development of the
word *romantic. Romantic,* with its foundation in the
imaginative world of romances replete with heroes
and ladies, went on to develop senses such as "chival-
ric, gallant," "exotic," and "imaginary, ideal." From
1728 onward, *romantic* is recorded in association
with words such as *love, lover,* and *friendship,* used
to express the idealistic quality of these relationships.
Use of *romantic* in this way influenced the development of *romance* in the senses "a love affair," "the
idealistic quality in a love affair," and "a love story."
Now perhaps one can see why it would be appropriate to have a romance in Rome, etymologically at
least. Anyone for a Roman holiday?

rubber   The noun *rubber,* "a substance made from the sap of
the rubber tree," is derived from the verb *rub.* Central American Indians are believed to have made rubber balls for their games, but one of the first uses of
the substance was discovered by Europeans rubbing
out pencil marks. Although many other uses have
since been found, the name *rubber* has stuck.

rubber stamp
Rubber Stamp Maker
—Extract from *Instructions to the Clerks of the Census of England and Wales*, 1881

Thus reads the first recorded instance of the expression *rubber stamp*, referring to a stamp made of rubber, not to someone who approves a piece of legislation without reading it simply because a political leader or the chief executive tells him or her to do so. Owing to the fact that rubber stamps were used to confer official approval, approval that could at times be given rather automatically, the expression *rubber stamp* took on the figurative sense "a person or body that approves uncritically." This sense is first recorded in a passage referring to William Howard Taft in William R. Thayer's 1919 biography of Theodore Roosevelt: "He may have heard the exhortation 'Be your own President; don't be anybody's man or rubber stamp.'" Taft, unlike other rubber stamps, seems to have acted on this exhortation, since he ran against Roosevelt, whose rubber stamp he had been, in 1912, thereby opening the way for Woodrow Wilson's victory.

The expression *rubber stamp* has not vanished totally into a figurative world of political yes men and yes women, however. The verb derived from the noun is first recorded as early as 1922, when the May 13 issue of *Hotel World* noted primly, "No hotel would rubber-stamp its stationery." Back in the political world, members of Congress—and even chief executives—use autopens, not rubber stamps, for their signatures. Will the first autopen please step forward?

runcible
They dined on mince, and slices of quince,
Which they ate with a runcible spoon.
—Edward Lear, "The Owl and the Pussycat," 1871

Edward Lear, who gave us the runcible spoon, also mentions such things as a runcible cat, runcible hat,

(continued

runcible goose, and runcible wall. Lear liked the nonsense word *runcible*, which is supposed to be a fanciful form of *rounceval*. *Rounceval* is a curious word in its own right. It means or has meant things like "a large variety of pea," "a wart," "a monster," "a woman of large build and boisterous or loose manners," and "gigantic, huge." Most of its senses have to do with largeness, which is explained by its etymology. *Rounceval* comes from the place name *Roncesvalles* (in Spanish) or *Roncevaux* (in French), a mountain pass in northern Spain where Roland and the rear guard of Charlemagne's army were slain by the Saracens. Giant bones found in the area were said to be the bones of the slaughtered.

However, the bones were not what they were said to be, and neither was Lear's runcible spoon necessarily what a runcible spoon is now. The Washington *Post* of March 25, 1979, tells us that "a runcible spoon . . . is a large, slotted spoon with three thick, modified fork prongs at the bowl's end, and a cutting edge on the side." Lear's illustrations for his books give us no evidence for this. Only the owl and the pussycat know for sure.

rune   A rune is a letter in one of several alphabets used by ancient Germanic peoples from about the third to the thirteenth century. It is thought that runes developed from alphabets used by peoples who lived in Greece and Italy. The word *rune*, although referring to an old thing, is not an old word in English. It is probably a modern borrowing of the Danish word *rune* with the same meaning. The Old Icelandic equivalent of Danish *rune* is *rūn*. It too meant "runic character," but it also meant "mystery" and "secret lore." The sense "letter" belongs to this group because in early Germanic times the ability to read and write was a mysterious skill possessed by a select few, who used runes to write magic spells and charms and to convey secret messages.

Rx It may be printed on the prescription pad, but etymologically speaking, there is no *x* in *Rx*. The spelling *Rx* is an attempt to represent in ordinary letters the symbol ℞, which is merely a capital *R* with a slash through its elongated tail. It is a symbol used as an abbreviation for *recipe*, a form of the Latin verb *recipere*, "to take, receive." In Medieval Latin *recipe*, meaning "take," was usually the first word in medicinal prescriptions directing one to take a certain quantity of a preparation. The English word *recipe* originally meant "a medicinal prescription"; only later did it acquire the meaning "a formula used in cooking."

sacred cow   There is a close connection, as well there might be, between a cow wandering down a street in India and an institution considered immune from criticism. *Sacred cow*, meaning "a cow as an object of veneration among Hindus," is first found in English in the late nineteenth century. This cow, having crossed the ocean, is next found wandering through the pages of the March, 1910, edition of the *Atlantic Monthly:* "In the office these corporations were jocularly referred to as 'sacred cows.' " And one of the two journalistic uses of the term *sacred cow* is illustrated here: "someone who is not to be criticized." Another sense in journalism is "copy that is not to be changed or cut." From the world of journalism it was an easy amble into the wider world and greener pastures where sacred cows are found today.

sad sack   *Mr. Goldman's movie sweeps up a dustpanful of young Village sad sacks and patronizes them.*
                      —*The New Yorker*, April 15, 1967

This quotation illustrates well how a term can become generalized in use. *Sad Sack* was originally the name of a cartoon character, invented by George Baker, that first appeared in *Yank* magazine in 1942. Since the Sad Sack, an army private, was the epitome of inept, ineffectual blundering, his name became a general term for all such unfortunate misfits in the armed services, as is seen in this quotation from the December 28, 1943, issue of the Baltimore *Sun:* "A forlorn look, a G.I. haircut, an oversized fatigue uniform and all the paraphernalia that goes with them branded me as a typical 'sad sack.' " The term was then extended far beyond the barracks, where it applies to people who might be highly unlikely candidates for military service to begin with.

salt   Salt is a hidden ingredient not only in many foods but in many words as well. From the Latin word for "salt," *sal*, and the related verbs for "to salt" in Latin and Latin-based languages, English has acquired the words *salami* and *sausage* for salted meats, and *salad* and *sauce* for salted dishes that accompany a meal. *Saucer*, originally a plate for holding sauce, is also a descendant of the Latin word *sal*.

Indeed, *salt* has hardly lost its linguistic savor. Our word *salary*, as indispensable to modern life as salt itself to the ancients, was also once directly related to *salt*. Its Latin source, *salārium*, first meant "money given to soldiers to buy salt" and later came to mean "a stipend, wages."

saltcellar   A saltcellar is not a basement storehouse for sodium chloride; in fact, the word has nothing to do with the word *cellar* at all. The spelling of the element *–cellar* is an alteration of the obsolete English form *saler*, which meant "saltcellar." The word *saler* was ultimately derived from Latin *sal*, "salt."

salver   At your next party should you think twice before taking that canapé or cocktail from a salver? The history of the word will give you a hint. Thomas Blount was on the right track when he defined the word in a

218

1661 edition of his *Glossographia*, one of our earliest
English dictionaries: "*Salver* (from *salvo*, to save) is a
new fashioned peece of wrought plate, broad and flat,
with a foot underneath, and is used in giving Beer, or
other liquid thing, to save the Carpit or Cloathes
from drops." However, this type of tray was not originally used because of concern for the condition of
the carpet or of one's clothing. *Salver* is an adaptation
of the French word *salve*, "a tray used for presenting
certain objects to the king," or its Spanish source,
salva, which meant "the sampling of food or drink to
see whether it is safe to eat or drink." Thus *salva* became a name for the tray on which the tested item of
food or drink was served. *Salva* was derived from *sal-
var*, "to save, render safe, test food or drink." Rest as-
sured, then, that anything on a salver should be
entirely wholesome, etymologically speaking.

samovar The setting is a bitter Siberian night, punctuated by
the intermittent howls of wolves. The landscape is
obscured by swirling mists of blowing snow. Imagine
an exhausted, fur-swathed traveler parking his sled,
gratefully entering a cozy cottage, and settling himself
before a glowing, hissing, boiling samovar. As his
Samoyed takes a snooze and our traveler opens a
banned book distributed through the ingenuity of samizdat, we might ask: What is the relationship
among *samovar*, *samizdat*, and *Samoyed*? The linkage
between the first two words is established, but the
story behind *Samoyed*—whether man or beast—is a
matter unto itself.

The Russian emphatic definite pronoun *sam* (mascu-
line) or *samo* (neuter), meaning "–self," can combine
with other Russian words to yield new words, as in
samovar, "tea urn," where *samo* joins with *var-*, a
root having to do with boiling (found, for example, in
the verb *varit'*, "to boil"). A *samovar*, literally a "self-
boiler," boils liquid by means of an interior tube that
is heated by burning charcoal. The same pronoun
sam also occurs as an element of the Russian word
samizdat, which in the last sixteen years has migrated into English with other Russian words such as

gulag. Samizdat, meaning "the secret publication and distribution of government-banned literature in the U.S.S.R.," is a shortened form of *samoizdatel'stvo,* literally "self-publisher" (with *izdatel'stvo* meaning "publishing house, publisher").

In the case of *Samoyed,* the name for a people who live in the northeastern European reaches of the Soviet Union and in northwestern Siberia as well, it was thought that the first element of the word was *samo-,* combining with *yed-,* a root having to do with eating, thus yielding *samoyed,* or literally "self-eater, cannibal." However, the Samoyeds—the people and indirectly their white or cream-colored sled dogs, which were named for the people—have been unfairly maligned. The name *Samoyed* has been traced to the Norwegian-Lapp word *Sāme-Ædnàma,* meaning "of Lapland."

Samsonite If your Samsonite suitcase can withstand a lot of wear and tear, it is only living up to its name. *Samsonite,* a trademark for a brand of luggage, is derived from *Samson,* the name of the Biblical hero who exercised his great strength on the Philistines, even when blinded.

His name has been used in allusion to parts of his story or to his strength, as in Shakespeare's *Henry VI, Part I,* when one of the French dukes says: "For none but Samsons and Goliases [another strong Biblical character, Goliath] It [England] sendeth forth to skirmish." The name is also found in the compound *Samson fox.* This fox, whose guard hairs are missing from its fur, giving it a singed appearance, was named for the story about Samson found in the King James Version of Judges 15:4–5: "And Samson went and caught three hundred foxes, and took firebrands, and turned tail to tail, and put a firebrand in the midst between two tails. And when he had set the brands on fire, he let *them* go into the standing corn [wheat] of the Philistines, and burnt up both the shocks, and also the standing corn, with the vineyards *and* olives."

sandwich Lunch on a hectic day? A sandwich, of course, the time-honored meal of the distracted diner. We owe our hasty repast to a somewhat less than honorable distraction, however. Our name for slices of bread with a filling comes from the title of the eighteenth-century English nobleman John Montagu, 4th Earl of Sandwich. An indefatigable gambler, he is reported to have asked his servant to bring him this easily handled refreshment (the original filling is said to have been roast beef) so that he might spend the wee hours in a particularly absorbing session at the gaming table. Word of the incident circulated, and the happy construction, dubbed *sandwich*, soon became a popular meal. Its endurance comes as no surprise: life is full of chances we can't afford to miss.

sarcasm The next time you feel the bite of somebody's sarcasm, get out the bandages. *Sarcasm* goes back to the Greek verb *sarkazein*, from *sarx*, "flesh." *Sarkazein* is first recorded in the senses "to tear flesh like dogs" and "to pluck grass with closed lips as horses do." The sense "to bite the lips in rage," recorded later, is thought to have developed into the sense "to speak bitterly, sneer." The noun *sarkasmos*, "mockery, sarcasm," is derived from the verb. This noun is the source, through Late Latin or French, of our word *sarcasm*. Flak jackets, anyone?

satellite A dead satellite moving through space might seem to be very much on its own. But it is still part of an interstellar relationship, so to speak, both in its orbit around another celestial body and in its name, as we shall see. *Satellite* goes back to Latin *satellit-*, the form of the noun *satelles* that is used to make most of the cases of the noun. *Satelles* meant "one of a bodyguard or escort to a prince or despot; henchman, attendant," and was often used contemptuously. In 1611 the astronomer Johannes Kepler applied the Latin word *satellitēs*, the plural form of *satelles*, to the recently discovered bodies revolving around Jupiter because he thought these bodies surrounding the planet, which was still considered a heavenly personality, were like ever-hovering attendants or bodyguards. *Satellite* then took on the sense "a relatively small body orbiting a planet." Thus it was natural to use the word *satellite* for a manmade object orbiting a celestial body. This sense was prefigured in 1880 in an English translation of *The Begum's Fortune* by Jules Verne: "A projectile [that will] revolve perpetually round our globe . . . Two hundred thousand dollars is not too much to have paid for the pleasure of having endowed the planetary world with a new star, and the earth with a second satellite." Tell that to the NASA budget analysts.

satin   Sinuous satin, originally made from silk, sheathes in its name a past in which East and West are inextricably interwoven. The term *satin* goes back through Old French to the Arabic word *zaitūnī*, which means "pertaining to the town of *Zaitūn*." *Zaitūn* is usually identified with Ch'üanchou (or Tsinkiang), China, a city described by Marco Polo as a thriving port during the thirteenth-century reign of Kublai Khan. The history of the word *satin* parallels the history of the importation of satin to the West: satin was carried to Europe by way of the Middle East from China, where it was first made.

satire   *Satire is a sort of glass, wherein beholders do generally discover everybody's face but their own.*
     —Jonathan Swift, *The Battle of the Books*, 1704

The word *satire* comes to us from the Latin term *satira*, a variant form of *satura*, denoting a long poem that held human follies and vices up to ridicule and scorn. *Satura* also meant "a dish of mixed ingredients, mélange," and appeared in the phrase *per* (or *in*) *saturam*, "collectively." The word *satura* used in these ways is clearly derived from *satur*, "full," which is related to *satis*, "enough," the source of our English words *satisfy* and *satiate*.

This derivation of *satura* accords with the sense "satirical poem," because satire traces its beginnings to a dramatic medley and throughout its development continued to be full of variety, like a dish of mixed ingredients. *Satura* in the dramatic or literary sense may, however, be a separate word derived from Etruscan *satr-* or *satir-*, "speech." Whatever the derivation of the word *satire*, Latin literary satire, which evolved from a number of traditions, focused on mocking vice and folly. Satire continues to mock, whether or not people recognize themselves in its glass.

saw   *It is an ever ready saw that an egg is equivalent to a lb. of meat; whereas it is not at all so.*
        —Florence Nightingale, *Notes on Nursing,* circa 1860

The noun *saw,* "a saying," goes back to the same Germanic ancestor as does the word *saga,* "a narrative." *Saw* is a native English word whose Old English form was *sagu. Saga* was borrowed from Icelandic in the eighteenth century as the name of the historical legends of the Scandinavian peoples. In Old Norse and modern Scandinavian languages *saga* basically meant "a story or legend transmitted orally"; the narratives now called *sagas* were written down several centuries after the events they recount. Both *saw* and *saga* are related to the verb *say.*

schmaltz   *"What we call honest sentiment," he says in equally honest puzzlement, "you call schmaltz."*
        —*The Observer,* November 19, 1978

If a diner thinks the mashed potatoes might be improved by a bit of schmaltz . . . he pours some out of a dispenser.
        —*The New Yorker,* June 3, 1974

Obviously we have two senses of *schmaltz* here, although the second sense might be unclear to those unfamiliar with the literal senses of the German word *schmalz* and the Yiddish word *shmalts,* "grease, fat, lard." (In the second quotation, *schmaltz* means "liquid chicken fat.") Both words developed the figurative sense "sentimentality," which can get rather greasy and thick. While our word *schmaltz* is not generally used in English with reference to fat (except in the compound *schmaltz herring,* "a kind of pickled herring"), schmaltz of the figurative variety is everywhere, although the word itself is first recorded in English as denoting ordinary or straight jazz. Aldous Huxley in his 1956 *Adonis and the Alphabet* offers an appropriate context for a general sense of *schmaltz:* "The Mother of the greeting cards inhabits a delicious Disneyland, where everything is syrup and Technicolor, cuteness and schmalz."

seal The noun *seal,* "a die or signet used to stamp an impression," is related to the word *sign. Sign* is derived, through Old French *signe,* from Latin *signum,* which meant, among other things, "a signet" and "the impression of a signet or the piece of wax bearing this impression." *Signum* formed the diminutive noun *sigillum,* which also denoted a seal or the figure in relief left by the impression of a signet ring. Latin *sigillum* then became Old French *seel,* which was borrowed into Middle English and was ultimately transformed into our Modern English word *seal.* There you have the relationship between the two words, signed, sealed, and delivered.

second How is a second second? Let's take a minute to find out. The noun *second,* meaning "a unit of time or of angular measure equal to 1/60 of a minute," is ultimately derived from the same Latin word as the adjective *second,* meaning "coming next after the first." The Latin word *secundus* was an adjective that meant "following" or "second." The sense of *secundus* referring to angular measure arose because of the method used to divide up degrees of a circle. Certain units, such as the degrees of a circle, were, and still are, divided into equal parts, and those parts were further subdivided. The first subdivision was called *pars minūta prīma,* or "first little part," and the subdivision of this unit was called *pars minūta secunda,* or "second little part." *Secunda* is the feminine singular form of the adjective *secundus,* agreeing with the feminine noun *pars. Secunda* alone was eventually used as a noun for the second subdivision of a degree and is the source of our word *second.*

semester   A semester of college is not as long as it used to be. Our word *semester* goes back to the Latin word *sēmestris*, derived from *sex*, "six," and *mensis*, "month." *Sēmestris* meant "of six months duration." The German word *Semester*, derived from *sēmestris*, referred to a period of about six months in German universities. English borrowed the term from German, but fortunately for students in the United States a semester is only about four months long. In fact, *semester*, according to Kemp Malone, writing in the October, 1946, issue of *American Speech*, "is no longer restricted to the meaning 'academic half-year' and is steadily becoming a mere synonym for *term*." Malone cites the use of the phrase "four-semester college," which indicates that the word has drifted a bit from its etymological basis.

sequoia   The giant sequoia acquired its name from a giant of another sort. George Guess (to most Americans of his time) or Sogwali (to his fellow Cherokees) was named Sequoya by missionaries. He devised a way of writing the Cherokee language, probably completing his work in 1821, and thus helped unify the members of his tribe. Stephan Ladislaus Endlicher, a nineteenth-century Hungarian ethnologist and botanist, probably knew of this achievement, and so used Sequoya's name for the genus that includes the redwood and the giant sequoia.

serendipity   What do you call the faculty of making fortuitous and unexpected discoveries by accident? We are indebted to the English author Horace Walpole for coining the answer: *serendipity*. In one of his 3,000 or more letters, on which his literary reputation primarily rests, and specifically in a letter of January 28, 1754, Walpole says that "this discovery, indeed, is almost of that kind which I call Serendipity, a very expressive word." Perhaps the word itself came to him by serendipity. Walpole formed the word on an old name for Sri Lanka, *Serendip*. He explained that this name was part of the title of "a silly fairy tale, called

The Three Princes of Serendip: as their highnesses travelled, they were always making discoveries, by accidents and sagacity, of things which they were not in quest of . . . One of the most remarkable instances of this *accidental sagacity* (for you must observe that *no* discovery of a thing you *are* looking for, comes under this description) was of my Lord Shaftsbury [Anthony Ashley Cooper], who happening to dine at Lord Chancellor Clarendon's [Edward Hyde], found out the marriage of the Duke of York [later James II] and Mrs. Hyde [Anne Hyde, Clarendon's daughter], by the respect with which her mother [Frances Aylesbury Hyde] treated her at table."

shadow   The meanings of *shade* and *shadow* are distinct enough to obscure somewhat the common origin of the words. Both are descended from the Old English word *sceadu*, which meant "shade" and also "shadow." *Sceadu,* the form used when *sceadu* was the subject of a sentence, as in "the *sceadu* is cool," is an ancestor of Modern English *shade*. Forms of *sceadu* containing a *w* were used, for example, when the word occurred in the plural, as in "I saw two *sceadwa*." *Shadow* is derived from such forms.

shampoo   *[A Mahratta wife] first champoes her husband, and fans him to repose; she then champoes the horse.*
               —James Forbes, *Oriental Memoirs,* 1813

What a commercial for hair products this scene would make. The one difficulty is that the word *shampoo* in the context quoted above means "to give a massage to." *Shampoo* in this sense comes from the Hindi form *cāpō* of the verb *cāpnā,* "to press, massage," used in giving commands to servants. An important part of the rubdown that the Mahratta wife gave her husband was a massaging of the head and hair. For this reason *shampoo* in English eventually came to mean "to rub and wash the scalp with a cleaning agent." One can still shampoo a horse, and now the Mahratta wife could shampoo a carpet as well.

sheriff   Like many ancient titles such as *coroner*, the word *sheriff* now means different things in different places. In Anglo-Saxon England the sheriff was the chief representative of the king in each county. The Old English form of the word *sheriff* was *scīrgerēfa*, a compound of *scīr*, "shire," and *gerēfa*, "officer," the ancestor of our English word *reeve*. Today in England a sheriff has chiefly ceremonial duties, such as presiding over elections and courts; in Scotland a sheriff is a local judge; and in the United States a sheriff is an important law enforcement officer. So plan to wear your best finery when you vote in England, tell the truth when you testify in Scotland, and never, never break the law when you travel around the United States—lest you have a not so pleasant encounter with the sheriff.

shyster   *For it presented no evidence in support of its malicious charges except a statement by a half-imbecile shyster, who is the butt of the town, of his feeble-minded suspicions, indorsed by another fool in full regimentals, who is the laughing-stock of the state, and who, without knowing anything about it, appended to Gribble's idiotic drivel his official signature.*
                                —St. Paul, Minnesota, *Daily Pioneer-Press*,
                                                          August 17, 1882

The word "shyster"—defined in Webster to mean "a trickish knave," "one who carries on any business, especially a legal business, in a dishonest way"—is evidently capable of having reference to the professional character and standing of a lawyer. Bailey v. Kalamazoo P. Co., 40 Mich. 251. The issue made in the pleadings as to whether the plantiff was a lawyer was therefore material, and hence evidence to show that he was a lawyer was in point.
                            —*Gribble* v. *Pioneer Press Co.* (December 8, 1885),
                                               25 N.W. 710, 34 Minn. 342

The origin of *shyster*, unlike that of *ignoramus* (also under scrutiny in this book), was not known for certain until recently. According to one etymology, *shyster* comes from the surname of one *Scheuster*, a disreputable and almost certainly nonexistent mid-nineteenth-century attorney. In his book *Human*

Words, a collection of words formed from the names of people, Robert Hendrickson says that Dr. Henry Bosley Woolf and others "list the N.Y. advocate as a possible source." But the actual etymology, according to Gerald L. Cohen, a student of the word, is less flattering. According to this etymology, the word is derived from the German term *scheisser*, meaning literally "one who defecates," from the verb *scheissen*, "to defecate," with the English suffix *-ster*, "one who does," substituted for the German suffix *-er*, meaning the same thing. *Sheisser*, which is chiefly a pejorative term, is the German equivalent of our English words *bastard* or *son of a bitch*. *Sheisser* is generally thought to have been borrowed directly into English as the word *shicer*, which, among other things, is an Australian English term for an unproductive mine or claim, a sense that is also recorded for the word *shyster*.

sierra The grandeur of the Sierra Nevada in California has inspired many visitors. Not to take away from this grandeur, one should nevertheless point out that the first part of the name of these mountains is rather down to earth in origin. *Sierra*—a Spanish word for a mountain range—refers to the geological configuration found in certain types of ranges. *Sierra*, which originally meant "saw," was applied to a range of hills or mountains rising in peaks that suggest the teeth of a saw. It comes from Latin *serra*, "saw," to which can also be traced our word *serrated*.

silhouette We are not certain why a silhouette is named for Louis XV's controller general, who was in office for eight months in 1759. Etienne de Silhouette's brief tenure leaves us with several possible reasons for this example of eponymy, that is, the naming of something after a person. Silhouette might be dubbed the David Stockman of his day, for, like Stockman, he failed to impose his ideas of responsible fiscal policies on his government. Nonetheless Silhouette managed to anger most of the French population, whose oxen he had gored. Various reasons have been given for the application of his name to shadow portraits, including his brief tenure in office, his tight-fisted economic policies, and the fact that he made these shadow portraits himself, recommending them for their cheapness. Whatever the reason, Silhouette has lent his name to such portraits and even to shadows themselves.

siren Sirens now shriek terribly as they warn of danger, their name evoking the Sirens who sang sweetly while they lured victims to danger and destruction. The Greek word *seirēn*, the ultimate source of our word *siren*, denoted mythical creatures, part women and part birds, who by their sweet singing enticed sailors to their death on rocks surrounding the shore. The use of the word *siren* with which our ears are most familiar originated when the term was applied to an acoustical device invented in 1819 by the French physicist Charles Cagniard de la Tour. This device produced musical tones, and because it was "sonorous in the water," according to the *Annual Register* of 1820, it was called a *siren*. A larger device used on steamships to emit fog signals was given the same name, and the term was later extended to devices producing similar sounds, including the ones shrilling through our neighborhoods.

skeleton A skeleton, whether an artifact of medical interest, a frightening character in a horror movie, or an object rattling in the closet, is not an object commonly encountered by most people. However, the ultimate source of the word *skeleton* is quite matter of fact and rather dry, actually. Our word *skeleton* comes from the Greek expression *skeleton soma*, "dried-up body." In this expression *skeleton* is a form of the adjective *skeletos*, meaning "dried up, withered."

The notion of a skeleton in the closet alluded to above is first mentioned in the works of Thackeray in the nineteenth century, although the phrase was used

(continued)

earlier. It is interesting to compare Thackeray's remark, "there is a skeleton in every house" ("Punch in the East," 1845), with the mention in the December, 1883, issue of *Harper's* of "a household that . . . possessed no closeted skeletons."

skirt   The relationship between a skirt and a shirt is not just a matter of fashion but also a matter of etymology. The connections between England and Scandinavia in peace and war during the Middle Ages were always close, and the interaction between them added greatly to the vocabulary of English. Some words borrowed from Scandinavian did not completely supplant the native words with which they shared a common Germanic ancestor; rather, they existed alongside them. *Shirt* and *skirt* are one such pair. Both are descended from the Germanic word *skurtaz*, which became *scyrte* in Old English and *skyrta* in Old Icelandic, a dialect of Old Norse. *Skyrta* meant "a shirt or kind of knee-length tunic." Our word *skirt*, borrowed from Old Norse, came to denote the lower part of a garment or a lower garment by itself. The meaning of Old English *scyrte* is obscure, but *shirt*, its descendant, referred in Middle English to an undergarment worn on the upper part of the body. The downward drift of *skirt* and the upward hike of *shirt* fits with the fact that the original Germanic word denoted a short undergarment (wearable by itself in warm weather) that covered both parts of the body.

slogan   *Coke is it.*

You're the Pepsi generation.

The advertising slogans flying back and forth in the cola wars may be reminiscent in a trivial way of the history of the once-proud word *slogan*. *Slogan* is an adaptation of the Scots Gaelic word *sluagh-ghairm*, "war cry," from *sluagh*, "host," and *gairm*, "shout,

Siren

231

cry." Our word was first used in Scots to denote such a cry. Sir George Mackenzie's circa 1680 *Science of Heraldry,* for example, states that "the Name of Hume have for their Slughorn (or Slogan, as our Southern Shires terme it) a *Hume, a Hume."* *Slogan* went on to develop the senses "a word or phrase expressing the aims of a person or group" (such as "He kept us out of war!" in Woodrow Wilson's 1916 presidential campaign or "A chicken in every pot, a car in every garage," from Herbert Hoover's 1928 campaign) and "a catch phrase used in advertising or promotion" (such as the slogans above).

sneeze If it had not been for a combination of factors, you would fneeze rather than sneeze. The word *sneeze* is descended from the Old English word *fnēosan* by a combination of circumstances that caused the replacement of the initial *f* by *s.* The most important factor in the change was probably the similarity in appearance of *f* and *s* in some medieval manuscripts and printed books. An initial *s* looked like an *f* without the crossbar, so it was easy to misread one letter for the other. Contributing to the confusion was the rarity of the cluster *fn-* at the beginning of a word in English. Such a combination was uncommon even in Old English and had been all but eliminated by Middle English times. On top of all this, the sounds represented by *f* and *s* were very similar, a circumstance that would make the spelling change more acceptable. The original verb *fnēosan* is related to the Greek term *pneuma,* "breath," from which our word *pneumatic* is derived. Gesundheit!

soccer Soccer, which is probably the most popular team sport everywhere except in the United States, was invented in England. The word *soccer* is a shortening and alteration of the official name of the game, *Association Football,* that is, football as played under the rules of the Football Association of England, founded in 1863. *Assoc.,* the abbreviation for *Association,* was shortened and given an extra *c* and the suffix *-er* that also occurs in other words found in British public school and university slang, such as *footer* for *football*, *rugger* for *rugby*, and *wagger pagger bagger* for *wastepaper basket*.

souse

There Tostius hakked his brother servantes, and sowsede here lemes, and sente word to the kyng that . . . he schulde have salt mete i-now.

[There Tostius chopped up his brother's servants, and soused their limbs, and sent word to the king that . . . he should have plenty of salt meat.]

—John de Trevisa, translator, *Polychronicon Ranulphi Higden*, before 1387

An early meaning of the verb *souse* was "to pickle," and the earliest recorded meaning of the noun is "pickled meat." Various liquids can be used to pickle or preserve food, but a common one is brine, which is highly salted water. The etymology of *souse* reflects this fact, for the word is ultimately derived from the Germanic word *sultjo*. This word is derived from the same Indo-European root *sal-*[1] as is the Germanic word *saltam*, the ancestor of our English word *salt*.

spade

A spade on a playing card is not called a spade because of its resemblance to a digging tool. The word *spade* meaning "a tool for digging" is only a distant etymological relative of *spade* meaning "a suit of playing cards."

The first *spade*, the implement, is descended directly from the Old English word *spadu*, which meant "a digging tool." The second *spade* was borrowed into English from the Italian word *spada*, which meant "sword." *Spada* is derived via Latin *spatha* from the Greek word *spathē*, both words meaning "broad blade." *Spathē* goes back to the same Indo-European form *spadh-* as does the Germanic ancestor *spadan* of Old English *spadu*, so the two words spelled *spade* are indeed distantly related.

A broad-bladed sword was used on Italian playing cards as the symbol of a suit, and this suit was called *spades* in English. However, the symbol for spades on English playing cards was borrowed not from the Italian sword but from the French pike (*pique* in French). The shape of this pike was probably fashioned after the leaf symbol that appeared on early German playing cards.

speed The fable of the tortoise and the hare teaches us that speed does not always spell success. Historically in English, however, it does: the Old English word *spēd*, from which our word *speed* is descended, originally meant "prosperity, successful outcome, ability, or quickness." A corresponding verb, *spēdan*—in Modern English the verb *speed*—meant "to succeed, prosper, or achieve a goal"; and an adjective, *spēdig*—the ancestor of our word *speedy*—meant "wealthy, powerful." Except for archaic uses the words today relate only to the general sense of "velocity." The meaning "success" is retained chiefly in the compound *Godspeed*, a noun formed from the phrase "God prosper you."

spell Two of the words spelled *spell*—the noun *spell*, "an incantation," and the verb *spell*, "to give the letters of a word in proper order"—are etymologically related. Let us now attempt to spell out the intricacies of this relationship. Both words are derived from the Indo-European root *spel-*[3], which means "to say aloud, recite, pronounce." The noun *spell* comes from Old English *spell*, which had a much wider meaning than its modern descendant; it was used with the senses "discourse," "narration," "sermon," and "story." Old English *spell* also appears as the second element of *gospel*, meaning literally "good tidings." The meaning "incantation" did not appear until late medieval or early modern times. The verb *spell* is borrowed from Old French *espelier*, "to interpret, explain, spell." The French word came from a Germanic derivative, *spellōn*, of the same Indo-European root as the English noun *spell*.

234

starve   *And loveth hym [Christ], the which that right for love*
Upon a crois [cross], oure soules for to beye [save],
First starf [died], and roos, and sit in hevene above.
—Chaucer, *Troilus and Criseyde*, circa 1380

The verb *starve* is descended from the Old English word *steorfan*, which simply meant "to die," the sense in the quotation given from Chaucer (containing a past tense, *starf*, of *sterven*, the Middle English descendant of Old English *steorfan*). Only in modern times did the verb develop more specific meanings. In standard English *starve* became restricted to the meaning "to die from lack of food." In northern English dialects *starve* also acquired the sense "to die of cold," but this usage no longer occurs in the standard language.

story   The history of *story* and the story of *history* are related. Both words go back to the Latin word *historia*, which meant primarily "the recording of past events," but which could also designate any narrative, factual or fictional. *History* was borrowed into English directly from this Latin word, as well as from an Old French intermediary, *estoire* or *estorie*, also descended from Latin *historia*. But *story* came into English from the Old French intermediary alone. At first English *story* referred, as did its Old French predecessor, principally to narrations of actual past events, or to what were then perceived as factual accounts (although, of course, the medieval sense of "fact" does not always conform to modern standards of verification). Already during the Middle English period *story*, like the Latin word *historia*, had a secondary application to any relation of events, real or imagined, intended for entertainment. Gradually the word shifted toward the sense of "fiction" generally associated with it today, leaving to *history* the sense "a remembered or researched account of observable phenomena." As the opening of this paragraph suggests, the two words can still be used interchangeably in some contexts, but usually they are differentiated into virtually opposite senses.

235

subjugate An ancient Latin custom required that when an army
was totally defeated, the survivors were forced to pass
under a symbolic yoke made of two upright spears
and a third spear used as a crossbar. The Latin word
subjugāre (derived from *sub-*, "under," and *jugum*,
"yoke") literally meant "to bring under the yoke,"
which the Romans regarded as the worst possible hu-
miliation. Our word *subjugate* is derived from the
Latin word.

suede Suede is very haute couture, and the word *suede*,
fashionably enough, is very French. However, the
French word that we borrowed in the nineteenth century originally meant something quite un-French,
namely "Sweden." It was used in the French phrase
gants de Suède, literally "gloves from Sweden," and
denoted gloves made of undressed kidskin, a material
that was native to Sweden. *Suede* is first recorded in
English with reference to such gloves. From this use
suede went on to mean undressed kidskin, then
leather with a napped surface, and later material that
resembled this kind of leather. Seude meatballs anyone?

sunbeam The period of European history from the fifth to the
eleventh century, although often called the Dark
Ages, in fact did much to preserve and extend the
light of civilization. One of the relatively minor contributions of the time, albeit a fortunate one for us, is
the addition of the word *sunbeam* to the English language.

The word is believed to have entered English in the
ninth century, through the work of the English king
Alfred the Great. A scholar as well as a king, Alfred
undertook a number of translations of great Latin
writings, rendering them into the English of his time,
now known as Old English. Among the works translated during Alfred's reign was a store of narratives
and information about England's earliest connections
with the Church, called the *Historia Ecclesiastica*

gentis Anglorum, or *The Ecclesiastical History of the English People,* a work composed by the Venerable Bede. Several times in his book Bede uses the Latin phrase *columna lucis,* which we would today translate as "a column of light." Since the Old English translator did not have the word *column* in his vocabulary, he substituted the word *beam,* which meant "a tree" or "a building post made from a tree." *Columna lucis* thus became *sunne beam,* or "sun post," which survives as our *sunbeam.*

If *sunbeam* is perhaps a less stately expression than "column of light," it has nevertheless served us well. From it the word *beam* alone came to mean "a ray or rays of light"; it subsequently became a verb meaning "to radiate." It now allows us not only to beam with pride or happiness but also to beam our broadcasts to other countries and ourselves, as some would have it, through space. *Column* would never do.

super– A hypermarket, which is a British combination of a department store and a supermarket, sounds like a superior, if not the supreme, commercial establishment, over and above just a plain supermarket. In this sentence, which words are derived from the same Indo-European root? The prefix *super–* comes from the Latin preposition *super,* "above." The comparative and superlative forms of Latin *superus,* "upper," an adjective dervived from *super,* also appear in English. The former is *superior,* "higher," which also meant "greater" and "better" (the English word *superior* derived via Old French from the Latin word has these meanings too). The latter is *suprēmus,* which meant "highest" as well as "last, ultimate, final." English *supreme,* borrowed directly from Latin *suprēmus,* preserves the sense "highest" in its figurative use. Latin *super* is descended from the Indo-European form *uper,* "over, above," which came into Old English as *ofer,* our Modern English word *over.* The English prefix *hyper–* is a borrowing of *huper,* "over, above," the Greek descendant of the same Indo-European form.

supercilious   It is never easy to bear "the proud man's contumely,"
as Hamlet put it, but the next time you run into supercilious people it might be helpful to know how the
word for their haughtiness originated. The Latin word
supercilium (from which *superciliōsus*, the source of
our word, is derived) meant "an eyebrow." *Supercilium* came to mean "the eyebrow as used in frowning
and expressing sternness, gravity, or haughtiness";
hence developing the senses "stern looks, severity;
haughty demeanor, pride." In Latin and Late Latin *superciliōsus* meant "full of stern or disapproving looks,
censorious, severe; haughty, disdainful." So the next
time you meet someone who is supercilious, don't
even raise a supercilium.

syphilis   In 1530 Girolamo Fracastoro, a physician, astronomer,
and poet of Verona, published a poem entitled *Syphilis, sive Morbus Gallicus*, translated as *Syphilis, or
the French Disease*. (Incidentally, in France syphilis is
called *le mal du Naples*.) In Fracastoro's poem the
name of this dreaded venereal disease is an altered
form of the hero's name, *Syphilus*. The hero, a shepherd, is supposed to have been the first victim of the
disease. Where the name *Syphilus* itself came from is
not known for certain, but it has been suggested that
Fracastoro borrowed the name from Ovid's *Metamor-
phoses*. In Ovid's work Sipylus (spelled *Siphylus* in
some manuscripts) is the oldest son of Niobe, who
lived not far from Mount Sipylon in Asia Minor. Fracastoro's poem about Syphilus was modeled on the
story of Niobe. Although the etymology involving
Sipylus was known to the editors of the *Oxford English Dictionary*, it was not accepted as their last word
on the subject. C. T. Onions, one of the *OED*'s editors, writing in *The Oxford Dictionary of English
Etymology*, says that "*Syphilus* [the shepherd's
name] is of unkn[own] origin." Fracastoro went on
to use the term *syphilis* again in his medical treatise
De Contagione, published in 1546. The word that Fracastoro used in Latin was eventually borrowed into
English. Have the movie rights been sold for the Fracastoro poem?

238

syringe Consideration of the etymology of the word *syringe* might make one's next visit to the allergist or other injecting physician a bit less daunting. The Greek word *surinx*, to which our word *syringe* goes back, meant "panpipe," a primitive wind instrument consisting of a series of pipes or reeds played by blowing across the open ends, and "anything like a pipe," including things such as pores or even the passage through an elephant's trunk.

tadpole   Although a tadpole has much more to do with toads than with politics, we can find both connections by studying the history of the word *tadpole*. *Tad* comes from a form of the word *toad* that is last recorded by itself in the seventeenth century. *Pole*, recorded from the sixteenth to the nineteenth century, is a form of our word *poll*, meaning "head." A *tadpole* is thus "a toad that is all head." *Poll* still means "head" and also "a survey of public opinion" or "the place where votes are cast," among other senses more familiar to us than "head." *Poll* probably developed these senses at least partly through the notion of the head as the prominent part of a person in a crowd, a part that could be counted.

taint   *Taint* has been tainted. The word *taint* as we know it comes to us by way of two paths of origin. If we look down one of these paths, we also see where our word *tint* comes from. *Tint*, whose earlier form is *tinct*, is a direct borrowing of the Latin word *tinctus*, "a dyeing," from the past participle of *tingere*, "to dip, dye" (*tingere* is also the source of our English word *tinge*). In Old French two nouns, *taint* and *tainte*, both meaning "a dye, tint, color," developed; they too can

Teflon

241

be traced back to the past participle *tinctus*. These Old French nouns are the partial source of our word *taint*. The other source of *taint* is a shortened form of *attaint*, which in Middle English meant "a charge of felony" and which by the end of the sixteenth century had come to mean "touch of dishonor." The shortened form *taint* denoted, among other things, a conviction. From the two paths of origin came two English words that could have become separate words both of which we would spell *taint*. But according to one way of looking at the matter, the words met and blended, which led to the development of the sense "moral stain" for our word *taint*.

talent The word *talent* is ultimately derived from the Greek word *talanton*, "an amount of money." The meaning "ability, aptitude," comes from the metaphorical use of *talanton* in the parable recorded in Matthew 25:14–30. This parable tells how a master entrusted money to each of his three servants in his absence. The servant with five talents and the one with two talents both doubled their money and were rewarded on their master's return. The servant who had been given one talent buried the money and returned only the original amount, and for this he was reproached. The parable has been interpreted to mean that everyone has a duty to improve the natural gifts and abilities that God has given.

tansy *Tansy*, a name for various plants, especially one having pungent, aromatic juice and clusters of buttonlike yellow flowers, was thought by some etymologists to have a (not the) secret of immortality. *Tansy* supposedly goes back by way of the Old French word *tanaisie* or *tanesie*, "tansy," to Medieval Latin *athanasia*, "tansy or other herb." The Medieval Latin word may have been adapted from the Greek word *athanasia*, "immortality," from *a-*, "without," and *thanatos*, "death," probably because tansy flowers last a long time.

242

Perhaps this etymology should not be immortalized, though. Walther von Wartburg, an authority on the history of the French language, does not think Old French *tanaisie* is connected with Medieval Latin *athanasia*. Instead, he traces *tanaisie* to a Late Latin and Medieval Latin name for the plant, whose earliest form occurs as *tanacitam* in the fifth century A.D. The word *tanacitam* in turn must come from a non-Indo-European Mediterranean language. Flowers and etymologies, even pretty ones, may last a long time, but they are not immortal.

tantalize The religions of ancient Greece and Rome were swept away by Christianity, but their gods and heroes live on in our language and culture. *Tantalize*, for example, comes from *Tantalus*, the name of a legendary king of Lydia. He stole the food of the gods and gave it to mortals, a crime punishable by death. Tantalus, however, could not die, because he had eaten the divine food and had become immortal. The gods instead condemned him to suffer eternal hunger and thirst in the presence of food and drink that remained just out of his reach. The verb *tantalize* means basically "to cause to suffer the torments of Tantalus," although in a much milder form. Tantalus's offspring, by the way, also suffered torments; his daughter Niobe, from whose name we derived our word for the element niobium, was the personification of grief in Greek mythology.

tavern In language history the step between the sublime and the ridiculous is often a very small one indeed. That slender interval separates, for example, words as apparently unrelated, and in some respects incompatible, as *tavern* and *tabernacle*. Both of these English words are ultimately derived from the Latin word *taberna*, "a hut or booth," a term that probably evolved in Latin from the word *trabs*, "a building post or timber." *Tavern* entered English during the Middle English period by way of Old French, where the Latin word *taberna* had developed into *taverne*. In Middle English the word meant primarily, as it does today, "an establishment dispensing alcoholic beverages." *Tabernacle*, similarly, was borrowed into Middle English either from Old French *tabernacle*, an adaptation of the Latin word *tabernāculum*, or directly from this Latin source. *Tabernāculum*, a diminutive form of *ta berna*, that is, "a small hut or booth; tent," had been used in Late Latin to name the tentlike sanctuary carried by the Israelites of the Old Testament. English borrowed the term in this context and has continued to use it nearly exclusively in religious senses. The once-intimate connection between *tavern* and *tabernacle* is no longer evident, although, historically, the distinction is but a step sideways.

tawdry   The word *tawdry* is an alteration of the name of Saint Audry, an Anglo-Saxon princess who died of a throat ailment. A fair was held annually in her honor at which cloth neckbands or neckties, called *tawdry laces*, were sold. These must have been showy but inexpensive souvenirs, because the word *tawdry*, meaning "gaudy and cheap," became an adjective in its own right.

teetotaler   *I'm only a beer teetotaler, not a champagne teetotaler.*
                   —George Bernard Shaw, *Candida*, 1898

A true teetotaler would have none of this, of course. The word is probably derived from the phrase *teetotal abstainer*, coined by temperance workers in the 1830's. People who were teetotalers abstained not only from hard liquor, as earlier supporters of temperance had advocated, but also from all alcoholic beverages, including champagne and beer. The syllable *tee–* in *teetotal* is simply a spelling of the pronunciation of the letter *t*, the initial letter of *total*. *Teetotal* was therefore a catchy way of saying "absolutely total."

Teflon   Gentle reader, in illuminating interesting facts and exploring unresolved mysteries involving English words, it is sometimes necessary to debunk misconceptions, as is the case with two well-known trademarks, Teflon and STAR WARS. The proprietary trade name Teflon has nothing whatsoever to do with the fortieth president of the United States, Ronald Reagan. And STAR WARS, the trademarked title of a space adventure movie and the proprietary name of various spin-off products from that movie, in itself has no connection with Reagan's Strategic Defense Initiative.

A trademark is a name, symbol, or other device identifying a product that is officially registered and legally restricted to the use of the owner or manufacturer. A common problem with successful, highly visible trademarks is a tendency among some people to use them in contexts totally unrelated to the products they actually describe. For this reason and for many other reasons as well, the proprietors of trademarks watch certain changes in English usage very carefully, just as dictionary editors do, but not for linguistic purposes; rather, they monitor such developments to protect the proprietary status of their assets.

Teflon, a registered trademark owned by E. I. du Pont de Nemours and Company and coined by Du Pont's marketing people nearly fifty years ago, applies to a large family of Du Pont products, including plastics, films, and fibers. While the public knows Teflon best as a nonstick coating for cookware, its uses are in fact much broader. For example, Teflon is used to replace damaged parts of the body, such as heart arteries and vocal cords. It was also used as an insulator and a lubricant in the renovation of the Statue of Liberty. *Teflon* stands for the polytetrafluoroethylene resin discovered by now-retired Du Pont chemist Dr. Roy J. Plunkett. According to Du Pont, the word *Teflon* was simply made up.

How did Teflon jump from the frying pan into the Oval Office? Boston *Globe* writer Michael Kenney has noted that United States Representative Patricia Schroeder (a Democrat from Colorado) was the first to use *Teflon* in connection with Ronald Reagan. According to an article by Kenney in the October 24,

1984, issue of the *Globe*, it all began, appropriately or inappropriately enough, in Schroeder's kitchen in August of 1983. Schroeder was annoyed that the president had managed to escape unsinged after having made a series of what she felt were political blunders and "misdeeds." In his *Globe* article Kenney quoted Schroeder to this effect regarding that fateful August day:

"I was cooking breakfast this morning for my kids,"
Schroeder said, "and I thought, 'He's just like a Teflon
frying pan: nothing sticks to him.' "

(This citation is particularly interesting to lexicographers, for it freeze-frames the actual moment of word association and sense extension as it occurs in the language.) Schroeder's usage was picked up by the *Congressional Record* from the written text of a speech she made in Congress soon thereafter (although Kenney points out that she never uttered the word *Teflon* during the oral delivery). The reportage in the *Congressional Record* undoubtedly provided the impetus toward subsequent widespread use of *Teflon* in the Reagan context by the press, especially during the 1984 presidential race.

What does the president think of all this? Du Pont will be gratified to learn that Reagan doesn't think the description applies to him at all. When asked at a June 19, 1985, press conference if the Teflon coating was beginning to slip off his presidency, Reagan replied, "I never thought there was any Teflon on me anyplace."

Ironically, the trademark designating a nonstick surface coating has stuck around, as is indicated in passages such as this one, taken from the citation files of *The American Heritage Dictionary, Second College Edition*. This passage appeared in the December 2, 1985, issue of the Boston *Globe* in an article by writer Linda Charlton:

If Ronald Reagan can be said to have a "Teflon presidency"
in which negatives don't stick, then [the judge's] political
and judicial careers can be described as "polyester"—not
pretty, but durable and able to shed wrinkles.

We decided to ask Dr. Plunkett what he thinks about the extension in meaning of the word *Teflon* to refer to public officials like Ronald Reagan and even Andrei Gromyko, because it isn't often that lexicographers can ask such questions of people intimately involved with the evolution of new words. "In the first place, I don't like it," responded Dr. Plunkett. When pressed further he added, "It's a very inappropriate term for a national figure and of course it's an improper use of the trademark."

Having delved into one sticky subject, let us turn to another usage, also associated with the Reagan administration in recent press reports—a usage that can be said to have put Lucasfilm Ltd., the owner of the registered trademark STAR WARS, into intergalactic orbit. STAR WARS, as mentioned earlier, is Lucasfilm's trade name for a space adventure film (released in 1977) and for a multitude of spin-off products. When we checked into the origin of the term STAR WARS, we were informed by Lucasfilm that George Lucas alone came up with the title of the movie. There is no connection at all between the trademark STAR WARS and President Reagan's Strategic Defense Initiative (SDI), a plan for a network of satellites armed and programmed to destroy incoming enemy missiles and satellites. Nonetheless, printed evidence from press reports indicates that many writers have gone ahead and used the term *STAR WARS* as a synonym for, or as an adjective modifying, the SDI ("his commitment to Star Wars antisatellite and space-based missile defense," a citation taken from the December 31, 1984, issue of *Newsweek* being an example).

But according to yet another citation from our files, "President Reagan doesn't like to have his favorite space project referred to as Star Wars and neither does the company that made the movie of the same name. . . . complaints [were] filed by LucasFilm Ltd. [*sic*] to prevent the use of the 'Star Wars' movie title as a synonym for Strategic Defense Initiative" (Springfield, Massachusetts, *Morning Union*, December 2, 1985). Concerned that their trademark STAR WARS would be taken "out of the congenial realm of fantasy and entertainment and [thrust] into the frightening world of nuclear holocaust and death," as Lucasfilm's attorney Arthur J. Levine put it, Lucasfilm brought suit against the Coalition for the Strategic Defense Initiative, which planned to use the lower-cased term *star wars* in a series of commercials supporting the proposal.

Federal district court judge Gerhard A. Gessell stated in a November 26, 1985, memorandum in response to briefs, affidavits, and oral arguments from counsel in *Lucasfilm Ltd.* v. *High Frontier, et al.*, and *Lucasfilm Ltd.* v. *Committee for a Strong, Peaceful America, et al.*, that "STAR WARS has . . . become a strong trademark owned by plaintiff [Lucasfilm Ltd.]," but that "since Jonathan Swift's time, creators of fictional worlds have seen their vocabulary for fantasy appropriated to describe reality." Although the judge stated that "courts . . . cannot regulate the type of descriptive, non-trade use involved here without becoming the monitors of the spoken or written English language," he nonetheless made a strong statement affirming the status of the trademark STAR WARS itself, to wit: "The proof presented at this stage leaves no doubt that STAR WARS is still a strong trademark . . . Now the phrase star wars has acquired a double meaning, but it has not become a generic term, that is a term associated with an entire class of goods or services. Continued non-trade, noncommercial use cannot take the mark away from plaintiff Lucasfilms [*sic*]." The judge went on to say, "The new meaning of the phrase in the political or scientific context does not affect the distinct, and still strong secondary meaning of STAR WARS in trade and entertainment. Plaintiff's right to prevent an infringing use of its mark remains intact."

Even though printed citational evidence indicates that Reagan, more so than his predecessors, seems to generate a sort of "semantic attraction" for proprietary names (witness his "Rambo response" to terrorist attacks), he is not the only Chief Executive to have been so described: we need only recall Jimmy Carter's "Chiclets smile"—a usage that, unlike the

Cheshire Cat's famous grin, proved totally ephemeral. All this illustrates the simple fact that people—the users of English—like to employ the language just as they please. That's how changes in the language and changes in the meanings of words come about. But the phenomenon ceases to be the stuff of lexicography and can become a point of legal contestation when changes in the meanings and applications of proprietary names are involved. Therefore it is safer and really more precise to describe a president as *critic-repellent, potshot-proof,* or even *acrylic* than as *Teflon.* It is likewise safer and more precise to describe a space-based weapons initiative as a *space weapons system,* a *defensive space weapons system,* or even *space weaponry* than as *STAR WARS.* Otherwise, watch out: Darth Vader or Rambo may step out from behind the nylon curtain and zap you.

tele- Where would we be without the telephone or television? We might also ask where we would be without the highly productive prefix *tele-* or *tel-.* This prefix comes from the Greek form *tēle-* or *tēl-,* which combines with other words to create new words. Greek *tēle-* or *tēl-* is a form of *tēle,* meaning "afar, far off." Thus our prefix often refers to distance. The telescope enlarges distant objects, making them appear closer. Messages travel over a distance by means of the telegraph, sound by the telephone, and visual images by television.

Languages such as English, French, and Italian make free use of prefixes descended from Greek *tēle-;* new compounds are often formed in one language and then borrowed into another (the English word *telegraph,* for example, comes from French). It is interesting to compare German with English in the use of *tele-* words. Such words also exist in German, but because native terms are preferred in German, we find many words that are created with the prefix *fern-,* meaning "long distance." Besides *Teleskop,* we have *Fernrohr* (literally, "long-distance tube"), besides *Telephon,* we have *Fernsprecher* ("long-distance speaker"), and one word for *television* is *Fernsehen* ("long-distance seeing").

testicle   The word *testicle* might seem at the outset far removed from the language of the law. Nevertheless, it
may have etymological connections with the words
testimony and *testify*, both of which go back to the
Latin word *testis*, meaning "witness." *Testicle* is from
a diminutive, *testiculus*, of a second Latin word *testis*, which meant "testicle." It is thought that this *testis* is probably a special use of *testis*, "witness," a
testicle being a witness to virility.

thesaurus   In etymological terms a thesaurus is truly a treasury
of words, for the word itself comes from the Greek
term *thēsauros*, "treasure." The Romans borrowed
the Greek word, and Latin *thesaurus* developed into
Old French *tresor*, which was borrowed into English
as *treasure*. The Latin word *thesaurus* was used in titles of English books in early modern times, as in
Robert Ainsworth's *Thesaurus linguæ Latinæ com-
pendiarius*, or *A Compendious Dictionary of the
Latin Tongue*, published in 1736. We first find *thesaurus* used as an English word in the nineteenth
century, when it denoted both a treasury, as of a temple, and a "storehouse" of knowledge. In that latter
sense Peter Mark Roget used the word for the title of
his major work, *Thesaurus of English Words and
Phrases*, published in 1852. Roget's work was meant
not to discriminate between synonymous words but
rather to organize words by categories, so users could
find words they needed by looking up the proper
category. People did, however, see Roget's work as a
collection of synonyms, and because of this misunderstanding and the far-reaching influence of Roget's
work and its successors, the most common modern
sense of *thesaurus*, ironically enough, is "a book of
synonyms."

thimble   A thimble belongs on the thumb; the history of the
word leaves no doubt about that. The Old English
word *þȳmel*, the ancestor of *thimble*, is derived from
Old English *þūma*, the ancestor of our word *thumb*.
The suffix *–el*, used for appliances or instruments,

survives as -*le* in *thimble* and in similar words such as *ladle* and *bridle*. (The *b* after the *m* in *thimble* developed later in English.) The earliest sense of *thimble* was "a covering for the thumb or finger." In Middle English *þȳmel* came to mean "a sheath of leather that protects the finger pushing the needle in sewing." Leather has since been replaced by metal, ceramic, and plastic.

thing Let's say a thing or two about *thing*. This word is perhaps derived from the Indo-European root *tenk-*[1], "to stretch, pull or draw (together)," although we have found descendants of *tenk-*[1] only in the Germanic languages. It is hard to imagine how other language families do without descendants of this root, since the Germanic word *thingam*, "assembly," derived from *tenk-*[1], was so important and appears in some form in all the Germanic languages. In Old English *thing* meant "a judicial assembly" and hence "a legal matter." These Old English meanings of *thing* are now obsolete, but the related senses "a matter of concern" and "a circumstance" survive. The sense "an entity" has always been a meaning of the English word.

third The ordinal number *third* and its corresponding cardinal number, *three*, exhibit what was once a very common linguistic process in English, that of metathesis. The word *metathesis* literally means "change of position." In the case of *third*, the *r* sound changed its position with respect to the vowel. The Indo-European root from which both *three* and *third* are derived is *trei-*. *Three* preserves the original position of the letter *r*; *third* represents a change. The usual form of the ordinal number in Old English was *thridda*, although the form *thirdda* was also used. Both the forms *thrid* and *third* occurred throughout the Middle English period, and *thrid* did not die out until modern times. Metathesis of *r* is exhibited by other pairs of related words, among them *burn/brand* and *work/wrought*.

Thursday Should you expect thunder on Thursday? The English name of the fifth day of the week is actually a translation of its Latin name, *diēs Jovis*, "Jupiter's day."
The Old English form of *Thursday* was *Thunresdæg*; *thunres* is the genitive of *thunor*, the ancestor of our modern word *thunder*. *Thunor* was also the name of a Germanic thunder god; the Norse form of *Thunor* is *Thor*. Since Jupiter, too, was associated with thunder, the two gods were linked together, and Thor's or Thunor's name was given to Jupiter's day.

tide *Tyde nor tyme tarrieth no man.*
—Robert Greene, *A Disputation Betweene a Hee Conny-catcher and a Shee Conny-catcher, 1592*

The words *tide* and *time* are related, both going back to the Indo-European root *da–*, "to divide," and were once synonymous, both meaning "an interval or division of time." This sense for *tide* is now obsolete. The usual sense of *tide*, "the periodic variation in the surface level of the earth's waters," is a development of the original meaning of the word, since the tides rise and fall at predictable times of the day.

tittle *For verily I say unto you, Till heaven and earth pass, one jot or one tittle shall in no wise pass from the law, till all be fulfilled.*
—Matthew, 5:18

Tittle has gained a legitimate title to its sense "the tiniest bit." *Tittle*, like *title*, is derived from the Latin word *titulus*, which originally meant "label, title." But how did the meaning "the tiniest bit" develop for such a word?

During the Middle Ages *titulus* came to have somewhat the same meaning as the Latin word *apex*, which meant "a long mark placed over a vowel" and also "the tip or angle forming part of a letter." In a Middle English translation of the Bible produced before 1382, Latin *apex* was translated *titil*. *Apex* in the context of Saint Matthew's gospel referred to a small part of a letter; in other words, not even a small por-

252

tion of the written law would pass from it. The Middle English translator is said to have substituted *titil* for *apex* because *apex* and *titulus* had become more or less synonymous. *Titil* at this point was simply a form of the word that became our Modern English word *title*. But this Biblical use of *titil* seems to have contributed to the separate development of our word *tittle*, in senses referring both to writing and to the figurative notion of a small bit. And that's not diddleysquat, if you'll forgive an old Southern expression.

torpedo The original meaning of *torpedo* in English was "electric ray," a fish that produces an electric charge and causes numbness with its sting. The term was borrowed from the Latin word *torpēdō*, which denoted the same fish but which basically meant "numbness." *Torpedo* in English came to be used figuratively for someone or something with a numbing effect, as in Oliver Goldsmith's remark in *The Life of Richard Nash*, published in 1762: "He used to call a pen his torpedo whenever he grasped it, it numbed all his faculties." The torpedo we are most familiar with is self-propelled and not numb at all; the original form of the weapon, which was a drifting underwater mine, was probably so named because, like the fish, it could "sting."

torte *Torte*, *tortellini*, and *tortilla* may share a common ingredient, that is, derivation from the Late Latin word *torta*, "a flat, round bread." Over time Late Latin *torta* became *torta* in Italian, with the meaning "cake." It is thought that German *Torte*, "a rich cake," which is the source of our word *torte*, may have come from Italian *torta*. Having finished dessert, let us move on to our main course. From Italian *torta* was derived *tortelli*, "a kind of pasta"; this word's diminutive, *tortellini*, denotes small, stuffed pasta dumplings. Now for the pièce de résistance. The Late Latin word *torta* also became the Spanish word *torta*, "round cake," and its American Spanish diminutive, *tortilla*, means "a thin, round unleavened bread, usually made from cornmeal and served hot with various toppings of ground meat or cheese." Bon appétit!

toxic If you shot an arrow into the air and it landed at the site of a toxic waste dump, you would have hit an etymological bull's eye. The word *toxic* goes back by way of Late Latin *toxicus*, "poisoned, poisonous"— from Latin *toxicum*, "poison"—to Greek *toxikon* in the phrase *toxikon pharmakon*, "poison for smearing arrows with" (*pharmakon* here means "poison"). *Toxikon* is a form of the adjective *toxikos*, "of or for the bow," from *toxon*, "bow." Users of Greek started to think that the word *toxikon* in the phrase *toxikon pharmakon* meant "poisonous" and began to use the word by itself as a noun meaning "arrow poison" and then "any poison." *Toxikon* in this sense was borrowed into Latin, becoming *toxicum*, the ancestor of our word *toxic*.

trapeze The daring young man on the flying trapeze may not realize that the name of the apparatus on which he performs comes from the science of geometry. The French word *trapèze*, the source of our word, is derived from the Latin word *trapezium*, which comes from the Greek geometric term *trapezion*. *Trapezium* in Latin could refer to an irregular quadrilateral with two parallel sides, and from such use the trapeze seems to have acquired its name in French. The word was originally used for a gymnastic apparatus that consisted of a crossbar hung by ropes from a beam supported by posts. The beam and crossbar formed the two parallel bases of a geometric figure and the ropes formed the sides. The ropes possibly came down to the crossbar from points on the beam that were spaced farther apart than the width of the bar. Hence, the beam, the crossbar, and the ropes formed a *trapezium*.

travel The hardships of making a journey in earlier times are reflected in the etymological identity of the words

254

travel and *travail*. Both are derived from the Old French word *travaillier*, which comes from the Vulgar Latin word *tripāliāre*, "to torture on the rack," from *tripālium*, "a kind of rack." *Travaillier* originally meant "to torture, torment, trouble," and thus "to suffer, be troubled, become tired or worn out." *Travaillier* hence came to mean "to tire out by a journey" and "to journey." *Travaillier*, borrowed into English, has given birth to two separate words. *Travail* still refers to pain and suffering. *Travel*, originally only a variant form of *travail*, now exclusively describes only one kind of pain—and pleasure.

treason   One person's treason is another person's tradition, at least from the etymologist's point of view. Our word *tradition*, which refers to things that are handed on from generation to generation, goes back to the Latin word *trāditiō*, which described the same sorts of things. But *trāditiō* could also denote a handing over, a surrender, or a betrayal of persons or territory. In this sense *trāditiō* passed into Romance languages such as French and, according to one possible etymology, was reshaped in form, becoming Old French *traison*, which was borrowed into English and became our word *treason*. And so, to paraphrase Patrick Henry, if this be *treason*, let us make the most of its etymological tradition.

trove   Have you found a trove lately? The origin of our word *trove* is *trové*, the past participle of the Old French verb *trover*, "to find." The word entered English by way of the French phrase *tresor trové*, literally "found treasure," which was borrowed into English and became *treasure-trove*. *Treasure-trove* came to apply specifically in English law to treasure that had been certainly or presumably hidden, as opposed to treasure that was lost or abandoned. Lost or abandoned treasure, which was likely to be of little value, could be kept by the finder, but treasure-trove, which could be valuable, materially as well as historically, belonged to the Crown, although the finder would be compensated in order to encourage him or her to turn it in.

Besides its legal sense *treasure-trove* also developed the figurative sense "a valuable discovery." *Trove*, a shortened form of the compound, has the same sense, or simply the sense "a discovery." It has also developed new senses such as "a valuable collection" and "a haul or take."

tulip   Although we associate tulips with Holland and windmills, the history of the word takes us on an odyssey to the Middle East, where the tulip is associated with turbans and whence the flower was brought to Europe in the sixteenth century. The word *tulip*, which earlier in English appeared in such forms as *tulipa* or *tulipant*, comes to us by way of French *tulipe* and its obsolete form *tulipan* or from Modern Latin *tulipa*, from Turkish *tülbend*, "tulip, turban," derived from Persian *dulband*, "turban." (Our word *turban*, first recorded in English in the sixteenth century, can also be traced back through Turkish to Persian *dulband*.) The word for turban in Turkish was used for the flower because a fully opened tulip was thought to resemble a turban.

turkey   The bird commonly known as the *turkey* and familiar as the centerpiece of the Thanksgiving feast is a native of the New World. It acquired the name of an Old World country as a result of two different mistakes. The name *turkey*, or *turkey cock*, was originally applied to an African bird now known as the *guinea fowl*, which at one time was believed to have originated in Turkey. When European settlers first saw the American turkey, they thought it was the same bird and gave it the name *turkey*. The two species, however, are quite different.

Turkey

256

tuxedo   Does a tuxedo have anything to do with a wolf? Read on. The tuxedo takes its name from Tuxedo Park, New York, the site of a country club where this fashionable evening attire was supposedly first worn. It has been said that the place name *Tuxedo* came from a word that in the modern Oklahoma Delaware language has the form *Túkswīt*, literally meaning "one who has a round foot" and denoting a member of the wolf family. But a number of factors make this etymology impossible. Among them are the fact that the word does not occur in the Native American language spoken in the vicinity of Tuxedo Park. Also, the etymology does not explain the final vowel in *Tuxedo* (or *tuxedo*). Be that as it may, better a wolf in a tuxedo than a wolf in sheep's clothing—especially on the dance floor at the country club.

tycoon   Those of you who are business tycoons may consider yourselves captains or even princes of industry, but by virture of being called *tycoons*, you have already achieved princely status, at least from an etymological point of view. *Tycoon* came into English from Japanese, which had borrowed the title, meaning "great prince," from Chinese ta^4, "great," and $chün^1$, "prince." Use of the word was intended to make the shogun, the commander in chief of the Japanese army, more impressive to foreigners (his official title *shōgun* merely meant "general"). In fact, the shogun actually ruled Japan, although he was supposedly acting for the emperor. When Commodore Matthew Calbraith Perry opened Japan to the West in 1853, he negotiated with the shogun, whom he thought was the emperor. The shogun's title, *taikun*, was brought back to the United States after Perry's visit. Abraham Lincoln's cabinet members used *tycoon* as an affectionate nickname for the president. The word soon came to be used for business and industry leaders—perhaps at times for those who had as much right to such an impressive title as did the shogun. The word itself now has an old-fashioned sound, but when we encounter it, we should think back to the days of

Commodore Perry and President Lincoln, both of whom were real tycoons in their own ways.

tyrant Nobody likes a tyrant, and apparently this feeling goes back a long way. The Greek word *turannos*, to which our word *tyrant* goes back, denoted an absolute ruler who was not constrained by law or constitution. The word was frequently used in a negative sense, as its English descendant is, whether referring to a ruler or to any martinet. In *The Gentleman's Magazine* of December, 1792, we learn, for example, of "a man of republican levelling principles, who was the greatest of tyrants to his wife and family."

ukulele   The ukulele, which we usually associate with Hawaii, is actually a modification of the braguinha, a small Portuguese instrument of the guitar family. This instrument was probably brought to Hawaii in 1879 by Portuguese settlers from Madeira. It is possible that Hawaiians first heard the braguinha when one of the new settlers played it while celebrating a safe arrival in Hawaii. Some of the Portuguese families began manufacturing the instrument, which over time was modified in various ways, as by using native Hawaiian wood, so that it ultimately became the ukulele as we know it today.

How the instrument came to be called a *ukulele* is disputed. One story has it that a British army officer, Edward Purvis, who helped popularize the instrument, was nicknamed in Hawaiian *'uku-lele*, literally "the jumping flea," from *'uku*, "flea," and *lele*, a form having to do with jumping. Purvis was given this name because he was small and nimble, and the name was then transferred to the instrument. This explanation, based on oral tradition, may well be correct. Another, less colorful, explanation is that the player's fingers moving rapidly over the strings called to mind a jumping flea. John Henry Felix, Leslie K.

Undertaker

Nunes, and Peter F. Senecal in *The 'Ukulele: A Portuguese Gift to Hawaii*, published in 1980, say that "this simple explanation . . . is quite possibly the most accurate one."

uncouth The history of the word *uncouth* reveals the propensity of human beings to react with hostility and aversion to something unknown or strange. *Uncouth* is the descendant of the Old English word *uncūth*, which meant simply "unknown, unfamiliar." It was descended from a Germanic combination of the negative prefix *un-* and *kunthaz*, the past participle of *kunnan*, "to know." The rather neutral meaning "unfamiliar, strange," for *uncouth* eventually developed into the meaning "odd, awkward," which further developed into "crude, unrefined," probably the most familiar modern sense of the word. *Couth*, meaning "known, familiar"—the descendant of Old English *cūth* from Germanic *kunthaz* by itself—did exist at one time, but is now obsolete. A new adjective *couth* has very recently been formed as an antonym of *uncouth* in the sense "crude, unrefined." We find both words in this sentence taken from the March 28, 1963, edition of the Manchester *Guardian*: "Modern idiom and slang is used with reckless abandon and the couth and uncouth punch each other about the ears with unrelenting monotony."

undertaker The subject of death has always inspired euphemism; the word *undertaker* is but one example of many. Derived from the verb *undertake*, "to take upon oneself," *undertaker* early on simply denoted one who undertakes any kind of task, first recorded in this sense in a work written about 1400. Samuel Butler in *The Genuine Remains of Mr. Samuel Butler*, in a passage written before 1680, uses the word in this sense when he says that "The Devil . . . was the first bold Undertaker Of bearing Arms against his Maker." Around 1700, during a period of general refinement of speech and manners, the word *undertaker* was applied specifically to those who undertake to prepare the dead for the grave.

262

unkempt If your lawn is unkempt, you could try running a comb through it. *Unkempt* is a variant form of *unkembed*, derived from the past participle of *kemb*, "to comb." *Kemb* survives only in dialect except for its past participle, which is still used, as in "a nicely kempt beard." The verbs *kemb* and *comb* are closely related. The noun *comb*, from which the verb is derived, and the verb *kemb* go back to the Germanic word *kambaz*, "comb." *Kambaz* became *camb* in Old English, which in turn became our Modern English word *comb*. The Germanic verb *kambjan*, meaning "to comb," was derived from *kambaz*. The *j* in *kambjan* caused the first *a* to take on a different sound, which explains the *e* in *unkempt*.

unmentionables *A fine lady can talk about her lover's inexpressibles, when she would faint to hear of his breeches.*
                    —Farmer's Magazine, 1809

Whatever *unmentionables* and other such euphemisms may mean today, they once merely meant trousers or breeches. First recorded in 1830, *unmentionables* joined a crowd of similar terms for such kinds of male attire: *inexpressibles* (1790), *ineffables* (1823), *inexplicables* (1836), and *unutterables* (1843), not to mention (shh!) *unwhisperables* (1837). Trousers were, at least to nineteenth-century minds, quite disreputable, and for this reason they were subject to prolific, and yes, very coy euphemism. By 1870 one writer predicted that "at the rate of purity at which we are advancing, "legs" will soon walk off into the limbo of silence and unmentionableness." Clearly we have reached the downside of this particular trajectory.

upbraid *Upbraid* is a compound formed in Old English of the prefix *ūp-*, "up," and the verb *bregdan*, which had a variety of meanings derived from the idea of turning. In Old English the compound *ūpbregdan* meant "to turn up a matter against someone as a reproach." In later times the word came to mean "to find fault with" (as in William Wordsworth's lines in *Descriptive Sketches*, published in 1793: "There might the love-sick maiden watch at eve her lover's sun-gilt sail Approaching, and upbraid the tardy gale") and "to reproach" (as in Charles Darwin's *The Expression of the Emotions in Man and Animals*, published in 1872: "As she upbraided him, her eyebrows became extremely oblique").

upholster   The word *upholster* has a tortuous history that begins with the simple English verb *uphold*, meaning "to support" and apparently also meaning "to keep in repair." The noun suffixes -*ster* and -*er* were added to this verb, producing *upholdster* (or *upholdester*) and *upholder*, which originally meant "a dealer in or repairer of furniture." A new noun, *upholdsterer* or *upholsterer*, with much the same meaning, was formed by adding the suffix -*er* to the noun *upholdster*. The verb *upholster* was formed from *upholsterer* by deleting the suffix -*er*. Although the noun *upholsterer* is recorded from the seventeenth century, the verb *upholster* is not recorded until the nineteenth century.

urbane   Can one be urbane without being urban? *Urban* and *urbane*, once synonymous, come from the Latin word *urbānus*, "belonging to a city," derived from *urbs*, "city." *Urbane* was borrowed first, from Latin *urbānus* or its Old French descendant *urbain*. *Urbane* developed the more specialized sense of "refined, polite, elegant," already present in French and Latin. These desirable qualities were considered to be characteristic of urban rather than country folk.

utopia   A true utopia is probably not to be found anywhere, as an analysis of the word *utopia* suggests. Sir Thomas More named his imaginary island *Utopia*, the inhabitants of which enjoyed a perfect society. *Utopia* is a modern Latin word formed from Greek *ou*, "not, no," and *topos*, "place." *Utopia* lives on in general usage as a term for "an impractical, idealistic scheme for social and political reform" and "an ideally perfect place or condition." Many of its uses in the second sense suggest that these utopias cannot be real. For example, the Manchester *Examiner* of November 22, 1883, mentions "ingenious speculators who hope to reach Utopia by the nationalisation of the land."

vaccine   The first vaccine was prepared from the virus that causes cowpox, as the derivation of the word *vaccine* from Latin *vacca*, "cow," suggests. Cowpox is a mild bovine disease that can be transmitted to human beings. In the late eighteenth century Edward Jenner discovered that someone who has had cowpox is almost always immune to smallpox—a related but much more serious disease. Jenner was the first to inoculate human beings with the cowpox virus, although the method itself had long been used with matter from smallpox pustules, a far more dangerous procedure. Jenner called the inoculating agent he used *vaccine virus*. Many other diseases are now prevented by inoculation, and the word *vaccine* is applied to the inoculating agent in all such cases.

vandal   Vandals are nothing new, and the term describing them proves it. Originally, *Vandal* was the name for a member of a Germanic people who overran Gaul, Spain, and North Africa in the fourth and fifth centuries A.D. and in 455 A.D. sacked Rome. Our word *Vandal* or *vandal* is derived from the Latin form, *Vandalus*, of a name that in Germanic was *Wandal–*.

Vine

Although the Vandals did do their share of plundering and raiding, they do not seem to have engaged in trashing others' property, in the manner of their modern namesakes. But the Vandals acquired a sufficiently destructive reputation for their name to be used as a lower-cased term meaning "one who willfully or maliciously defaces or destroys public or private property."

vanilla The common household flavoring vanilla comes from an exotic source, which gives it its name. *Vanilla* is extracted from the seedpod found in some tropical American orchids. Both the seedpod and the orchid bear the name *vanilla*. The word *vanilla* originally came from the Spanish word *vainilla*, denoting the flower, the pod, and the flavoring. *Vainilla* is a diminutive of *vaina*, meaning "sheath or pod," the orchid having been named for its pod. The Spanish word *vaina* comes from the Latin word *vāgīna*, "sheath of a sword or similar thing; a natural structure resembling a sheath, especially the leaf sheath enclosing an ear of corn." Latin *vāgīna* has been borrowed into English, but its common English sense is found only once in Classical Latin. It occurs in Plautus's comedy *Pseudolus*, in which he makes an obvious joke about a sword fitting in a sheath.

varsity The varsity team of a university represents the school more than one might imagine, for the word *varsity* is a colloquial shortening of *university*. Our form *varsity* is first found in the nineteenth century, although in the seventeenth century two instances of the spelling *versity* are recorded. The new word *varsity* was not always highly regarded, however. In Henry Kingsley's 1872 novel *Hornby Mills* we find the statement, "never use that horrid word 'varsity, my lad; don't vulgarise the old place." *Varsity* is still used in British English to mean "university," but in the United States the word usually denotes the principal team representing a school in sports or other competitions.

vaudeville   To bring vaudeville back to prime time might require a long journey in space and time, that is, to fifteenth-century France. Our word *vaudeville* denotes stage entertainment that includes various short acts in a program similar to a television variety show. The word earlier referred to a light comic theatrical piece including songs, pantomime, and dance, a sense first recorded in the nineteenth century. In the eighteenth century *vaudeville* simply meant "a light, popular, often satirical song." These senses, or rather the things they denote, show an obvious development from the earliest, the song, to the latest, the variety show, but the development occurred in French, from which English originally borrowed the word, continuing to borrow the new senses and new vaudevilles that developed in France. The French word originated as a name for such a popular song in the phrase *chanson du Vau de Vire*, "a song of the valley of Vire," which is in northwest France in the Calvados region of Normandy.

venom   It should come as no surprise that love has a close connection with venom. Our word *venom* ultimately comes from the Latin word *venēnum*, "a potent herb or other substance used for such purposes as magic or medicine; poison." *Venēnum* in turn is derived from the Indo-European word *wenesnom*, "love potion." The form *wenos-*, from which *wenesnom* is derived, gives us the name for the goddess of love, Venus. Both *wenesnom* and *wenos-* descend from the same Indo-European root, *wen-*[1], "to desire, strive for," the common ancestor of other words such as *win* and *wish*.

vermicelli   *With Oysters, Eggs, and Vermicelli,*
She let Him almost burst his Belly.
   —Matthew Pryor, *Paulo Purganti and His Wife*, 1709

We are now going to open an etymological can of worms by discussing the origin of the word *vermicelli*. This word, like the food itself, is Italian in origin. In Italian *vermicelli* is the plural of *vermicello*, a diminutive of *verme*, "worm," from the Latin word *vermis*, having the same sense. Perhaps you might prefer spaghetti instead; the word *spaghetti* is derived from the Italian plural of the diminutive of *spago*, "string," possibly ultimately via the assumed Late Latin form *spācus*, "string," from Latin *scāpus*, a term used for a variety of long, thin objects, including a plant stalk and a cylinder on which a papyrus could be rolled.

vesper   *Vesper* shares the senses "evening star" and "evening" (the latter now archaic) with its Latin source *vesper*. The Latin word is descended from the Indo-European form *wespero-*, which meant "evening, night." Our word *Hesperus*, "the evening star," goes back to the Greek descendant *hesperos* of this same Indo-European form. From *wespero-* was derived the form *westo-*, which has come down through Germanic into English as *west*, "the direction of sunset."

victual   *Terence, this is stupid stuff;*
You eat your victuals fast enough.
There can't be much amiss, 'tis clear,
To see the rate you drink your beer.
               —A. E. Houseman, *A Shropshire Lad*, 1896

Victual was borrowed from Old French *vitaille*, the normal development of which is represented by the present pronunciation (vĭt'l) of the English word. As early as circa 1300 the Old French word was spelled with a *c* in the form *victaille*, reflecting the fact that the word goes back to Late Latin *victuālia*, "provisions." Forms of the English word, including *victual*, contain this *c*. They also contain the *u* in Latin *victuālia*, which is first reflected in French and English forms in the fifteenth century. However, the pronunciation of *victual* does not correspond to its Latinate spelling, and the written form *vittle*, which adheres more closely to the actual sound of the word, is still sometimes used.

270

villain   The villain of this piece is the word itself—a word that exhibits in its history the low opinion in which peasants were held by their social superiors. *Villain* is ultimately derived from Latin *villa*, "the headquarters of a farm or country estate." From *villa* came the Vulgar Latin word *villānus*, denoting one who worked on a farm or estate. This Vulgar Latin word was the ancestor of Old French *vilain*, "feudal peasant, low rustic or common person." The Old French word has given us *villein*, "feudal peasant," and *villain*, "feudal peasant, wicked person," both originally the same word in English. *Villain* at first meant "low rustic or common person," but this sense developed even more pejoratively into "a wicked person."

vine   Had it not been for a pronunciation change, we would be drinking wine made from the fruit of the wine. The words *vine* and *wine* illustrate the history of the Latin sound represented by the letter *v*. Classical Latin had no *v* sound like the initial sound of *vine*; the letter *v* represented the sound of the consonant *w*. The Latin word *vīnum*, "wine," was borrowed by the ancestral Germanic tongue, probably before the birth of Christ; it appears in Old English as *wīn*, "wine," with the original sound of Latin *v*. *Vīnea*, "vineyard," a derivative of Latin *vīnum*, became Old French *vigne* or *vine*. The Old French word contained the *v* sound that developed in later Latin speech, which was the source of the Romance languages. Thus, we have *vine* instead of *wine*, and a vintage explanation of how words change over the centuries.

vitamin   Take your vitamins, even though their name is based on a mistake. Our English word *vitamin*, originally spelled *vitamine*, was borrowed from the German word *Vitamine* (now *Vitamin*), which is a compound of Latin *vīta*, "life," and the scientific suffix *–amine*, "amine; an organic compound of nitrogen." It was at first believed that all vitamins were amines. This was later found to be untrue, and the spelling (both in

271

German and in English) was modified slightly. The rather thinly disguised name *vitamin* remains with us today.

vixen Let us not be outfoxed by the etymological truth about *vixen*. The Middle English word *fixen*, "she-fox," comes from an Old English source or sources beginning with the letter *f*. The spelling of *vixen* with a *v* instead of the expected *f* comes from the pronunciation of the Middle English word. Dialects in the southern part of England during the Middle English period, and perhaps during the Old English period as well, regularly changed the *f* sound at the beginning of words to the closely related *v* sound. But the Old English spelling system had no separate letter for the *v* sound. The letter *v* was only introduced by French scribes after the Norman Conquest, and in Middle English the dialect form probably became orthographically distinct, although the first instance of the spelling *vixen* is found in the sixteenth century. The form *fixen* survived until the eighteenth century, but in Modern English the form *vixen* has replaced it.

volcano The word *volcano*, meaning "a mountain pouring out molten lava and gases," can be traced back to the ancient Roman fire god Vulcan. Vulcan (called *Volcā-nus* or *Vulcānus* by the Romans) was a god of destructive fire, no doubt including volcanic fire, who was worshipped chiefly to ward off fires. On his festival at Rome, the Volcanalia on August 23, a burnt offering of fish, fresh from the Tiber River, was made in his honor. Apparently, his worshippers hoped that by giving him offerings of water creatures they could induce him to spare things that were in danger of fire at this hot time of year. Vulcan's name became our word *volcano* by means of a complex process. His name was applied to certain volcanic mountains, their fiery exhalations being seen as outpourings of the god. The Latin word was borrowed by Arabic travelers and became the Arabic word *burkān*. The

Spanish word *volcan* and the Portuguese word *volcão* developed either from Arabic *burkān* or from Latin *vulcānus*. The Spanish or Portuguese word was borrowed into Italian, where it became *volcano*, the source of our English word, a long journey indeed for Vulcan.

walrus   *"The time has come," the Walrus said,*
"To talk of many things:
Of shoes—and ships—and sealing-wax—
Of cabbages—and kings—
And why the sea is boiling hot—
And whether pigs have wings."
   —Lewis Carroll, "The Walrus and the Carpenter," from
         Through the Looking-Glass, 1872

Putting aside for a moment the question of whether
pigs have wings, we might consider instead the composition of the speaker himself, the Walrus, keeping
in mind that this is an etymology worthy of a long
conversation and that what is said here does not reflect all that has been written about this word. Etymologically, the walrus is a "whale-horse." The
English word *walrus* was borrowed directly from
Dutch (first recorded in English in the eighteenth
century). The word came into Dutch from a Scandinavian source. Although we do not know the Scandinavian source, a look at the word for "walrus" in
several modern Scandinavian languages reveals that it
is a compound of the words for "whale" and "horse."
Thus in Swedish, for example, the word *valross,* "walrus," combines *val,* "whale," and *ross,* a word meaning "horse" that still survives in dialect and descends
from the Old Norse word *hross,* "horse, mare."

Walrus

275

But why call the animal *whale-horse?* Etymologists disagree about how these elements came to be combined. Some have suggested that a now unknown word for "walrus" may have sounded to Scandinavians very much like their words for "whale" and "horse" put together. Because of this resemblance in sound, Scandinavians began to use their combination as a name for the animal. It is possible that the second element (the "horse" part) of this unknown word is a counterpart of *rosm*– in the Old Norse word *rosmhvalr,* which means "walrus." In this word we find *hvalr,* "whale," but *rosm*– is mysterious in sense and derivation. It may have come from the Lapp word *morša,* from which we get *morse,* a rather uncommon English name for the walrus. Other etymologists believe that the animal was, in fact, originally called *whale-horse* or perhaps *horse-whale.* They cite the Old Norse word for "walrus," *hrosshvalr,* and the Old English word *horshwæl,* both of which are compounds of words for "horse" and "whale." According to this theory, Swedish *valross* may have arisen from an inverted form of Old Norse *hrosshvalr.*

Still, the question remains, why think of the animal as a cross between a whale and a horse? Possibly its amphibious habits or some combination of its physical features made it seem to share aspects of both the large sea creature and the large land creature. The answer may one day be clearer, but for now the field of speculation is certainly open. It might be easier to determine whether pigs have wings.

wanderlust   Wanderlust is perfectly innocent, although our notions of lust may cause us to doubt that. The word *wanderlust,* "passion for traveling, desire to see the world," is a direct English borrowing of the German word *Wanderlust* having the same meaning. *Lust* in German still means such things as "wish, desire," as well as "carnal desire," while *lust* in English, which shares the same Germanic ancestor, *lustuz,* "wish, desire," with its German counterpart, narrowed in

meaning to refer only to sexual desire; to any overwhelming desire, as indicated in the phrase *lust for
power*; or simply to eagerness.

warlock   The history of *warlock* can be traced to Old English,
and the word may be even older. There is, however, a
discontinuity between the Old English and Modern
English words in both form and meaning. The Old
English ancestor of *warlock* was *wǣrloga*, whose
meanings were probably derived from *wǣr*, "pledge,"
and *lēogan*, "to lie," or from the Germanic ancestors
of these Old English words. *Wǣrloga* meant "oath
breaker," "wicked person," "damned soul," and
"devil," especially and specifically Satan. These meanings persisted until the end of the medieval period.
The regularly derived modern form of Old English
wǣrloga would be *warlow*, which actually does occur
in Middle English. During the Middle English period
warlow developed the meaning "sorcerer, wizard." It
had its greatest currency in northern England and
Scotland, where it survived well into the modern period. *Warlock* in its current sense, "wizard," acquired
new life throughout the English-speaking world
through its appearance in the works of Sir Walter
Scott and Robert Burns. The precise reason for the alteration of the second syllable is unknown. And now
on to another matter—*wedlock*.

wedlock   Wedlock, however indissoluble its bonds are considered to be, has no etymological connection with locks
of any kind. The element –*lock* is a respelling, perhaps influenced by the word *lock*, of the Old English
suffix –*lāc*, which forms nouns of action expressing
the practice or performance of something. It occurs
in only a handful of Old English compounds and has
not survived except in the word *wedlock*. The Old
English term *wedd* denoted a pledge or a security of
any kind, but the compound *wedlāc* seems even in
Old English times to have been restricted to marriage
vows.

weird
Macbeth: *Saw you the weird sisters?*
Lennox: *No, my lord.*
. . . .
Macbeth: *Infected be the air whereon they ride?;*
And damn'd all those that trust them!
—Shakespeare, *Macbeth,* Act IV, Scene 1

When Macbeth referred to the witches on the heath as the "weird sisters" he was not being insulting; he was being etymological and innovative at the same time. The phrase *weird sisters* originally referred to the Fates, the three women of classical myth who controlled the destiny of each person. The phrase was also extended to include women who prophesied or possessed other attributes of the Fates. *Weird* by itself was a noun originally meaning "fate" or "destiny" pure and simple, and in medieval times the word was used to translate *Parca,* the Latin name for one of the Fates. We owe our adjective *weird* to Shakespeare's use of the noun in the phrase *weird sisters,* where it was interpreted as an adjective. The great prestige of Shakespeare preserved this use of *weird,* which was picked up and extended to its probably most current meaning, "strange," by nineteenth-century poets and writers, notably Shelley and Keats. The recent coinage *weirdo* derives solely from this extended sense of *weird.*

Welsh
The Welsh are the descendants of the Celts who lived in Britain before the Roman and Germanic invasions. The Welsh call themselves the *Cymry,* but the invading Anglo-Saxons called them *Wealas* (the plural of *Wealh*), which in Old English meant "foreigners." *Wealas* became *Wales* in Modern English. *Wælisc,* the Old English adjective derived from *Wealas,* became modern *Welsh.*

whiskey
Whiskey, vodka, and water seem a potent, incompatible combination. However, all three words share a common Indo-European root, *wed-¹,* "water, wet." The differences between their present forms are partially explained by the fact that under certain condi-

278

tions the Indo-European *e* could appear as *o,* or both *e* and *o* could disappear. *Water* is a native English word, which goes back by way of Germanic *watar* to the Indo-European form *wodō(r),* with an *o. Vodka* is borrowed from Russian, in which *vodka* is a diminutive of *voda,* "water." *Voda* goes back to the same Indo-European form as does *water. Whiskey* is a shortened form of *whiskybae,* a variant form of *usquebaugh,* both meaning "whiskey." English borrowed *usquebaugh* from Irish Gaelic *uisce beatha* and Scots Gaelic *uisge beatha,* a compound of Gaelic *uisge,* "water," and *beatha,* "of life," meaning literally "water of life." *Uisge* comes from the Indo-European form *udskio–* (without *e* or *o*). Do you want your whiskey, vodka, and water on the roots, excuse me, on the rocks?

wizard The Wizards of Id and Oz might find the origin of their title somewhat less than complimentary. *Wizard* is a compound formed from the adjective *wise,* "learned, sensible," and the suffix *–ard.* The word originally meant "a wise man, philosopher." The suffix *-ard,* however, almost always has a pejorative or disparaging sense, as in the words *coward, drunkard, laggard,* and *sluggard. Wizard* was therefore often used contemptuously to mean "a so-called wise man," and from this use it came to mean "sorcerer" and "male witch."

woman *Woman is the glory of all created existence.*
—Samuel Richardson, *The History of Sir Charles Grandison,* 1753–54

Although the word *woman* is basic to the vocabulary of English, it was not always so, for the word was coined in relatively late Old English times. *Woman* is actually a compound word formed from *wīf* (the Old English ancestor of our word *wife*), meaning "adult human female," and *man,* which meant in Old English, as it still does today, "human being" and "adult human male." The compound thus literally means

279

"woman-person." During Middle English times *wīf-man* became *wimman*, the pronunciation and spelling of which varied from dialect to dialect. The irregular plural *women* preserves the irregular plural *men* for *man*, as used in the original compound; it is not the same plural as the *-en* of *oxen* or *children*. Why the Anglo-Saxons felt a need to create a new word cannot be known, but the coinage was successful and eventually supplanted *wīf*, which now, as *wife*, is almost completely restricted to denoting a married woman.

world

All the world's a stage . . .
And one man in his time plays many parts,
His acts being seven ages.

— Shakespeare, *As You Like It*, Act III, Scene 7

In this passage Shakespeare comes close to the etymology of the word *world*. *Weorold*, the Old English form of *world*, consisted of two syllables, and this fact provides us with a clue to its origin. *World* was originally a compound word, but one formed so long ago that its etymological meaning has become obscured. It was formed in the Common Germanic period, the time before the Germanic language broke up into separate dialects, which scholars date to the millennium before the birth of Christ. *World* is ultimately made up of Germanic *weraz*, "man," and *alð-*, "age." The literal meaning of the Germanic compound *werald-* would have been "the age of man" or "the period of human life." Old English *weorold*, the descendant of the Germanic word, was often used to translate Latin *saeculum*, "generation, age." The common current sense of *world*, "the physical globe of Earth," was also found in Old English, but it most likely represents an extension of the word's original sense.

wormwood

Absinthe drinkers, take heart. There is no distasteful connection between worms and *wormwood*, which refers especially to the plant *Artemesia absinthium* that yields an extract used in making the alcoholic beverage absinthe. The etymology of *wormwood* is a good example of the process of folk etymology operating at an early period. The Middle English form *wermode* was descended from Old English *wermōd*, which is of unknown origin. By the fifteenth century, however, the first syllable was incorrectly interpreted as the word "worm," and the ending *-ode*, which did not make much sense in the new analysis, was reinterpreted as the word *wood*. The plant was used as a remedy for worms in the body, and hence *wormwood* made sense as its name.

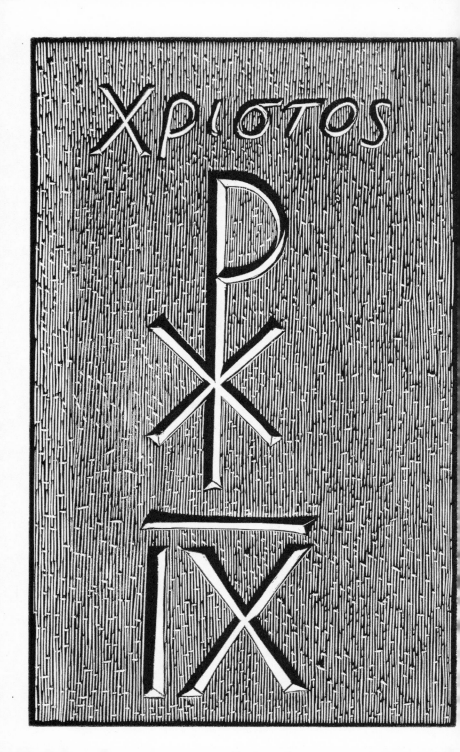

xenon   Xenon may not be a familiar gas—at least to the average person—a fact that is etymologically justified, for
the name of this gaseous element came from the neuter form of the Greek word *xenos*, meaning "strange,"
"stranger." More people may be familiar with the
form *xen-* or *xeno-*, which also goes back to the
noun *xenos*, "guest, stranger," and the adjective
xenos, "foreign, strange." This form, which is found
as part of words in Greek, Latin, and English, as well
as other languages, is perhaps most familiar to us in
the word *xenophobia*, "fear and hatred of strangers or
foreigners." However, one can also love foreign things
and be a *xenophile*; in fact, one can even suffer from
xenomania. To take the point further, if one could
be reincarnated as an ant, one might try to engage in
xenobiosis, a form of symbiosis in which ants of two
species live in the same nest but raise their young
separately.

Some *xeno-* words have died out in English. *Xenodochy*, which meant "entertainment of strangers, hospitality," is found recorded only in a seventeenth-
century dictionary and in a book by John Josselyn,
An account of two voyages to New England, published in 1674. Josselyn describes "Sincere and relig-

ious people . . . descryed . . . by their Zenodochie or hospitality." Apparently Josselyn did not necessarily expect his readers to know this word, which is never recorded again. One could, however, count on finding xenodochy in a xenodochium. *Xenodochium* has been an English word since 1612 with the general sense "a place for strangers and pilgrims to stay." In his book *The History and Antiquities of the Anglo-Saxon Church*, published in 1845, John Lingard tells us that "within the precincts of the monastery stood an edifice, distinguished by the Greek name of *Xenodochium*, in which a certain number of paupers received their daily support, and which was gratuitously opened to every traveller who solicited relief." No xenophobes there.

Xmas   The character x in *Xmas* represents not the letter x in the Roman alphabet but rather the Greek letter chi. The Greek form of chi is χ (minuscule) or X (capital). Chi is the first letter of the Greek form of *Christ*, which in Greek is χριστός, transliterated as *Khristos* or *Christos*. The symbol χ or X has long been used as an abbreviation for *Christ*.

x-ray   Wilhelm Roentgen, the nineteenth-century German scientist who discovered x-rays, gave them the name *X-strahlen*, which was translated into English as "x-rays." He used x, the symbol for an unknown quantity, because he did not completely understand the nature of this kind of radiation.

xylophone   *Xylophone* is a word one expects to encounter in the X section of any children's alphabet book. It is there because it is one of the few words beginning with x that a child or most anyone else would know. Do you recognize *xerophagy*, "the eating of dry food, especially as a form of fasting practiced in the early Christian Church and chiefly in the Eastern churches today," or *xylotomy*, "the preparation of sections of wood for microscopic study"? Most of the English words beginning with *x*, including these obscurities, are of Greek origin, the *x*, pronounced (z), representing the Greek letter xi. In the case of *xylophone*, *xylo*– is a form meaning "wood," derived from Greek *xulon*, "wood," and –*phone* represents Greek *phōnē*, "voice, sound," the same element found in words such as *telephone*, *microphone*, and *megaphone*. Our famous *x* word is first recorded in the April 7, 1866, edition of the *Athenæum*: "A prodigy . . . who does wonderful things with little drumsticks on a machine of wooden keys, called the 'xylophone.'"

yahoo Yahoo, "a crude or brutish person," is a generalized use of the name Yahoo, invented by Jonathan Swift for his imaginary race of brutes in human form in *Gulliver's Travels*. The Yahoos lived in a society where the civilized, rational inhabitants were horses. These creatures were called *Houyhnhnms*, whose name suggests the whinny of a horse. Swift's vision of this society gains force when we realize that in his time horses were as important as cars are today.

yardstick A yardstick is literally a "stick-stick," for the word *yard* is the descendant of Old English *gird*, which meant simply "a stick." Since sticks make convenient measuring devices, a stick of a certain length became used as a standard of linear measure. The length of this unit varied over the centuries. A statute of uncertain date, probably enacted during the thirteenth century, decreed that "the Iron Yard of our Lord the King" should contain exactly three feet. The compound *yardstick* is a relatively recent coinage, using the word *yard* in the sense "a unit of length."

Yahoo

ye The word *ye*, which is sometimes used in pseudo-archaic phrases such as *ye olde curiosity shoppe*, is actually a variant spelling of the definite article *the*. The variant arose from a confusion of the letter *y* with the letter *þ*, or thorn, which was used in medieval times to represent the sounds now spelled *th*. Early printed English books retained *ye* for *the* and the common abbreviation *yt* for *that*.

yoga Yoga is no yoke, but it is close to one etymologically. The word *yoga* is from Sanskrit *yogaḥ*, "union; the uniting of the self with the universe." This word literally meant "a yoking together" and is descended from the Indo-European root *yeug-*, "to join, yoke." *Yeug-* descended into Germanic as *yuk-*, represented in Old English by *geoc*, the ancestor of Modern English *yoke*.

yolk Etymologically speaking, there's a lot of yellow in the word *yolk*. This word, meaning "the yellow part of an egg," is descended from Old English *geolca*. *Geolca* is a noun derived from the adjective *geolo*, the ancestor of *yellow*. *Yolk* and *yellow* go back to the Indo-European root *ghel-²*, meaning "to shine." From this root are derived words denoting color, such as *yellow* and Greek *khlōros*, "pale green, greenish-yellow," the source of the form *chloro-* in *chlorophyll*. From *ghel-²* also come words denoting gold, including *gold* and *gild*; words denoting bile, including *gall*; and words having to do with light or shining, such as *gleam, glint, glimmer, glitter, glisten,* and *glow*. We finish up this list of related words in a glow of contentment, with our words *glee* and *glad*.

Yule *Yule*, in Old English *gēol*, was originally the name of the midwinter season or possibly of a pagan festival held in midwinter. Among early Germanic peoples only the Scandinavians are known to have held such a celebration—as attested by the Old Norse word *jōl*. The festival may well have been named for the season, rather than the other way around. After the English were converted to Christianity, the name *Yule* was used for the feast of Christmas. The use of native words for Christian terms was encouraged in the Anglo-Saxon church; another example is the use of the term *Easter* for the feast of Christ's resurrection.

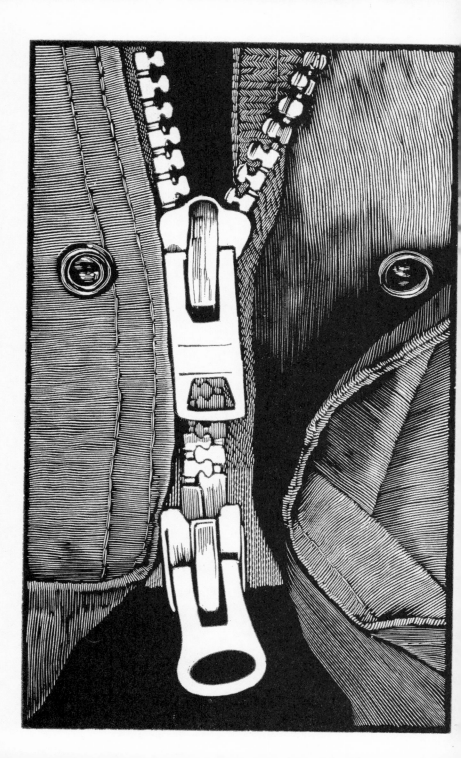

zero The word *zero*, "the numeral 0," is not only synonymous with the word *cipher* but goes back to the same source, the Arabic word *ṣifr*, which meant "empty" as well as "zero." *Zero* came into English from Italian *zero*, a contracted form of earlier *zefiro*, while *cipher* came into English via Old French from Medieval Latin *cifra*. Although *zero* was borrowed as a synonym of *cipher*, the two words have diverged in meaning. *Cipher* has developed the sense "a code," whereas *zero* is used primarily as the name of the numeral, especially in scientific use.

zest The knowledge that the origin of the word *zest* is a mystery ought not detract from your zest for life. *Zest* can be traced back only as far as French *zest* (now *zeste*), which meant both "the skin that divides the inside of a walnut" and "orange or lemon peel." English borrowed this second sense of *zest*, a sense first recorded in the fourth edition of Thomas Blount's *Glossographia*, published in 1674: "Zest (Fr.) [French] the pill [peel] of an Orange, or such like, squeesed into a glass of wine to give it a relish." *Zest* was then extended figuratively (a sense first recorded

Zipper

in 1709) to mean "something that adds flavor or interest," as in "That sweet minor zest Of love, your kiss," from Keats's 1819 poem "To Fanny." *Zest* also came to mean "gusto," first recorded in Boswell's 1791 *Life of Johnson* in an entry dated September 20, 1777: "If I were to reside in London, the exquisite zest with which I relished it in occasional visits might go off."

zipper   The word *zipper* is an example of what the owners of trademarks try to prevent. Coined in 1925, *zipper* was originally a B. F. Goodrich trademark for overshoes with fasteners. A Goodrich executive is said to have slid the fastener up and down on the boot and exclaimed, "Zip 'er up," from the zipping sound made by the device. The noun *zip* and the verb *zip*, referring to a light sharp sound or to motion accompanied by that kind of sound were already in existence (*zip* as a noun was first recorded in 1875; as a verb in 1852). The two words owed their origin to the imitation by speakers of the sound made by a rapidly moving object. As the fastener that "zipped" came to be used in other articles, its name became generalized. B. F. Goodrich sued to protect its trademark but was allowed to retain proprietary rights over it only for its *Zipper Boots*. *Zipper* had moved out into the world of common nouns, where it then spawned the verb *zip*, "to fasten with a zipper."

zither   What do the zither and the guitar have in common, etymologically speaking? A zither is a stringed musical instrument from Austria. The German word *Zither* comes from Latin *cithara*, borrowed from Greek *kithara*, which also denoted a kind of stringed instrument. Greek *kithara* has other descendants in Modern English, such as *cittern* and *guitar*, musical instruments in the same family as the zither.

zombie   People who are told that they are behaving like zombies may wish to ask for a second opinion. As devotees of horror films know, a *zombie* is a reanimated corpse, one of the living dead. Such devotees may not know, however, that *zombie* is also the snake god of voodoo cults as well as a supernatural force that is believed to have the power to reanimate a corpse. The word for these different entities, *zombie*, like the word *voodoo*, comes to the New World from Africa, where we find similar words in the Bantu language group, such as Kongo *zumbi*, "fetish," and Kongo *nzambi*, "god." In Haiti, where voodoo is still widely practiced, zombies are still believed to exist, although recent field work by Wade Davis, a graduate student in ethnobotany at Harvard University, seems to confirm that zombies are people who have been placed in a deathlike state by the use of a poison. The zombies are then buried alive and afterward dug up to be used as the slaves of voodoo priests. Davis also says that zombification is dealt out as a punishment by secret voodoo societies.

zoo   Lovers of zoos everywhere owe the name of this institution to one zoo, the Zoological Gardens in Regent's Park, London. The name of this pioneering animal park was colloquially shortened to "the Zoological" and then to "the zoo." The new name was subsequently extended to other similar exhibitions of animals. The word *zoological* ultimately goes back to the Greek word *zōion*, "living being, animal."

zugzwang   The German borrowing *zugzwang*, though it may sound as if it were the name of a snow-capped Alpine mountain, is actually a chess term. *Zugzwang* denotes a situation in chess when all moves contemplated by a player are equally disadvantageous to that player. In German the term is made up of the words *Zug*, "a move in chess," and *Zwang*, which means such things as "compulsion," "coercion," and "force." Thus the compound expresses the notion of a player being compelled to make a disadvantageous move. But at least in chess, a zugzwang is only temporary; there's always another game.

THE LAST WORD

We have intended this collection of mysteries and histories of English words to be absorbing and entertaining in its own right, word by word. More generally, we have hoped that it would deepen your appreciation of the people and forces shaping our language. In the words of the great scholar George Harley McKnight, taken from his definitive work *English Words and their Background*, "Above all, words are interesting on account of the human nature revealed. In the creation and use of words there appears not only the sense of beauty and the sense of humor, but a human fallibility exhibited in the inexactness of knowledge and in seemingly capricious modes of procedure. In fact the variety of interest to be found in words corresponds with the variety of interest in complex human nature. All in all, the history of words introduces so much of the unexpected and strange that the subject matter becomes often less that of science than of romance."

Beauty. A sense of humor. Human fallibility. The unexpected. Romance. These qualities run through the complex tapestry of English—a tapestry the details of which range from the ordinary (*cat*) to the extraordinary (*butterfly*); from the learned (*cynosure*) to the colloquial (*funky*); from the sublime (*genius*) to the ridiculous (*fizzle*); from the known (*algorithm*) to the unknown (*posh*); from the legal (*asset*) to the lawless (*desperado*).

In its fullest sense the story, or the history, of a word encompasses everything known about that word: its current spelling, its pronunciation, and its meaning or meanings, together with all its past forms and meanings. However, having all this knowledge about a particular English word is often insufficient because many English words have come into our language from Latin, French, German, Chinese, Russian, and many more languages. Still other

Self-portrait as Lexicographer

words in our lexicon go back to Common Germanic, the ancestor of languages such as German, Dutch, Icelandic, Swedish, and of course, English. But the stories of individual words are simply footnotes to a much bigger story—the history of the English language, its prehistory, and the histories and prehistories of languages contributing to its development and structure. Words like *dog* and *gossip* are examined in terms of the three major historical stages in the development of the English language: Old English (700–1100), Middle English (1100–1500), and Modern English (1500–present). The book also studies words borrowed from or descended from French (*quiche*), Latin (*alibi*), Greek (*skeleton*), Scandinavian languages (*iceberg*), Italian (*paparazzo*), and Russian (*samovar*), and words coming to us from many other languages, including Chinese (*tycoon*), Hindi (*shampoo*), and Arabic (*algorithm*). You are also introduced to loan translations (*gospel*) and words borrowed along with their descendants (*lacuna*).

Many Latin words were borrowed into English during the medieval period because of the pre-eminence of Latin as the language of Church, State, Scholarship, and Literature. Having mentioned Latin, we should note that we have differentiated the various stages of later Latin in our book as follows: Late Latin (A.D. 200–700), Medieval Latin (700–1500), and Modern Latin (1500–present). We also refer to Vulgar Latin, the chiefly unrecorded common speech of the ancient Romans, which is distinguished from standard literary, or Classical, Latin and is the ancestor of the Romance languages. English has borrowed heavily from one particular Romance language—French—partly because of the Norman Conquest of England in 1066. The English language, having been brought into intimate, sustained contact with French, began to borrow words in great numbers from Old French, that is, the French language from the ninth century to the beginning of the sixteenth century. Many of these borrowings were from Anglo-Norman, the dialect of Old French that was spoken in England after the Conquest.

But even before the advent of the French Connection, English had been influenced by the influx of other invaders, specifically, by Scandinavians—chiefly Danes and Norwegians—many of whom settled in the eastern and northern parts of England. The Scandinavians' contributions to the English language were substantial, with the word *skirt* being a prime example.

Another important element contributing to the richness of English is the development of words and meanings within the language itself. New words are formed through a host of processes: compounding (*daisy*), clipping or shortening (*mob*), reduplication (*namby-pamby*), blending (*brunch*), functional shift (*contact*), folk etymology (*hangnail*), and back-formation (*asset*). Other words are acronyms (*laser*), coinages (*runcible*), and trademarks (*Teflon*). Still other terms come from the names of people, real (*lynch*) or fictional (*syphilis*), or from places (*satin*). Words are also formed through prefixation and suffixation (*remacadamize*) or are constructed on the basis of existing words (*bureaucrat*). Processes subjecting new words and old to changes in meaning include extension, or generalization, of meaning (*chauvinism*); restriction, or specialization, resulting in a narrowing of meaning (*meat*); elevation, or melioration, of meaning (*prestige*); degeneration, or pejoration, of meaning (*lewd*); and transfer of meaning (*foot*). Other processes change the shapes or sounds of words but not their meanings; they include dissimilation (*colonel*), metathesis (*argosy*), and respelling (*debt*).

Major sources of evidence used in compiling this book are the great historical dictionaries, such as the *Oxford English Dictionary* (*OED*), the *Middle English Dictionary* (*MED*), and the *Dictionary of American Regional English* (*DARE*). When we have given dates at which words or meanings entered the English language, we have often given the dates recorded in these large historical dictionaries. Such dictionaries exist for other languages, too, including *Trésor de la Langue Française* and *Deutsches Wörterbuch*. To the editors—past and present—of all these great works we are heavily indebted.

Another important resource in the study of the history of words is the work of linguists who analyze recorded languages and reconstruct unrecorded languages, such as Germanic and Indo-European. Calvert Watkins's *The American Heritage Dictionary of Indo-European Roots* has been especially helpful to us in this respect. Still other valuable sources of information for our own work are etymological dictionaries such as *The Oxford Dictionary of English Etymology*, the *Französisches Etymologisches Wörterbuch*, and the *Etymologisches Wörterbuch der deutschen Sprache*.

All this may seem highly technical, and some of it is very much so. The serious study of the historical development of our lexicon requires skilled, sharply honed methodology. Mere guesswork and unsubstantiated allegations have been scrupulously avoided in this work. On the other hand, though words are the object of scholarly investigation, they are obviously not the sole preserve of scholars. The words in our lexicon express our needs, hopes, and fears; our happiness, laughter, grief, and tears; our love and hate; our lies and truths. The ever-changing language that expresses all this and more deserves our attention, for a heightened awareness of its development adds an extra dimension to our use and understanding of it. We also come to appreciate more deeply the inextricable linkage of our language to our own past, and to the pasts of other peoples and nations and their relationships with us. In Emerson's words, "Language is the archives of history."

David A. Jost, Ph.D.
Editor

INDEX

Page numbers for main entries are in boldface.

bastard, **18-19**, 228
bathroom, **19**
bay, **19-20**
bead, **20**
beam, 237
beatnik, 164
Beaumont, Francis, *Vertue of Sack*, 119
bed, **20-21**
Bede, *Historia Ecclesiastica gentis Anglorum*, 236-37
bed of Procrustes, 189
beef, 55-56
belly, **21**
Berlin, Irving, "Puttin' on the Ritz," 209
Bertram, James M., *Shadow of a War*, 111
B. F. Goodrich Company, 292
Big Bertha, 102-03
black, 21
blackball, 17
blackmail, **21**
Blackmore, Richard, 68
Blanding, Don, *Hula Moons*, 158
bleachers, 70
Blount, Thomas, *Glossographia*, 218-19, 291
blue chip, **21**
bluestocking, **22**
blurb, **22**, 26
board, 1
Boccaccio, Giovanni, *Il Filostrata*, 174
bodega, 24
bodice, **22-23**
bohemian, **23**
book, **23-24**; illustration, 16
boss, **24**
Boston *Globe*, 73, 245-46
Boswell, James, *Life of Johnson*, 291
boutique, **24**
Bovay, A. E., 207
bovine, 111
Bowdler, Thomas, 25
bowdlerize, **25**
boycott, **25-26**
Boycott, Charles C., 25-26
Boyle, Robert, 57
bridal, **26**
bridegroom, 101
brobdingnagian, 45
bromide, **26**
brunch, **27**
Buenos Aires, 150
Bulwer-Lytton, Rosina, *Cheveley*, 80
bureau, 27
bureaucrat, **27**
Burgess, Gelett, *Are You a Bromide?*, 22, 26
Burnet, Gilbert, *History of My Own Time*, 141
bus, **27-28**
bus boy, 28
business, **28**
Business Week, 123
Butler, Samuel, *The Genuine Remains of Mr. Samuel Butler*, 262
butterfly, **28**
buxom, **29**

cacao, 45
Caesar, Julius, 167
Cagniard de la Tour, Charles, 229
caldron, **31-32**
camouflage, **32**
canapé, **32-33**
candidate, **33**
candy, **33**
cannabis, 34
cannibal, **33-34**
canopy, 32
canvas, 34
canvass, **34**
Čapek, Karel, *The Insect Play*, 209; *R.U.R.*, 209
Cape Times, 9
Capgrave, John, *Chronicle of England*, 143
capital, 38
caprice, **34-35**
car, **35**
cardinal, **35**
career, **36**
Carey, Henry, 161
Carroll, Lewis, *Alice's Adventures in Wonderland*, 54; *Through the Looking-Glass*, 27, 275
carton, **36-37**
cartoon, 36
casserole, 32
cat, **37**; illustration, 30
catch, **37-38**
cathedral, 39
cattle, **38**
Catton, Bruce, 113
Cervantes, Miguel de, 197
chair, **39**
chaldron, 31
Charles, Prince, 170
Charlton, Linda, 246
charming, **39**
chase, 37-38
chattels, 38
Chaucer, Geoffrey, 131; *Canterbury Tales*, 52, 60; *Legend of Good Women*, 98; *Troilus and Criseyde*, 69, 174, 235
Chauvin, Nicolas, 39-40
chauvinism, **39-40**
cheap, **40**
check, **41**
checkmate, 41
chess, 41
Chesterfield, Lord, *Letters*, 188
child, **41-42**
children, 41-42, 280
chlorophyll, 288
chocolate, 45
chowder, 31
Christ, 284
Churchill, Winston, 125, 196
cipher, 291
city, **42**
Clancey, Tom, *The Hunt for Red October*, 204-05
class, **42-43**
classic, 42
classical, 42
classy, 42-43

305